Correctional Management and the Law

A Penological Approach

Correctional Management and the Law

A Penological Approach

Lior Gideon

JOHN JAY COLLEGE OF CRIMINAL JUSTICE,
NEW YORK, NY

O. Hayden Griffin III

THE UNIVERSITY OF ALABAMA AT BIRMINGHAM

WITH

David Caspi

SOUTHWESTERN COLLEGE,
SAN DIEGO

CAROLINA ACADEMIC PRESS

Durham, North Carolina

Library of Congress Cataloging-in-Publication Data

Names: Gideon, Lior, author. | Griffin, O. Hayden, III, author.
Title: Correctional management and the law : a penological approach / Lior
    Gideon and O. Hayden Griffin, III.
Description: Durham, North Carolina : Carolina Academic Press, LLC, 2017. |
    Includes bibliographical references and index.
Identifiers: LCCN 2017012445 | ISBN 9781594609930 (alk. paper)
Subjects: LCSH: Correctional law--United States.
Classification: LCC KF9728 .G53 2017 | DDC 344.7303/5--dc23
LC record available at https://lccn.loc.gov/2017012445

e-ISBN 978-1-53100-536-8

Carolina Academic Press, LLC
700 Kent Street
Durham, North Carolina 27701
Telephone (919) 489-7486
Fax (919) 493-5668
www.cap-press.com

Printed in the United States of America

For their continuing love and support,
which is the fuel to our doing,
we dedicate this book to our families—
Hila Shalev-Gideon, Jonathan and Eithan Gideon,
Vanessa Woodward Griffin, and
Asher and Evan Caspi

Contents

Preface

Correctional practices and management are constantly changing and evolving. Such a process reflects changes in penological ideologies and perceptions of judicial interpretations of these ideologies. As such, changes in correctional management policies and practices can be viewed as a direct result of inmates' litigation that evoked judicial response to existing correctional policies and practices.

Many believe that upon conviction, offenders should lose their rights. These offenders should be punished and incapacitated by being removed from society, and if placed on community supervision, such supervision should restrict their basic rights. After all, those who side with a severe punitive approach will argue, these are convicted offenders and they deserve to suffer. Furthermore, many agree that convicted offenders do not deserve to be treated fairly, and many more will argue that inmates today receive far too many rights; rights that cost taxpayers enormous sums of money that could be funneled to more deserving populations. These advocates of harsher punitive policies and practices will also argue that our penal system is too soft. While people may disagree about issues that aim to protect the rights of convicted offenders, the Supreme Court has held that offenders retain certain procedural and substantive rights. However, such a judicial approach has experienced numerous shifts during the past four decades during which the Supreme Court began to defend the civil rights of the incarcerated by extending some form of the protections guaranteed by the U.S. Constitution to people under correctional control. The impact of these decisions has significantly influenced correctional practices. Moreover, the issues of prisoner rights continue to evolve and thus continue to shape current and future correctional practices while guarding basic rights and dignity. It is within this context that *Correctional Management and the Law: A Penological Approach* offers readers an in-depth penological examination of the issues and challenges related to the constitutional and legal aspects of correctional management and the ways in which current correctional practice has been shaped by the various rulings of the U.S. Supreme Court in its quest to protect the constitutional rights of a powerless and unpopular minority, while also debating serving the needs of correctional administrators tasked to deliver prescribed court punishments.

Accordingly, *Correctional Management and the Law: A Penological Approach* explores and discusses the legal challenges that affect correctional practices and management. It does so by analyzing how key Constitutional provisions, landmark and significant Supreme Court decisions, and important Federal and State laws have impacted current correctional practice, and the ways in which convicted offenders are treated by the system.

The Current Book in Context

Prisons, in one form or another, have been in existence throughout the centuries. After the American Revolutionary War, the United States adopted not only Britain's common law legal system but also its correctional practices. While American prisons have changed and evolved over the years in terms of objectives, methods, and philosophical foundations, prisons, by and large, have been used to punish and incapacitate offenders.

Once in prison, inmates become members of a self-contained society where their lives are controlled by the state or federal government, as provided by the 13th Amendment to the U.S. Constitution. Prison administrators, as agents of the government, not only deprive the inmates of liberty but also dictate the details of daily life, including the administering of discipline for those inmates who violate prison rules. The fact that prison personnel control virtually every aspect of an inmate's life raises a number of questions and concerns. Should prison administrators have unfettered control and freedom to act as they deem fit, or do prisoners have rights that must be respected? If prisoners have rights, what is the justification for such rights? Where do these rights come from? Who is responsible for deciding the rights to which a prisoner is entitled? How will such rights be enforced? Whose responsibility is it to protect those sentenced from arbitrary and capricious conducted? Who is to decide when a punishment is cruel and unusual and why?

If you ask the average American citizen, you will likely find that most are not overly concerned with these questions and with issues concerning prisoners' rights. In fact, many would probably indicate that a prisoner should have no rights at all, as this is the price that one must pay for violating the law and harming society. The Supreme Court, however, has held that prisoners do in fact have certain constitutionally protected rights, even if not as broad as those rights belonging to free citizens. Prisoners are considered to be a minority group, and an unpopular minority group at that; the exact type of minority group that needs protecting.

Federal courts and state courts did not always see themselves as the proper guardians of prisoner rights. Prior to the 1960s, for a variety of reasons (federalism, separation of powers, work load concerns, etc.), courts were reluctant to hear prisoner complaints of inhumane conditions or treatment. This is known as the "hands off" era. Consequently, prisoners could do no more than complain to prison officials who had little incentive to listen or respond. Similarly, legislatures also had little motivation to address prisoner concerns. The 1960s ushered in the civil rights era which provided more receptive courts and prisoner legal aid groups staffed with attorneys who knew how to properly draft and file a legal complaint. In 1964, the Supreme Court in *Cooper v. Pate* (378 U.S. 546) held that the Civil Rights Act of 1871 (42 U.S.C. § 1983) applies to state inmates thereby giving state inmates standing to sue in federal courts when a constitutional right was denied by an agent of the state. Considering that 90% of inmates are held in state prisons (Fliter, 2001), this was an important procedural holding. Subsequent cases, as will be discussed throughout the chapters of this book, reinforced the Supreme Court's view that federal courts had a duty to protect prisoner procedural and substantive constitutional rights (see *Wolf v. McDonnell*; *Procunier v. Martinez*; *Palmigiano v. Garrahy*; *Kahane v. Carlson*; and *Ruiz v. Estelle*).

The newfound accessibility to courts, along with a continually increasing prison population, resulted in a dramatic surge in inmate initiated lawsuits. In 1975 there were 6,600 lawsuits filed in federal courts, but by 1995 there were nearly 40,000 new federal civil lawsuits, which represented nineteen percent of the civil docket (Wall Street Journal, 1996). Access to the courts provided an important means by which prisoners could seek redress for inhumane treatment or denial of protected rights. Unfortunately, many of the lawsuits lacked merit. These so-called "frivolous" lawsuits were perceived by many as clogging up court dockets and wasting taxpayer dollars. One estimate, by the National Association of Attorney Generals, found that the states spent over $80 million dollars addressing frivolous lawsuits (Kuzinski, 1998). This led to the period known as the "Retrenchment Period" where Congress began to take steps towards curtailing the number of prisoner initiated lawsuits. In 1996, the Prison Reform Litigation Act (PRLA) was enacted. This act was designed to limit access to the courts and reduce the number of frivolous lawsuits.

Prisoner rights and correctional law are dynamic and evolving areas of law that extend not only to the incarcerated but to others under the control of the criminal justice system as well, such as those on probation and parole. In light of the millions of individuals under the criminal justice system on any given day and in light of the fact that this number is on the rise, prisoner rights is a highly relevant topic to the general study of criminal justice, and to the study of corrections in particular. Prisoner rights, in addition to affecting the incarcerated, also impact correction officers, institutional administrators, courts, judges, legislatures, taxpayers, and the executive branches of federal and state government. Rights given to prisoners and guaranteed under our Bill of Rights are also a mirror that reflect our society and the level of humanity by which we value the life of others, and expect our government to treat us. Consequently, the aim of this book is to present a comprehensive examination of prisoners' rights and correctional law in a penological context, and their impact on others within the broader criminal justice system.

Innovation of the Current Book

Most existing books about prisoners' rights and correctional law are fairly narrow in scope and do not situate the discussion of prisoner rights into a broader penological context of corrections or criminal justice. Other texts are appropriate for law students but too sophisticated for an introductory level college course. Furthermore, those texts that do integrate prisoner rights and correctional law into a broader discussion of corrections tend to do so in a cursory manner, thus leaving out many important legal issues, relevant federal statutes, and significant cases. Furthermore, a theoretical framework that will enable readers to better understand the rationale behind the laws that pertain to correctional practice is absent.

With over two million individuals currently incarcerated and another 5.1 million under community supervision (both probation and parole), the nation's correctional population reaches an astonishing number of over 7.3 million people under some form of correctional supervision/treatment. This is about 1 in every 31 adults. As a consequence of this reality, there are tens of thousands of lawsuits, both civil rights and torts based, filed every year by convicted criminals. Aside from the impact on the prisoners, the holdings of those cases with merit (as well as the sheer number of lawsuits) affects the lives of correction officers, correction administrators, judges, attorneys, and the general public. In this regard, a comprehensive discussion of prisoner rights is necessary to any textbook on corrections. *Correctional Management and the Law: A Penological Approach* integrates a broad and detailed discussion of prisoner rights in a manner not previously offered, while proposing a theoretical framework that will enable readers to better understand the social, penological and administrative rationale behind relevant laws and judicial decisions, as well as their impact on current and future correctional practices.

In terms of prisoner rights, *Correctional Management and the Law: A Penological Approach* begins with a short discussion on the goals of punishment, and those of corrections. Such discussion is followed by a chapter that will discuss the history of correctional law in the United States. It then discusses the structure and issues that revolve around community supervision—probation and parole—as well as issues of jail and prison structure and administration. The following chapters then address the constitutional issues and relevant legal cases as they pertain to prisoners and prisons, making distinctions between substantive rights and procedural rights. Next, chapters discuss relevant federal statutes that have been used to broaden or limit prisoner rights while explaining the context of prisoner rights, the relationship between federal and state court rulings as well as the applicability of federal and state statutes. A special chapter is then devoted to the discussion of prisoners with "special needs" (i.e., mentally and chronically ill, prisoners with HIV/AIDS, women with special needs, LGBTQ, and the elderly). Two separate chapters discuss the impact of prisoner rights litigation on correction officers (including liability), correction administrators, courts, and the costs to general public. These chapters also examine the political context of judicial interventions as well as issues of race and its effect of judicial intervention. These chapters further address legal issues associated with correctional operations. The final chapter examines the importance of judicial intervention in correctional management while integrating knowledge acquired from previous chapters in an effort to develop a theoretical framework that will enable readers to better understand the rationale behind the laws, and court decisions affect and shape current and future correctional practices. This chapter closes a circle to the first discussion of the goals of punishment and the aims of corrections presented early on in the book.

Lior Gideon & O. Hayden Griffin, III
December 2016

Acknowledgments

Teaching correctional courses for over fifteen years often requires us to expand the discussion beyond the boundaries of the course curricula. Many times, students are eager to understand why some policies and practices are the way they are, and why some Justices decided the way they did. Attempting to explain such decisions always leads back to basic penological explanations and basic correctional concepts. It is within this context that the idea of this book came to life. For this, we are thankful to all our corrections and penology students who challenged us through the years, and placed their intellect and curiosity in the forefront of their learning. We are also thankful to our colleagues at John Jay College of Criminal Justice, and the University of Alabama at Birmingham for their mental support and advice during the daunting stages of writing.

Beth Hall, from Carolina Academic Press, deserves special recognition and applause for her critical role in bringing this project to publication. Without her support the authors of this book would have not met, collaborated and produced this book. Beth also demonstrated a deep sense of understanding and forgiveness for our deadline deviation, and was always available for consultation and good advice. Special thanks are appropriate to Zora O'Neill, who worked studiously on the edits of this book. With her infinite knowledge and wisdom, she guided us in making each word, sentence, paragraph and idea clear and coherent. We are thankful for her hard and prompt work.

We also want to extend our gratitude to those who reviewed the book in its original stages, and gave some helpful comments on its proposed organization and chapter coverage. It is always challenging to address the many opinions of our colleagues, but we hope we were able to rise to the task.

Lior Gideon & O. Hayden Griffin, III
December 2016

Correctional Management and the Law

A Penological Approach

Chapter 1

Introduction: The Goals of Punishment and Aims of Correctional Institutions

Those who have offended us, betrayed our trust, and violated the equilibrium of our daily lives: these are the very ones we seek to protect. A seeming paradox, a dim irony many will find too difficult to grasp, yet we do it. We embrace the folly, and at times, to a level of absurdity, ignore the inner voice to harm those who harmed us. Why do we do this? Why do we feel compelled to protect those who refuse to obey our laws? And most of all, why do we use such laws that were viciously violated to protect those same individuals who violated them? These questions are at the heart of this book, and these questions are used to guide our search for understanding why and how correctional practices are affected by our laws, in particular the Bill of Rights. Furthermore, we direct additional focus to an attempt to explain how these practices are being shaped by legislation, and landmark court cases.

Early correctional practices were characterized by "*civil death*" statutes that were common in many states as a natural part of punishing the offender. According to this practice, convicted offenders were stripped of most, if not all, of their civil rights. Once incarcerated, inmates lost all rights and many times found themselves at the mercy of those who guarded them. Such a practice was not so different for those sentenced to community supervision—probation or house arrest—as their right to life and liberty were violated as well. Once the convicts were sentenced, society seemed to want very little to do with them. "Throw away the key" and "let 'em rot" were common sentiments that dominated society's way of dealing with its offenders. These perceptions were self-serving, and many were perfectly comfortable with not dealing with those who had been effectively shunned from society. In fact, a common belief was that once convicted and incarcerated, offenders became "slaves of the state," as can be understood from the Thirteenth Amendment, which states:

> Neither slavery nor involuntary servitude, except as punishment for crime whereof the party shall have been duly convicted, shall exist within the United States, or any place subject to their jurisdiction.

Prison administrators, as agents of the government, not only deprive the inmate of liberty but also dictate the details of daily life, including the administration of discipline for those inmates who violate prison rules. Inmates became "nonpersons," and thus it was easy not to think of them. Furthermore, two underlying principles are essential to this approach: (1) under the separation of powers inherent in the Constitution, the judicial branch of the government should not meddle with the operations of the executive branch, and thus in the affairs of correctional facilities; (2) judges should leave correctional administration to correctional experts (Cole, 1987). Consequently, state and federal government neglected prison inmates, enabling prison administrations to run their facilities in whatever manner they saw fit. This was all done in the name of punishment, society's reaction to those who offended it. How, then, do these practices collide with the stated goals of punishment and those of corrections?

The Goals of Punishment

The process of apprehending, prosecuting, sentencing, and sanctioning those who have committed crimes is a calculated, rational process orchestrated by the government and done in the name of its sovereignty. This is the logic rooted in Hobbes's *Leviathan*, in which people mutually agree to surrender some of their liberties in order to have a government that will deter potential wrongdoers, while protecting law-abiding citizens' safety and property. Such punitive practices, according to Shoham and Shavit (1995), reflect the philosophy and social ideology of a given society, and it is within this context that the goals of punishment should be clearly identified and discussed, as it provides a lucid connection to the *modus operandi* of society's executive branch, and thus to correctional operations.

The goals of punishment also reflect the way in which a society is structured, as well as its needs and cultural values at different points in time. Shoham and Shavit (1995) argue that the goals of punishment can be viewed according to utilitarian goals of given societies at a given time. According to this approach, they argue, the purpose of punishing offenders is to benefit and protect society. They further differentiate between three main groups of goals that lay on a utilitarian scale that ranges between non-utilitarian, semi-utilitarian and highly utilitarian. The goals are laid out in Table 1.1.

Table 1.1 Goals of Punishment According to Utilitarianism within Society

Non-Utilitarian Goals	Semi-Utilitarian Goals	Highly Utilitarian Goals
Reconciliation (Restorative justice) Purification Atonement	Deterrence (specific & general) Reparation Treatment & Rehabilitation Prevention Incapacitation Banishment	Retribution/ Retaliation

Reconciliation

In highly cohesive societies, crimes were perceived as harmful to social balance and as contaminating social purity and harmony. Accordingly, social responses to deviant and criminal behavior were concerned with regaining this tranquility while restoring social harmony—that is, they pursued the practice of restorative justice. Such reconciliation is achieved by repairing the harm caused in collaboration with all members of the community who were directly harmed by the act. Under this aim, society holds a stake in the punishment and reintegration of the offender. As the first step in restoration, the offender needs to face his wrongdoing and acknowledge the damage done. Then that offender must make peace with members of his community in an effort to restore the balance that was disturbed. According to Braithwaite (1989), reconciliation by *reintegrative shaming* will reduce further criminality, as it presents the offender with the chance to regain status, while also building society's trust. In fact, such an approach focuses on rehabilitating both the community and its individuals, considering both to be victims. Supporters of this approach argue that the needs of the victims must not be ignored, since crime has a harmful effect, and justice requires that this harm be removed and minimized as much as possible.

Atonement

This non-utilitarian goal of punishment has roots in religious ideology, according to which a criminal offense is identified with sin. Consequently, the goal of punishment is to help the offenders/sinners to repent and atone for their sins. Such punishment, by definition, involves physical and mental hardship, as suffering is the only perceived means for making amends. The ideology of atonement governed the modern penitentiary of the 18th century. *Eastern State Penitentiary*, built in 1829 in Pennsylvania, was designed to serve this specific purpose of penitence. It was expected that inmates would reflect on their life of wrongdoing, make amends, and change their ways. Inmates were kept in isolation from one another and spent most of their day in their cells either working or studying the Bible. Eastern State Penitentiary operated on the *silent system*, which meant that inmates were prohibited from talking to one another. Such a practice increased the goal of atonement, and it was documented that many inmates in that prison developed some form of mental illness. This occurred because humans are typically social creatures who need interaction with other humans. Such extreme periods of isolation can cause considerable damage on the human psyche.

Deterrence

Building on the principles of rationality, this utilitarian goal of punishment is most desirable when it comes to evaluating sentencing policies and court intervention in correctional practices. According to Cesare Beccaria, who is considered the founder of *classical criminology* and a visionary of modern criminal justice philosophy, punishment should have celerity (that is, it should be swift), certainty, and severity (i.e., be proportional to the offense). By adhering to these three principles, Beccaria argued, individuals can make a rational calculation of pain versus gain, and thus should be responsible for their own consequences. Specifically, by knowing that upon committing an offense one will be caught and punished with no delay, people could make the rational decision of whether to violate the rules or adhere to the norm, to commit a crime or not. Using the three principles of celerity, certainty, and severity, offenders can be deterred specifically and generally. Thus the ultimate goal of punishment is to prevent future crimes by letting potential offenders know the consequences they will be held for, and as a result, reduce the likelihood of offending (Gibbons, 1992). Furthermore, *specific deterrence* is based on the premise that individuals will be deterred from committing future crimes if they experience the pains of a specific punishment. Only once individuals have paid the price of their wrongdoing can they rationally evaluate the advisability of committing another crime. By contrast, *general deterrence* is based on the logic that witnessing the pain of others is sufficient to scare individuals away from engaging in criminal activity. The logic is that those who witness the pain suffered by others who commit crimes will desire to avoid such pain and will refrain from criminal activity. Deterrence is also the foundation of modern criminal justice policy that aims to reduce crime rates and recidivism.

Reparation

Reparation is the act of paying off the damage caused by a crime, as a means of amending the wrongdoing, but it also has an element of punishment and suffering to it. Through the payment, some of the pains caused to the victim are believed to be alleviated, and the offender is also being punished for his or her wrongdoing. Shoam and Shavit (1995) identify three aspects of reparation and compensation:

1. Emotional reparation: This is the most basic form of granting satisfaction to the victim, in which the offender who caused the harm is forced to pay for the wrongdoing. Such emotional reparation serves to ease the need to avenge the crime. Under this form of reparation, the offender is forced to pay a sum that is considered to be equal to the damage caused, thus ease the victims emotional need to retaliate.

2. Direct reparation: The offender is allowed to better the damage caused to the victim. In direct reparation, the sum paid is not equal to the damage caused, and often will be simply symbolic, as a way of saying, essentially, "I am really sorry for what I did." By paying this sum, the offender is considered to have acknowledged wrongdoing while also acknowledging the suffering caused to the victim. Recent research on the role of victims in the sentencing stage recognizes the importance of this phase, as victims are often searching for a public affirmation of the wrong that they suffered (see Des-Rosiers, Feldthusen, & Hankivsky, 1998; Erez, 1999; Shoham, 2004; Shoham & Regev, 2008; Yanai, 2003). In fact, Shapland (1984) argues that victims are interested in the affirmation of damage caused by the criminal act more than they are concerned

with the actual monetary compensation. It is further argued that this form of reparation has an educational effect on the offender and on the relationships between the offender and the victim (Docker-Drysdale, 1953).

3. Creative reparation: This form of reparation is probably one of the most interesting developments of modern criminal justice sanctions. Under this form of reparation, the offender is required to acknowledge his or her criminal act not by paying the victim but by serving the community. The aim is to make the offender acknowledge the harm caused by his action, not just to the victim but to the entire society or community and its values. The offender is offered the opportunity to compensate the society by contributing to it. The aim is not to put an additional burden on the offender, nor does it aim to further punish him or her. The aim is to edify the offender about the damage caused by the wrongdoing, while directing him or her toward greater social responsibility and tightening ties to the community. This form of compensation is achieved through community service under community supervision (e.g., probation and parole). In fact, many criminal justice researchers believe this strategy to be a good substitute for short-term incarceration (Muiluvuori, 2001; Bouffard & Muftic, 2006; Killias, Aebi, & Ribeaud, 2000).

Reparation thus is a form of easing the victim's pain from the crime, and of educating and directing the offender to become a socially responsible member of society and the community while also making amends.

Treatment and Rehabilitation

Using a medical approach to dealing with offenders, this contemporary goal of punishment views offenders as ill individuals who need to be treated and rehabilitated. The basic assumption in this approach is that offenders are suffering from a variety of ills that cause them to deviate and commit crimes. Consequently, the aim of punishment should be to address such ills in an attempt to target the causes of the illness, and to enable offenders to be rehabilitated so that they will not recidivate. According to Fagin (2005: 337), "*rehabilitation* calls for criminal sanctions to 'cure' the offender of criminality." As in previous goals, treatment and rehabilitation are reactions to crime; however, it is hoped that by addressing the needs and risks of current offenders, future crimes will be prevented. Under this approach, convicted offenders are treated for their non-normative behavior by receiving psychological counseling, substance abuse treatment, and educational and vocational guidance, as well as pre-release consultation that will prepare them for life after incarceration. Although there is empirical evidence to support the effectiveness and efficiency of substance abuse programs (Gideon, Shoham, & Weisburd, 2010; Shoham, Gideon, Weisburd, and Vilner, 2006; Simpson, Wexler, & Inciardi, 1999; Welsh, 2011), educational and vocational programs (Bouffard, Mackenzie, & Hickman, 2000; Guerrero, 2011), many challenge the actual success of these programs in reducing recidivism and rehabilitating offenders. According to Braithwaite and Mugford (1994: 139), "[t]he specter of failure haunts modern criminology and penology. Deep down many feel what some say openly—that nothing works." Nevertheless, public support for correctional-based treatment and rehabilitation programs geared toward successful reintegration of offenders is gaining strength and has recently resulted in the approval of the Second Chance Act (see Gideon & Loveland, 2011). In fact, several studies that aimed to examine public support for reintegration services to released prisoners demonstrate consistent and high levels of support in the community, based on the belief that such services will grant a second chance to convicted offenders released after having served their sentences (Petersilia, 2017). For example, a poll of Oregon residents that was conducted by Sundt and colleagues found that about 90% of respondents supported Second Chance Act-related services such as housing assistance, education, job training, drug treatment, and mental health services for convicted offenders (Sundt, Cullen, Thielo, & Jonson, 2015). Similar high support was also found in an earlier study of New York residents, with 83.1% of respondents supporting the Second Chance Act (Gideon & Loveland, 2011).

Prevention, Incapacitation, and Banishment

Under these approaches to punishment, it is assumed that offenders cannot be treated or rehabilitated, nor can they be deterred. The only deterrence that may be achieved is *general deterrence*, through hard punishment that will remove and isolate the offender from society, and thus prevent the person from committing further crimes. It is assumed that such a practice will deter other potential offenders, who are assumed to be rational decision-makers. By incarcerating offenders, we hope to diminish the ability of offenders to commit further crimes, as they are being removed and isolated from society. This also acknowledges the fact that we do not know how to effectively deter and prevent crimes. Indeed, James Q. Wilson (1975) expressed skepticism about evidence that suggested that rehabilitative programs had any value. Consequently, he argued that the function of the corrections system should be to isolate and to punish, as there is not much hope for anything else. Accordingly, he argued that incarceration "is also frank admission that society really does not know how to do much else" (Wilson, 1975: 173). This same idea governed the older practice of banishment, which demanded that offenders be removed from society so that they will not be able to cause any more harm. However, unlike incarceration, banishment demands that those who are sentenced are expected never to return, and if they do, they face death. Incarceration/incapacitation and banishment are utilitarian by appealing to a cost-benefit calculation. These sanctions symbolize society's ability to control its subjects by fear of isolation, and it is due to this logic that incarceration has become the most prominent form of punishment in modern society. Incarceration is the most severe form of punishment, and according to Zimring, Hawkins, and Kamin (2001), people have a tendency to choose more severe punishments simply to express their hostility toward those who commit a crime. It is via this assumption that Zimring and his colleagues explain the massive incarceration rates that characterize the American prison system.

It is interesting to note that although treatment and rehabilitation are fundamentally different from incapacitation and banishment, they nonetheless share a similar concern with prevention. According to Victor Hassine (as cited in Johnason & Tabriz, 2011:73), "prison confines, punishes, and sometimes deters. It is neither designed nor inclined to foster, cure, or rehabilitate." However, those who support the treatment and rehabilitation of offenders argue that by addressing their offenders' needs and risks, future crime will be prevented. Successful rehabilitation and reintegration of offenders may also have a positive effect on communities that in turn expand the circle of normative behavior in decaying neighborhoods, and ultimately reduce crime. These practices can be seen as long-term prevention strategies, a kind of investment in social health. By contrast, incapacitation and banishment are concerned with prevention as more of a short-term goal, by taking away the offender's ability to commit crimes in the community. Supporters of this approach believe that incapacitated and banished offenders will be blocked from inflicting more harm for the time of their sentence, with the hopes that they will also be deterred from committing future crimes. Unfortunately, this is not a foolproof solution. There are cases, for example, of incarcerated gang members who continue to use violent methods inside the correctional setting against other inmates, and at times even order violent actions from the inside against specific members of rival gangs in the community outside prison.

In American society today, incapacitating and isolating offenders is done by incarceration, which is considered the harshest form of punishment, with the exception of the death penalty. Such punishment is implemented by correctional institutions. Seiter (2011) argues that the most traditional mission of corrections is "to implement court-prescribed sentences for criminal violators or to carry out the sentences of the court" (pp. 5–6). However, this is just a narrow definition, and many correctional practitioners will argue that the broader mission of corrections is also to protect society by providing 24/7 surveillance and control of offenders, which is a short-term goal defined by individual lengths of sentences. With that in mind, correctional administrators also acknowledge the importance of treatment and rehabilitation of incarcerated offenders as an integral part of their mission to protect society. These are long-term goals, in that they are designed to ensure successful reintegration, which in turn is hoped to increase public safety.

Retribution and Retaliation

Punishment is, in its most basic form, a normal human reaction that is based on vengeance, and as such is associated with cruelty (Darrow, 1922), which often requires the involvement of the legislature to mediate, soften, and offer forgiveness. These approaches to punishment argue that offenders should be punished because they deserve it, as they harmed another member of the society/community. This is the logic behind the "*just deserts*" principle, meaning they deserve that kind of justice. More than any other approach to punishment, this one is associated with the "get tough on crime" movements, and it calls for harsher mandatory sentencing. The rationale is to let offenders know that crime will not be tolerated and offenders will be punished according to the crime they committed. Under this philosophy, offenders are expected to consider the harm they imposed on others as their own punishment, as they will be exposed to the same harms. The *Code of Hammurabi* did just that, by publishing the exact "price" for each violation and crime. This ancient Babylonian code, established more than 4,000 years ago by King Hammurabi, had 282 laws that regulated civil and criminal behavior. These laws were carved in stone and erected in a public place for all to see, read, and follow. Each law had a clear punishment for its violation, and thus it was expected that people acting in a rational manner would be deterred from violating the laws, and if they were to violate one, they would know what would be coming to them. Accordingly, the *Code of Hammurabi*, to which contemporary laws are very similar, operates on the premise of literal accountability, and in this way, retribution and retaliation are rendered as a "price list" to those who choose to violate the laws. Under these approaches, offenders carry the full responsibility of their wrongdoing by experiencing the consequences. It is assumed that by punishing according to the crime, offenders will develop accountability as they weigh their actions according to a known consequence. Originally evolved from the need of victims to avenge their attacker, such approaches serve two aims: make the offender experience the actions of his or her wrongdoing, while also providing the offender with a sense of the "price" that he or she will have to pay for wrongdoing. Such a known-in-advance "price" was assumed to address rational decision-making, as presented in the principles of the *Classical* and *Neoclassical School* of thought (as in the early works of Cesare Beccaria and Jeremy Bentham during the 18th century), and thus makes it highly utilitarian, in that offenders are assumed to calculate the utility of their wrongdoing in terms of the consequences of their actions. Nowadays, incarceration, rather than a literal cash "price," has become the most visible form of retribution and punishment, so that individuals who are convicted of a crime are punished with jail and prison terms, with about 2.3 million individuals currently under the supervision of correctional institutions. It is believed that by isolating the offender from society for a defined period of time, society takes vengeance on the offender and his crimes. According to Branham and Hamden (2005), retribution in correspondence with the principle of "just deserts" will place limits on sentence lengths, as it provides an important checks against tyranny. Under the rationale of retribution, only those who deserved to be punished, are being punished.

Each goal of punishment represents a different level of utilitarianism, and each aims to serve a specific social and cultural purpose. However, when punishing, we need to consider the strength of the punishment and its potential effect on the other goals of punishment. Duffee (1985) noted that sometimes achieving one goal of punishment may undermine another goal that may be equally important. May and Wood (2010) explained this by discussing the increase in mandatory incarceration sentences that also became harsher and longer. They argue that such punishments are retributive in nature; however, they undermine the utilitarian goals of deterrence and rehabilitation as offenders who spent longer terms in prison become less resistant and deterred by a prison sentence. No matter what the goals of punishment are, the fact remains that the idea of punishment originated in the feeling of resentment, hatred, and vengeance (Darrow, 1922). With that in mind, Darrow (1922:15) also argued:

> "Neither the purpose nor the effect of punishment has ever been definitely agreed upon, even by its most strenuous advocates. So long as punishment persists it will be a subject of discussion and dispute."

Although this was written almost 90 years ago, Darrow's words still remain relevant to today's discussion of the goals of punishment and the way in which they pertain to prisoners' rights. We cannot ignore the true nature of punishment, but given the massive scale of incarceration today, we rarely seem to have room to ask, what is the real goal of punishment? And, what do we, as a society, achieve by incarcerating masses of people?

Conclusion

Incarceration rates in the United States have quadrupled in the last 30 years (Gideon, 2011), leaving us with the highest rate of incarceration in the industrialized world. According to May and Wood (2010), America incarcerates about one quarter of the world's prisoners. In fact, the Bureau of Justice Statistics (2008) indicated that on June 30, 2007, there were 2,299,116 prisoners in federal, state, and local jails, an increase of 1.8% from year-end 2006. On December 2008 that number increased to a staggering 2.4 million incarcerated people, with another 5.1 million under community supervision, both parole and probation (Bureau of Justice Statistics, 2010). These data translate to a grim reality: one in every 100 adults in America is incarcerated, and, grimmer still, 1 in 31 American adults are under correctional supervision and control (Gideon, 2011; May & Wood, 2010). At yearend 2015, an estimated 6,741,400 persons were supervised by U.S. adult correctional systems. This reflects a decrease in the rate of incarceration to 1 in 37 American Adults under correctional supervision. The incarcerated population at yearend 2015 was at its lowest since 2004, and measured at 2,136,600 people in federal, state and local jails. Still these are far higher rates compared to most western societies. (Bureau of Justice Statistics, 2016: Published Dec. 31st 2016: available at: https://www.bjs.gov/index.cfm?ty=pbdetail&iid=5870). With such dismal rates of incarceration in recent decades comes an increased responsibility to evaluate our punitive practices, and with that an increased responsibility on the part of the legal system to make sure that punishments are administered according to constitutional and legal guidelines. It is within this context that we seek to examine current correctional practices and the law, while considering the goals of punishment that we have previously discussed. Such an examination is important as it reflects the perception of fairness in punishment as perceived by the offender. Sherman (1993) related this to what he called "*defiance theory*," according to which punishments that are perceived as unjust, unfair, excessive, and in the case of this discussion, violations of basic rights, can backfire, so that offenders become more defiant and rebellious, which in turn increases future criminal behavior.

It is within this context that a discussion of correctional management and law, as its guide, becomes crucial to our understanding of the different rulings and judicial intervention in correctional practices, and the management of incarcerated and supervised offenders. However, our examination cannot ignore court rulings that have strengthened the hands of correctional officials, as they are the ones who understand best how these institutions operate, and are thus most able to ensure institutional security and meet correctional goals. Further, we must consider in our discussion how the perceived goals of punishment and society's views of the crime problem have shifted, and how this has affected the treatment of offenders. Being aware of these changes over time is pivotal to guiding any judicial intervention in correctional management, as they reflect changes not only in penological philosophy but also, and maybe more importantly, in social and political attitudes toward such penological ideologies.

Discussion Questions

1. Discuss the goals of punishment in regard to their utilitarian aim.

2. What is the common goal of deterrence and rehabilitation? Discuss each of the goals while focusing on their expected final outcome.

3. What is the underlying logic that guides prevention, incapacitation, and banishment? Define each of these goals, and discuss how they relate to the utilitarian approach.

4. Discuss the difference between non-utilitarian goals of punishment and highly utilitarian goals of punishment. In what ways do you think such penological approaches were affected by the understanding of what causes deviant and criminal behavior?

5. In your opinion, how does judicial interference in correctional management relate to penological ideologies? Discuss in the context of the different penological goals and their developmental stages.

6. How does the Thirteenth Amendment to the United State Constitution help us understand the status of many convicted offenders? Discuss the penological ideology that this amendment represents.

7. Read more about the Second Chance Act, and discuss it in lieu of the penological goal of rehabilitation. How supportive is the public of such legislation, and how do you think this will affect future judicial intervention, if at all?

Chapter 2

Historical Account of Correctional Law

The courts' involvement in correctional practices, conditions of incarceration, and prisoner matters is an important indicator of sentencing policies and the way in which they have affected community supervision and the nation's prison population. One cannot fully understand correctional law and court involvement without carefully examining trends in incarceration, as these correspond to the nation's idea of "getting tough" on crime, and more punitive approaches as reactions to criminal behavior. These policies set the tone for what goals must be achieved when dealing with convicted offenders, and thus what actual sentences should be imposed, as discussed in the previous chapter, in order to maximize their utility. It is within this context that we must understand and view the development of the American correctional system and the laws that govern its operations, as these laws reflect the various punitive ideologies for dealing with offenders, and their corresponding judicial intervention in correctional management.

The Hands-Off Era (Prior to the 1970s)

In an examination of the history of punishments, it becomes clear that incarceration was not society's initial response and form of punishment. In fact, when looking at the more common forms of punishing offenders, one can see that in cases where the culprit was stripped of his or her rights, this was done in order to avenge and deter. Offenders were ridiculed, flogged and whipped, dunked in rivers or lakes, and at times even branded or mutilated. These forms of punishment sent the message that once a person harms the community, he or she is no longer protected by it, and as a result, loses his or her right to protection from the state. Consider, for example, public ridicule, in which an offender is placed in a public location for all to see and punish. Offenders were stripped of their rights so that law-abiding citizens could be secure in their own persons, while offenders were treated as less than human by their community.

Not surprisingly, the Thirteenth Amendment, ratified on December 6, 1865, states, "Neither slavery nor involuntary servitude, except as a punishment for crime whereof the party shall have been duly convicted, shall exist within the United States, or any place subject to their jurisdiction" (Section 1). The language of this amendment suggests that convicted offenders are no longer free men, and can be treated like slaves, with no rights. This may seem logical to many who believe that after a person betrays the trust of society and his or her community by committing a crime against its members, he or she no longer has rights, and thus should not be treated equally and enjoy the protections of the same society whose peace that criminal offender violated. Protection and equilibrium under the law and the Bill of Rights can thus not be applicable to those convicted of a crime, as they themselves violated such rights. Consequently, once convicted of a crime, that offender forfeits his liberty and for the time of his sentence he becomes the slave of the state (Branham & Hamden, 2005). Branham and Hamden also argue that once convicted and sentenced, the offender becomes *civiliter mortuus* and all his or her possessions may be treated as if he or she was dead. This goes back to the perception of the state as the victim in *Leges Henrici,* written as early as 1116. King Henry I issued these laws to identify certain offenses as a violation of the "King's peace." Those found guilty of such acts were considered enemies of the kingdom, or state, and thus this shifted the responsibility for dealing with them from the victim to the state, which assumed the responsibility of apprehending, prosecuting, and punishing the offender (Fagin, 2005).

It is around this pivotal issue, of whether convicted offenders are and should be entitled to some protections and rights, that the current book discusses different correctional practices and the way in which they relate to legislation, the Constitution, and Supreme Court rulings.

Prisons emerged as the more visible form of punishment in the late 1700s, as part of a reform movement that called for easing the harsh and sometimes cruel capital punishments that were previously described. Prisons as we know them today were called *penitentiaries* and were designed to encourage offenders to express penitence and seek God's forgiveness for their sins. It is not surprising that early penitentiaries followed the system of silence, solitary confinement, and reading of the Bible (the only book allowed in each cell). In that regard, early prisons operated without any judicial intervention. Penitentiaries were designed for repentance, and executed punishment. This was the essence of the "hands-off" doctrine that almost completely disregarded constitutional rights of convicted offenders, leaving the management of penitentiaries to the sole expertise and ideology of its administrators who were believed to be professionals in their field. However, the "hands-off" approach was about to take a turn with the rise of some civil-rights movements emerged in the late 1960s. The ideas of such movements began to penetrate the thick walls of prisons pointing to the poor and unconstitutional conditions inside these facilities. The end of the 1960s and early 1970s were characterized by an increase in crime rates which resulted in President Johnson's "War on Crime." As a result of the war on crime, increase in incarceration rates in the 1970s exacerbated the already dire conditions of prisons which led to prisoners' riots and increased public attention to what was going inside prisons and behind the walls. Such events further drew the attention of the courts.

Shifting Judicial Ideology in the Civil-Rights Era

Looking at incarceration rates and the growing prison population in the United States, West and Sabol (2008) noted a steep increase in incarcerated people during the first half of the 1970s, around the same time that the prisoners' rights movement emerged. Neubauer and Fradella (2011:383) argue that the "rapid increase in the size of the prison population occurred during the same time that federal courts began to demand improvements in prison conditions...." The reliance on incarceration as punishment still dominates our penological practices as the most visible form of punishment (although fines and probation tend to be more common). The increase in prison population resulted in overcrowded facilities that, along with strained budgets, magnified the inhumane conditions of confinement; conditions worsened with drained local and federal governmental budgets. The harsh conditions in many of the country's prisons resulted in disturbances and violent riots, the best known example being the 1971 uprising in Attica state prison in New York, in which 43 people were killed and many more injured. The media covered the uprising in detail, with broadcasts on national television, revealing widely for the first time the general distress of inmates and correctional staff in the face of overcrowding. Millions of Americans were exposed to the inhumanity that was widespread in the American correctional system, and this in turn had ramifications for how lawyers and judges viewed the nation's prisons as well. Some even say that the Attica riot is one of the cornerstones of the prison rights movement that emerged during the 1970s (Adler, Mueller, & Laufer, 2006; Anderson et al., 2010).

However, this was not the only reason for the increased interest of the courts in what was going on inside correctional facilities. Throughout the 1960s and into the 1970s, the social and political climate had been in turmoil. The civil rights movement, the war in Vietnam and antiwar protesters, riots in many minority neighborhoods, and the end of state-sponsored school segregation all came together to enable a climate of protest, which empowered inmates to be more outspoken and demand that their constitutional rights be protected. Additionally, during the public upheaval across America, antigovernment protesters were arrested and introduced into the prison system. They brought in with them a philosophy of penal reform and human dignity, while fighting against institutional oppression and in favor of the rights guaranteed by the constitution (Anderson, Mangles, & Dyson, 2010). Finally, the sudden interest in radical social movements from outside prisons inspired many attorneys, and people who eventually became attorneys, to take up the plight of society's disadvantaged peoples. As a result, there were many attorneys in this era who wanted to defend the civil liberties of incarcerated offenders. These circumstances enabled prisoners to file more lawsuits that were better prepared and adhered to court procedures, thus responding to an earlier concern by the courts about processing *pro se* complaints by inmates who did not have any legal training or knowledge of the law and related procedures. Due to the wave of prison litigation during the era of the civil rights movement of the 1960s and 1970s, prisons have changed in the decades that followed. While certainly a great many prisoners slip through the cracks, prisoners today overall are less isolated than prisoners in previous generations. As a result, inmates bring with them a lot from the outside into what used to be closed penal institutions. As more of the free world is being imported to the prison via media and press, so does prison become more transparent to the outside — most vividly in the case of the Attica riot. According to Cullen, Agnew and Wilcox (2014: 284) such incidents — as the Attica riot along with the Vietnam war, college student protests and the Watergate scandal — further signaled that a belief in a just society, and faith in the criminal justice system, "… had been replaced by a painful realization that inequality was deeply entrenched and that those in power wished to reinforce, not change the status quo." Around the same time, President Lyndon Johnson appointed Thurgood Marshall to be the first African-American Justice to the United States Supreme Court. Thurgood Marshall was known to be a strong advocate of civil rights. Before his nomination to the US Supreme Court, he argued the case *Brown v. Board of Education* in front of the US Supreme Court. Such an appointment came at the right time and in an attempt to reduce and control racial tensions. Indeed, President Johnson stated (regarding the nomination) "the right thing to do, the right time to do it, the right man and the right place." Hence, it is not surprising that Justice Marshall's nomination and appointment during a time of civil unrest and turmoil had an effect not just on the broader society but also on judicial involvement in correctional matters.

As the prison riots and the general unrest of the civil-rights era helped expose problems in prisons, entities emerged to address conditions of confinement and prisoners' rights under the Constitution, and attempted to change the behavior of prison officials and the justice system. For the first time, the courts took concerted interest in correctional issues. This shift in judicial intervention can be seen through the lens of *Interest Group Theory*, as proposed by Goode and Ben-Yehuda (2009). They suggest that whenever a public interest arises and forms an interest group, policy tends to change to reflect the demands of the group. Fundamentally, the theory holds, political change is enabled by competing groups and lobbies with special interests. Interest groups are key to change due to their efforts, Goode and Ben-Yehuda (2009: 67) say, but also because "once attention is focused on a particular issue by interest groups, broad sectors of the public … may become seized by its urgency, appropriating the issue for its own purposes." Thus, it is possible that the increase in attention to legal issues of incarcerated inmates stems not only from the efforts of prisoners and civil-rights activists but also from its own lobby within the criminal justice system, in particular the courts and prison administration, as a reaction to the growing number of people sentenced to prison. This, Goode and Ben-Yehuda say, is a natural part of the interest-group process, in which the system tries to regulate itself by inviting more "checks and balances" to correct the collapsing practices of the time. After all, someone is expected to benefit from such legal involvement and lawsuits filed against malpractice. Goode and Ben-Yehuda (2009: 67) ask:

The central question asked by the interest-group model is: *cui bono*? For whose benefit is it? Who profits? Who wins out if a given issue is recognized as threatening to the society?

This approach may be viewed as self-serving and somewhat cynical, but it dovetails with Becker (1963) and his analysis of the civil-rights movement. He characterizes the cause's major actors as "moral entrepreneurs" who launched crusades that also brought benefits to them. In the context of prisoner legislation and attempts and reform, then, it is important to remember that it may be more than just offenders who potentially benefit from these developments and court interest in correctional practices.

This model is important to our understanding of the shift in judicial intervention in correctional administration and as such, is highly relevant in the last three decades, when prison populations have "quadrupled, leaving us with the highest rate of incarceration in the industrialized world" (Gideon, 2011: 384–85). More and more we have heard of overcrowded prisons and the inhumane conditions under which inmates and correctional staff are required to operate. This information has also reached the attentive ears of many civil-right activists and resulted in the rejuvenation of interest groups that made it their goal to shift or develop policies to improve conditions of confinement and grant inmates more rights, while reducing jail and prison overcrowding. Members of the media, religious groups, educational organizations, and civil-rights activists have all taken an interest in confinement-related issues and have been alerting legislators to what goes on inside the nation's correctional facilities via appeals to the courts. The activity of these groups has driven a series of political and cultural adaptations that have fundamentally changed how governments and citizens think and act in relation to crime. Such a trend has also appeared in the United Kingdom (Garland, 2002).

In the 1970s, David Garland (2001) noted, trends took a correctionalist direction, meaning the ideology of rehabilitation, individualized treatment, and more criminological research was gaining strength. Simply locking offenders behind bars without addressing their needs was, in this thinking, a practice that must be revised. Thus, a new approach, dubbed *penal welfare*, became well established and contributed to dynamic and progressive change, which made its way through traditional correctional practices. Specifically, the penal welfare structure combined a liberal legalistic approach to the implementation of due process rights and proportionate punishment with a correctionalist commitment to rehabilitation, while tapping criminological expertise. In other words, as a result of interest groups' effects on how people view correctional practices, a shift in punitive approach emerged to focus on prisoners' rights and how to positively motivate them in ways that would enable them to gain opportunities for advancement within the criminal justice system. This approach aimed to reduce institutional disruptions while addressing the rights and needs of those individuals confined to them.

The collective turmoil of the civil-rights era crystallized into a driving force that gave the courts a reason to abandon the "hands-off" doctrine of not involving themselves in correctional affairs. As they directed more attention to the incarcerated pop-

**Figure 2.1 The Penological Balance between Security Needs and
Inmates' Constitutional Rights**

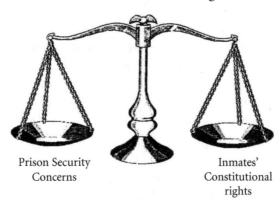

Prison Security
Concerns

Inmates'
Constitutional
rights

ulation, the courts began to resolve inmate-related disputes by examining the interests of each party to the dispute, and how such interests might affect the legitimate concerns that relate to the safety of the administration, guards, inmates, and the general public, as illustrated in Figure 2.1.

Another consideration is the potential negative effects of court decisions on prison and jail staff, as well as on other prisoners. It is important to note that although prisoners are entitled to their constitutional rights and the rights of due process—under the Fourth, Fifth, and Fourteenth Amendments—not all rights may be suitable to the management of correctional institutions, which need to achieve very specific penological goals, as discussed in the previous chapter. What guides the courts in their decisions are the best interests of prison officials and the policies created to maintain those interests. Often, the courts rule that prison officials are empowered to withhold and limit some rights in service to a much bigger necessity, which is maintaining prisoner and staff safety and general order inside the facility. Such interests may also have a farther-reaching effect on public safety. With that in mind, another question that guides the courts is, what steps can be taken to accommodate special needs, and are such steps within reason? Consequently, the model of the simple scale, presented above, cannot in fact provide an accurate illustration of the balance between constitutional and legal rights of incarcerated offenders, and the needs of the correctional administration, as the process of weighing interests is much more complex, balancing penological needs, security concerns, and the welfare of all parties involved. Given this complexity, in the end the scale often tilts in favor of correctional administrators, as they best understand how to run their facility.

With increasing crime rates, the subsequent war on crime and the war on drugs, and the somewhat misunderstood Martinson report of 1974 (which concluded, notoriously, that "nothing works" in rehabilitation), a major shift occurred in correctional thinking and practices later in the 1970s. The penal welfare movement of the 1960s through the early 1970s lost ground, and sentencing practices were adjusted to reflect this change in climate. More specifically, a general belief in the new era was that offenders need to be locked up for longer periods of time. However, some believed that by doing so, society was admitting that it had no other solutions (Wilson, 1975). This in turn caused a shift in inmates' rights, dictated in part through the Supreme Court's intervention in the treatment of convicted offenders behind prison walls. Meanwhile, the public's fear of crime during the late 1970s fueled political campaigns that were more punitive and less conducive to the ideas of corrections and rehabilitation. This deterred the courts from interfering with the management of correctional facilities, leaving correctional decisions to those trained practitioners. Consequently, it can be argued that once again, the government decided not to get involved with the management of convicted offenders and thus departed from the more liberal approach of correctionalism, and in so doing, put an end to the decade-long era of penal welfare, with its focus on rehabilitation and the rights and needs of inmates (Garland, 2001).

Nonetheless, the awareness that had emerged during the civil rights movement, as well as all the conditions in American prisons that had been exposed, had forced the courts to relax their approach somewhat, and the doors to inmates' litigation had been opened. However, while official policy remained in its preliminary approach of hands-off, the civil-rights movement of the 1960s and early 1970s had sparked a movement in prisons as well. Such movement evolved into a new era by the mid-1970s, which symbolized the beginning of a new approach, known as the "hands-on era."

The Hands-On Era (1970–80)

The idea that prisoners have rights was not entirely new. The notion that we incarcerate offenders but need to confine them in humane and cruelty-free conditions troubled some courts in the early 1960s, although such opinions and approaches were in the minority. The deadly 1971 riot in Attica Correctional Facility in New York was a turning point, alerting the public to the dreadful conditions in the nation's prisons. After the riots, more young civil-rights lawyers felt empowered to act on behalf of inmates. As a result, more lawsuits were filed on behalf of prisoners challenging their conditions of confinement, discrimination on the basis of religion and race, and further challenging common correctional practices used by prison administrators. These lawyers who joined the bandwagon of prisoner litigation could be called the "moral entrepreneurs" of the cause, as they served themselves while also serving those interest groups that aimed to challenge the traditional administrative approach of correctional institutions.

At the same time, prisoners became more vocal and at times even militant in their demand for better prison conditions and recognition of their constitutional rights. In this way, prison was a kind of microcosm of society, as the prisoners were aware of the social changes and protests outside, such as the ongoing protests against the Vietnam War and, of course, the civil-rights activism and school desegregation that had come in the previous decade. Together, activist lawyers and socially aware prisoners began filing more and more lawsuits for the vindication of inmates' constitutional rights. In the process, the courts were exposed to more constitutional violations. A landmark decision in this process, perhaps the peak of the hands-on movement, was *James v. Wallace* (1974), in which a federal district court ruled that the Alabama prison system violated prisoners' Eight and Fourteenth Amendment rights. The Alabama prison system was ordered to amend these wrongs.

Since then, the courts have established inmates' rights to be protected by the Constitution and the courts have demonstrated that they will uphold these rights. Yet, as the courts established in this hands-on era, for an inmate's petition to the courts to be successful, the plaintiff must prove *deliberate indifference* by correctional authorities, meaning that an inmate suffered intentional and deliberate discriminatory treatment by correctional staff. The courts also continued to balance inmates' constitutional rights with the need to maintain a safe and secure environment for the administrators, staff, and other inmates, as well as to maintain public health, in particular when dealing with inmates infected with contagious diseases, such as tuberculosis and HIV/AIDS. The "hands-on" period, which was most active for about a decade, set notable legal precedents, but it also resulted in an increase in prisoners' petitions to federal courts, petitions that were perceived by many as a way of letting bored inmates abuse the system. In fact, many would argue that the majority of prisoner litigation during this period was frivolous. It was this perceived abuse, coupled with the fear of crime in the general public, that caused yet another swing in the judicial approach to correctional management.

Shifting Back to a Hands-Off Policy

The decade following the "hands-on" era was characterized by the growing recognition from governmental agencies and vocal public interest groups in the legitimacy and utility of the right of prisoners to challenge the conditions of their confinement. According to Minor and Parson (2015), this recognition occurred in three temporal stages:

1. Some organizations began to call for a fair and effective grievance procedure;

2. Certain organizations engaged in research and developed models for grievance procedure; and

3. Other organizations, such as the American Correctional Association and the American Bar Association, subsequently adopted and disseminated the grievance model procedures to be followed.

These stages were important for establishing the grievance processes that are now in use. Additionally, the legislative branch shaped the evolution of correctional grievance even further when the U.S. Congress passed the Civil Rights of Institutionalized Persons Act (CRIPA) in 1980, in response to multiple violations of prisoners' constitutional rights. CRIPA authorized the justice department to oversee state and local institutions housing various populations, while establishing minimum standards for institutional grievance procedures and processes by which state and local authorities can submit procedures for federal certification.

The "hands-on" period came to a final end during the second half of the 1990s, when President Bill Clinton signed the Prisoners Litigation Reform Act (PLRA) in 1996. This act restricted prisoners from petitioning federal courts directly and required petitioners to first exhaust all options established in their institutions and at the state level. Some see the PLRA as an attempt to shift discretionary powers and professional judgment back to prison administrators and state agencies and, as such, a shift back to the "hands-off" doctrine, thus making it more difficult for prisoners to access the federal courts. The PLRA will be discussed at length in a later chapter (Chapter 11) that examines the access to federal courts. For now, we can simply say that the PLRA has dramatically increased the importance of internal mechanisms of grievances, in an effort to prevent prisoner litigation from overwhelming the courts. Although grievance mechanisms were in place in most correctional settings in America as far back as the early 1980s, the need to anchor these procedures in actual legislation resulted precisely from the politicization, militancy, and unrest of the hands-on period, as more and more (some say too many) prisoners availed themselves of the right to petition the courts, while the courts increasingly intervened in correctional matters. Thus, both CRIPA and PLRA introduced a revamped mechanism of checks and balances in which correctional institutions and states are the first to examine and address prisoner grievances.

The following chapters will examine how the courts handled various cases claiming violation of constitutional rights (the Fourth and Fourteenth Amendments, for the most part) and of Section 1983, the primary means of enforcing all constitutional rights. Section 1983 states:

> Every person who, under the color of any statute, ordinance, regulation, custom, or usage, of any State or Territory or the District of Columbia, subjects, or causes to be subjected, any citizen of the United States, or other person within the jurisdiction thereof to the deprivation of any rights, privileges, or immunities secured by the Constitution and laws, shall be liable to the party injured in an action at law, suit in equity, or other proper proceeding for redress....

The aim of this legislation was to provide a means for individuals and states to enforce, in both federal and state courts, the provisions of the Fourteenth Amendment. More specifically, many prisoners use Section 1983 to hold individual prison officials and staff directly liable for the conditions of confinement and for what inmates perceive as inadequate treatment and violations of their civil rights. This is also important to our understanding of many cases in which a prisoner files suit against a specific individual employed by the state as a correctional professional, usually the facility's warden or correctional commissionaire. More important, such regulations also place the employing government (usually the state) as liable for any redress that may be found as a result of the trial. Further, Section 1983 provides a much broader context in which violation of constitutional rights, in particular the Bill of Rights, was commissioned under the auspices of the government, and thus challenges social treaties in which the state is expected to protect its citizens. This has a much broader philosophical context of the right of governments to punish offenders while at the same time having the responsibility to protect their safety and well-being.

Conclusion

A shift in the social and political climate in the 1960s brought problems in correctional settings to the attention of the public. Prior to that, the courts had distanced themselves from correctional practices and practitioners, permitting correctional professionals to manage their facilities the best way they knew how. In their decisions, the courts signaled to correctional managers that they enjoyed the public trust in their abilities and professionalism. However, the increasing unrest of the public in conjunction with the civil-rights movement, the war in Vietnam and rising racial tensions, penetrated the isolation of prisoners from the outside world and introduced a new era of civil rights and engagement that led to violent prison riots, such as the one in Attica, New York. Footage of the riot was shown on television, and the incident received major national news coverage, which further fueled the movement for civil and human rights for the incarcerated. As a result, and in compliance with the overall social mode of the era, more attention was directed to conditions of confinement, prisoners' rights, and how prisons were managed and who managed them. Lawyers and judges who took an interest in civil rights began to focus more on these issues and brought prisoner litigation to the judicial spotlight, thus welcoming in the "hands-on era" in which the justice system and courts specifically were more involved with prisoners' status. However, after almost three decades of increased judicial involvement in correctional management, the courts had seen an influx of litigation from prisoners, much of which was frivolous, and this overburdened the system. As a result, a decision was made to allow prisoners to resolve their grievances within the context of the correctional institutions in which they are confined. Two pieces of legislation, CRIPA and PRLA, made it more difficult for prisoners to file suit against correctional employees and managers. This set the tone back to a "hands-off" approach, allowing prisoners to file grievance in state and federal courts only as a last resort.

Discussion Questions

1. Discuss the effects of the political climate on the judicial approach to correctional matters, and how this changed the way the courts intervened in correctional issues.

2. How can one characterize the years prior to the Attica prison riots in terms of judicial intervention? Discuss the potential views of justices that may have reflected this approach to prisoner litigation.

3. Find the language and definition of Section 1983, and discuss its importance in bringing suit against state and federal correctional employees. What effect did Section 1983 have on prisoners' access to the courts?

4. Discuss the importance of the Fourth and Fourteenth Amendments in regard to prisoner litigation. What are the main rights that appear in these amendments that make them helpful for prisoners challenging correctional practices and conditions, if any?

5. What factors led to the passage of the Civil Rights of Institutionalized Persons Act (CRIPA)? What effect did CRIPA have on the prisoners' access to the courts?

6. What factors led to the passage of the Prisoners Litigation Reform Act (PLRA)? What effect did PLRA have on prisoners' access to the courts?

7. Discuss the effects of CRIPA and PLRA on the shift in judicial intervention in prisoners' grievances.

List of Cases Cited

James v. Wallace, 1974. 382 F. Supp. 1177.

Chapter 3

The Administration of Probation and Parole

While jails and prisons are the more visible forms of punishment, many more convicted offenders serve their sentences in the community. This form of punishment is usually referred to as community supervision, with the most salient category being probation. Yet, parole, in which a prisoner is released in the community in lieu of remaining in prison, is also a form of community supervision, and it can be granted by correctional officials and early release boards, known as parole boards. Compared with prison, community supervision can seem like a "light" form of punishment, but in fact offenders lose significant rights while under supervision, and in some cases are not subject to the normal standards of due process. Moreover, the payment of fines or restitution may play a major condition of the imposed sentence. Accordingly, some will argue that under these conditions, parole and probation also serve the goals of restitution. And because offenders are living and visible in the community, their punishment can serve as deterrence both for themselves and for others.

The administrative structure of community supervision, in the form of both probation and parole, varies widely from state to state, and in some states, probation and parole are combined. There are state-administered probation systems and locally administered systems. For example, in New York, probation is locally administered under the general supervision of the state. This has some important judicial implications that relate to the legislation of that state, as probation is operating under different statutory frameworks. Further, comparisons across states and jurisdictions raise questions about the great variations in measures that characterize probation operations (Cushman & Sechrest, 1992) and how such variations affect modes of administration and operational management that makes them conducive to litigation and judicial intervention.

While the variations in structure and administrative operations of these agencies may be confusing to some, the terms are fairly consistent. *Probation* is a sentence requiring offenders to serve a period of correctional supervision in the community in lieu of incarceration (MacKenzie, 2011); essentially, it is the suspension of imprisonment, in which the judge often sentences the defendant to imprisonment but suspends the sentence in favor of community supervision, in order to minimize the potential harm that may be associated with removal from society and the family. The term "probation" was coined by *John Augustus*, who is considered the founding father of probation. The term comes from the Latin word *probare*, which means to test or to prove; thus, these elements guided community supervision through the years, testing and proving that offenders can remain in society as productive members. *Parole*, on the other hand, is a period of conditional supervised release in the community following a prison term. It includes parolees released through discretionary or mandatory supervised release from prison, those released through other types of post-custody conditional supervision, and those sentenced to a term of supervised release. Parole is considered an early release for the sake of rehabilitation and reintegration. It is usually granted to those offenders who demonstrate good behavior and make successful attempts at bettering themselves; it normally converts imprisonment time for those serving more than two-thirds of their sentence.

More so, probation is one of the most commonly imposed criminal sanctions (Branham, 2013). According to a report by Kaeble, Maruschak, and Bonczar (2015), at year-end 2014 there were 3,864,100 adult offenders serving time in the community under probation supervision. While probation supervision has experienced some decline in recent years (at year-end the number of offenders found under probation supervision was slightly lower than that found at year-end 2014, and was 3,789,800), early release on parole increased to an estimated 856,900, at year-end 2014 (additional increase was observed at year-end 2015, with 870,500 people under parole supervision). Such numbers add up to 4,708,100 adults serving their sentence in the community. These numbers are a clear indication that there are more convicted offenders in the community than are currently imprisoned in this nation's correctional facilities (estimated at about 2.2 to 2.3 million). Accordingly, it is of great importance and relevance to the discussion of laws and penological ideology that these two practices be examined. Accordingly, this chapter will aim to examine the administration of both probation and parole to better understand judicial intervention and legal issues that involve and revolve around the administration of community supervision.

Probation

As mentioned earlier, probation in its most basic definition is a suspension of an imprisonment sentence. When an offender is convicted of a crime and sentenced to serve his or her punishment in the community under probation supervision, a judge, taking recommendations made by a probation officer after he or she has completed a presentence investigation, will decide any conditions that a probation must abide by or fulfill. Often, judges will allow probation officers to set other conditions as deemed proper, and a probationer is required to abide by these additional conditions. which can include, for instance, abstinence from alcohol, compliance with curfew, employment, avoiding association with known criminals, etc. If the probationer violates any of these conditions, the terms of probation may become more restrictive (e.g., *intensive supervision*) or it may result in a complete revocation of probation, resulting in imprisoning the offender. According to Branham (2013: 122), "probation is not a monolithic sanction." Probation sentences may vary tremendously in their scope, conditions, and limitations imposed on the convicted offender. Many times, probation supervision requires only minimal/symbolic supervision, where the offender is required to meet with the probation officer once a month, or talk with the officer once a week over the telephone. Even less restrictive is the development in which offenders can fulfill their supervision-contact requirement by reporting to an automated kiosk report center, similar to an ATM—a response to an overcrowded and overburdened community supervision system (Hicks, 1995; Jannetta & Halberstadt, 2011). However, for those probationers who require *intensive supervision*, greater restrictions and more appearances before a probation officer may be required. Specifically, those sentenced to intensive supervision may be required to meet with their probation officer several times each week, and these probationers may further be subjected to unannounced home and workplace visits that may include random searches and/or compliance with urinalysis testing for drug use.

Because intensive supervision is designed to address the risk and needs of certain high-risk offenders and in particular those who suffer from substance abuse and mental illness, it may also include active reporting and participating in relevant treatment. Contrary to what many people may think, offenders sentenced to probation are not just those convicted of minor legal infractions, misdemeanors, and the like. In fact, the probation population includes many offenders who have been convicted of felonies and even sexual assault (Cushman & Sechrest, 1992; Siegal & Bartollas, 2016). According to Kaeble, Maruschak, and Bonczar (2015), 56% of offenders on probation were serving their sentence for a felony, with 42% of probationers serving a sentence for a misdemeanor. Considering this, it is not surprising that only 35% of the total probation population complete their sentence and exit from their probation status without any major infraction or difficulty.

While probation is considered by many as a "slap on the wrist" that does not punish but allows offenders to get off free, in actuality probation is an alternative sanction that carries with it varying degrees of restraints on liberty (Cripe, Pearlman, & Kosiak, 2013). Courts that sentence offenders to probation supervision usually enjoy very broad discretion regarding the conditions by which each offender must abide. However, the conditions judges set must follow some penological rationale that demonstrates the benefit of the sentence, and argues that the conditions reasonably relate to the crime committed. However, such conditions cannot violate constitutional rights. Examining seven years of studies completed by the National Association of Criminal Justice Planners (NACJP), Cushman and Sechrest (1992) argued that differences in the statutory frameworks among the states clearly account for some of the penological variation as it applies to sentencing offenders to probation. For example, they found that courts in states with determinate sentencing (that is, with no parole board) tend to use probation much more frequently than courts in states with indeterminate sentencing (with a parole apparatus). California, a determinate sentencing state, and its counties sentence offenders to probation in the range of 60% of cases, while states such as New York, an indeterminate sentencing state, and its counties sentence much lower, around 40% of cases.

Probation Responsibilities: Investigate and Supervise

Presentencing Investigation Report

A probation officer's work begins before the offender is sentenced in court, with the *presentencing investigation report (PSI)*. Within this scope, the probation officer is tasked with obtaining relevant information about the defendant, the circumstances of the crime, special considerations for sentencing, and even a recommendation to the judge on appropriate sentences. This occurs even in felony cases, when it is common for the court's probation staff to conduct a presentence investigation that includes details about the defendant's background, prior criminal record, education and employment history, family status, and family functioning. Specifically, probation staff will interview defendants for evaluation purposes with the aim of identifying the defendant's mental and/or physical condition. Interviews may also be conducted with the defendant's neighbors, employers, and acquaintances to evaluate ties to community and overall social functioning (see Figure 3.1).

Figure 3.1 Elements of the Presentencing Investigation Report

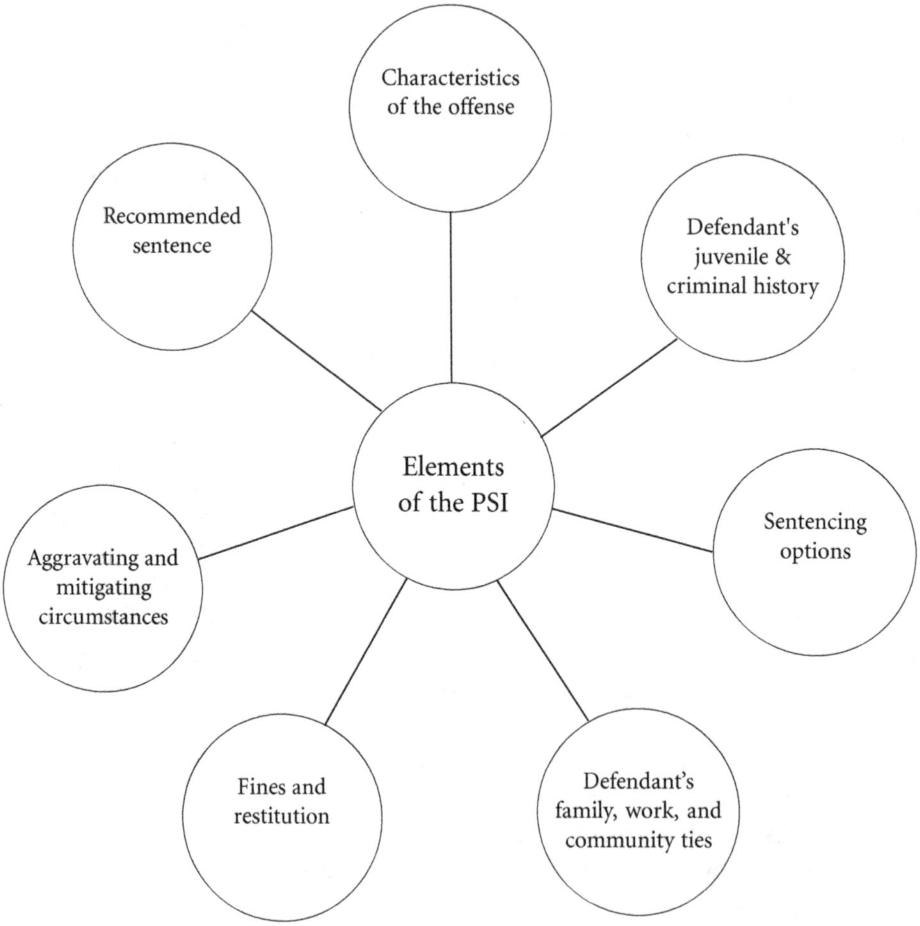

While information from the PSI is not available during the trial, it is important at the sentencing stages, as it allows judges to better evaluate the risk and needs of the defendant before sentencing. In that regard, a PSI serves as the basis for sentencing and has a significant influence on whether the defendant will be sentenced to confinement or community supervision/probation, and will further help the judge determine the conditions of supervision while on probation. It is in this critical context that an important judicial question takes center stage: should a defendant be allowed to have a defense lawyer present during the interview? In the case of *Minnesota v. Murphy* (1984), the court was asked to decide on the privacy of information shared between a probationer and the probation officer, and whether the Fifth and Fourteenth Amendments prohibit the introduction into evidence of the admissions in Murphy's subsequent criminal prosecution. Murphy, who was on probation, made incriminating admissions to his treatment counselor during his treatment at the Alpha House, where he was treated as a sex offender; specifically Murphy admitted to a rape and murder he committed in 1974. This information was shared with Murphy's probation officer, who then summoned Murphy to her office to further discuss the information she had received from the Alpha House counselor, while expressing her belief that this information evinced his continued need for treatment. Murphy became angry about what he considered to be a breach of his confidences and stated that he "felt like calling a lawyer" to which the probation officer's response was that he would have to take it outside the office. As a result, Murphy sought to suppress testimony concerning his confession on the grounds that it was obtained in violation of the Fifth and Fourteenth Amendments. The trial court found that he was not "in custody" at the time of the statement and that the confession was neither compelled nor involuntary despite the absence of warnings similar to those required by *Miranda v. Arizona* (1966). In evaluating Mr. Murphy's case, the Supreme Court held that probation officers are not obligated to provide Miranda advisement to defendants prior to interviews. Evaluating the rationale for such decision, one can argue that offenders under correctional supervision should not assume any privileges of confidentiality when it comes to delivering incriminating evidence of their own accord. Accordingly, in all states within the U.S., with the exception of Oregon, defendants do not have the right to an attorney during the course of their interaction with their probation officers, nor during a PSI interview.

A somewhat different scenario emerges when a defendant is accused of a capital crime, in which the death penalty may be a possible outcome. In such cases, defense attorneys have argued that the PSI should be disclosed to them as they seek the opportunity to challenge and dispute some of the information in the report that may lead to the administration of the capital punishment. In the case of *Williams v. New York* (1949), a jury in a New York state court found the appellant, Mr. Williams, guilty of murder in the first degree. The jury recommended life imprisonment, but the trial judge imposed the sentence of death. In giving his reasons for imposing the death sentence, the judge discussed in open court the evidence upon which the jury had convicted, stating that this evidence had been considered in light of the additional information obtained through the court's presentencing investigation report, made available by the probation department and through other sources. A different decision was rendered in later cases involving the death penalty. For example, in both *Gardner v. Florida* (1977) and *Booth v. Maryland* (1987), the U.S. Supreme Court decided that in cases of the death penalty, the PSI must be available to the defense and could not contain any victim statement impact reports that could inflame the jury and bias its decision. In a more recent case of *Wiggins v. Smith* (2003), Kevin Wiggins argued that his attorneys' failure to investigate his background and present mitigating evidence of his unfortunate life history and circumstance at his capital sentencing proceedings violated his Sixth Amendment right to counsel. The Maryland Court of Appeals, which first heard the case, observed that Wiggins' counsel knew of his unfortunate childhood circumstances, as it was available to them in the PSI report prepared by the Division of Parole and Probation, as required by Maryland law. In their decisions, Justices Scalia and Thomas vacated Wiggins' death sentence on the grounds that his trial counsel's investigation of potential mitigating evidence was "incomplete." Wiggins' trial counsel testified under oath; however, that he was aware of the basic features of Wiggins' troubled childhood that the court claims he overlooked. The court chose to question this testimony for reasons that do not withstand analysis. Moreover, even if this doubt could reasonably be entertained, that would certainly not establish that the Maryland Court of Appeals was *unreasonable* in believing it, and in therefore concluding that counsel adequately investigated Wiggins' background.

The PSI becomes a very important aspect in judges' sentencing decisions, as the report provides judges with information about the defendants that is usually not available to the jury. Studies have also shown that there is a very high correlation between the probation officer's recommendations for sentence in the PSI and the judge's sentencing decision (Petersilia, 1997). Further, probation officers will use the PSI for classification of risk and needs, which determines the intensity of the supervision while also helping probation officers better tailor treatment alternatives relevant to an offender's needs (e.g., mental health, sex-offender treatment, substance abuse treatment, anger management, etc.).

Supervision

Upon completion of the PSI and once sentencing is determined by the court to be served under community supervision in the form of probation, probation agents are tasked with the actual supervision of the offender. Depending on the supervision requirements as decided by the judge and, as discussed earlier in consideration with the PSI, the probation agent will meet with the convicted offender to discuss the terms of the probation supervision. It is not unheard-of that probation officers assist their clients in finding employment or a place to live, and even help them secure other needed social and medical services. This is done after the probation agent assesses the risk and needs of the offender that will also determine the level of actual supervision required and appropriate for each individual probationer.

Probationers may be supervised in the community in a variety of methods that can range from very basic appearances to reporting in day centers, electronic monitoring, scheduled call-ins, surprise visits, weekend supervision, and even split supervision, in which the offender is released only during the day and required to spend nights in a local residence. The extent and intensity of the supervision are determined by both the PSI and instruments such as the Level of Service Inventory Revised (LSI-R), which aims to identify static and dynamic factors associated with the risk and needs of the offender (Andrews & Bonta, 2000). Once conditions and frequency of supervision are established, probation officers are required to assure compliance with the conditions. To achieve such compliance, probation officers conduct home and work visits, collect information from neighbors, family, and friends, and in some jurisdictions require the offender to spend most of the time in the community. Some jurisdictions require their probation officers to carry handguns. Other important aspects of the conditions that must receive full compliance are restitution, abstinence from alcohol and drugs, and participation in assigned programs. Accordingly, probation officers are also required to administer drug tests via the collection of urine samples, visit and communicate with treatment personal, and make sure that fines and restitutions are paid according to plan. Such conditions of supervision may be considered draconian to some who are struggling to maintain their low-paying jobs. This is particularly true in cases where the conditions of probation require making monetary amends (restitution) to victims, paying governmental fines, or even paying for one's own supervision. Not surprisingly, the courts have been asked to intervene in many cases of probation revocation for noncompliance with certain conditions that have been constitutionally challenged. For example, probationers have challenged the legitimacy of home searches by probation officers without a warrant (*Griffin v. Wisconsin*, 1987; *United States v. Knights*, 2001) and probation revocation without the aid of counsel at the revocation hearing (*Mempa v. Rhay*, 1967; *Gagnon v. Scarpelli*, 1973) or due to failure to pay a fine and make restitution (*Bearden v. Georgia*, 1983). We discuss these cases at greater length in Chapter 12.

The Organization of Probation

Probation in the United States is administered by more than 2,000 separate agencies (Abadinsky, 2008) that supervise close to 4 million adult offenders (3,789,800 as of year-end 2015). As previously discussed, these agencies differ in their structure and in the services they offer, as well as in their relationship to the judicial branch, how they are funded, and whether these agencies are primarily a federal, state, or local function (MacKenzie, 2011). It is not uncommon for states to combine probation and parole into one statewide agency, while in other states probation is administered by the local court, or it is part of the county executive branch, under a chief executive officer, or under a city mayor. Probation services in the executive branch can be part of the state government under the office of the governor. In some states, such as Georgia, probation is a part of the larger department of corrections. When probation is placed under the judicial branch of the state government, these services are managed by county judges, as is in the case of New Jersey. In its neighboring state, New York, all local probation directors report to chief county officials or in New York City, to the mayor, although statewide oversight remains the responsibility of New York's Division of Probation and Correctional Alternatives (see Abadinsky, 2008).

Variation in Probation Workload

As previously mentioned, probation agencies vary greatly in their organization and administration. As such, different counties within one state can have very different challenges and accordingly face different workloads. An agency's workload is determined by the number and percentage of convicted felons, and those who require different levels of supervision, such as intensive supervision, and the length of stay. According to Cushman and Sechrest (1992), the volume of individuals under probation supervision and their unique characteristics will vary according to changes in the average length of stay in probation. This, in turn, translates into different modes of supervision, requiring probation agencies to tailor specific supervision packages to address the risk and needs of each client. When rates of admission and length of stay are combined with special supervision requirements and conditions, this can create a wide variety of workloads. This in turn has an impact on the staff and programming that needs to be provided for the offenders, particularly those convicted of a felony and those under intensive supervision. Consequently, comparing outcomes for probationers in different counties and jurisdictions can often be misleading, even if on paper, every agency is using the same probation measures. This is also important to this book's overall discussion of the legal rights of convicted offenders, as different jurisdictions will implement very different terms of violation and the disciplinary actions toward a violation of probation terms, and they may follow different procedures regarding noncompliance.

Variation in Probation Organization

The difference in workload and type of clientele assigned to probation department should have an effect on the resources available to each probation agency; departments with higher workloads should, presumably, have more resources, but this is not always the case. According to the National Association of Criminal Justice Planners (NACJP), there are five characteristics that differentiate probation agencies according to their working load and available resources:

1. Level of supervision of probationers and the corresponding number of contacts per month: As more probationers are assigned to a probation officer, the officer will, necessarily, have fewer meaningful contacts with each client. Accordingly, in agencies with a high workload and many felony probationers sentenced to longer periods of time, supervision may be less effective. It may also be less tolerant of violations, with a "finger on the trigger" to revoke probation status, as this requires less time and supervision. Thus, it can be expected that more litigation will emerge in such situations.

2. Ratio of probation officers to clients: Due to the great variation among probation agencies, this ratio is very difficult to obtain. So it is equally difficult to say what the preferred ratio should be.

3. Ratio of supervisors to probation officers: This ratio is more easily obtained, and it can often serve as a proxy measure to the quality of probation services in various jurisdictions. It can indicate a department's level of professionalism, and how much guidance and training the staff might receive.

4. Salary, benefits, and hiring and training criteria for probation officers: Studies have documented differences across departments in the education and experience required to apply for an entry-level probation officer position. While some agencies require a very short training period of about 38 hours, other places may have a more stringent requirement of 460 hours before one can become a probation officer. Additionally, jurisdictions vary by service training requirements. These further translate to differences in salaries and benefits, as well as in job satisfaction. Such metrics can help gauge such problems as overcrowded agencies, characterized by high clientele workload, and high turnover (and the constant need to hire additional probation officers), which in turn serves as an indicator of the department's overall level of professionalism. It should not be surprising then that jurisdictions characterized by high workload, rapid staff turnover, and poor training will be subject to more litigation from probationers.

Number, quality, and type of programs and services available to probationers: Probation agencies further vary by their expenditure per probationer. Such differences in spending are very rough indicators of the quality and amount of service each agency is able to deliver. While most agencies can provide intensive supervision (IS), drug testing and treatment, psychological counseling, alcohol treatment, family counseling, and vocation training referrals, it is extremely difficult to assess the quality, size, or effectiveness of these programs, and to compare them with services at other agencies. The variation in services and programs contributes to variation in supervision outcomes, and this may serve as another important criterion for understanding probationers litigation and judicial intervention.

These characteristics are important organizational dimensions that further our understanding of how convicted offenders are actually supervised in the community and what challenges probation agencies and probationers are facing. It is within this context that judicial interventions challenge the level of professionalism and effectiveness of supervision, while also indicating the rights and limitations of those offenders who are sentenced to probation supervision.

Variations in Disciplinary Policies

As previously established, probation agencies vary substantially in their client population, organization, and policies, which makes them hard to compare and evaluate. Further complicating the issue, they are not even consistent in the most basic terms they use to describe violations. For example, different agencies define the term "absconding" differently and as a result, they may apply different sanctions to such behavior. Agencies also report very different rates at which probationers satisfy conditions assigned to their supervision, such as payment of fines or restitution, and the agencies have different responses when such conditions are not met. This variation is then reflected in the policies that guide the agencies' operation and these policies lead to different revocation and rearrest rates, even when the population under supervision is identical across agencies and jurisdictions (Cunniff & Bergsmann, 1990; Cunniff & Shilton, 1991). For example, some departments use disciplinary hearings extensively and based on these hearings, they may modify the conditions of supervision (e.g., graduate sanctions) or revoke it entirely. Not surprisingly, agencies with high rates of disciplinary hearings tend also to be those with high workloads, less-trained personnel, and high rates of technical violations that lead to probation being terminated. On the other hand, agencies that administer policies that do not automatically trigger a disciplinary hearing tend to have fewer revocations and maintain a more manageable workload, with less litigation from probationers.

Parole

Parole is a period of conditional supervised release in the community following a prison term. While parolees serve the reminder of their sentence in the community, parole is not considered a community-based sentence like probation, but an extension of a sentence of incarceration. For this reason, it may include more stringent requirements for supervision, closer enforcement of rules, and little tolerance for violations (May et al., 2008). If convicted and imprisoned and offenders better themselves while in prison, they can then "buy" or accumulate "good" time credits that lead to the reduction of their time in confinement. The logic of parole is based on the concept of rehabilitation, so that offenders who show significant signs of changed behavior can reintegrate into their home communities while receiving guidance and supervision. Parolees, granted early release from prison, are given over to the authority of a community-based agency that will then supervise them for the remaining length of their original term of incarceration. If an offender was sentenced to six years in prison, for example, and was granted early release to the authority of a parole agency after completing 80% of the sentence, that offender will have to complete the remaining 1.2 years (20%) of the sentence in the community, while complying with certain conditions. Failure to meet these conditions will result in the offender returning to prison for the reminder of sentence (unless the parolee is convicted of a new crime, in which case the new sentence applies).

There are two main types of parole. *Discretionary parole* applies to prisoners who enter parole as result of a decision by a parole board that reviews the specific case and all the factors involved. On the other hand, there are those who receive *mandatory parole* as part of their sentence. This applies to prisoners whose release from prison was not decided by a parole board but instead was determined by sentencing status, good-time provisions, or emergency release set at time of sentencing by the presiding judge (Bayens & Ortiz-Smykla, 2013). These mechanisms result in the early release of about three-quarters of all prisoners, who end up under some form of parole supervision in the community (Ostermann, 2015). As many states are struggling to maintain the high costs of mass incarceration, an increasing number of prisoners have been released into parole supervision (see Kaeble, Maruschak, & Bonczar, 2015). So early release to parole supervision may have the goal of motivating and rewarding a prisoner for successful rehabilitation, but it also seems to serve the goal of relieving states from paying for their experimentation with the mass incarceration endeavor.

The function of parole agencies and parole officers is very similar to probation agencies and officers—which is to say, with a great deal of variation by state and county with regard to number of employees and caseloads. However, unlike probation, which is decided by a judge, parole is for the most part decided by parole boards, which are located in the heart of the corrections and parole system, and operate with a high level of discretion.

Parole Boards and Parole Hearings

Parole boards, also known as *parole authority*, are located in all jurisdictions of the United States and have the authority to pardon offenders who are sentenced to imprisonment, as well as grant and revoke parole and discharge offenders from parole supervision. Parole boards are also responsible for establishing conditions for supervision and for evaluating parolees' progress during their term of supervision. Parole boards vary in size and composition, as well as in the terms of tenure. In almost all states, the governor appoints at least one member of the parole board; in some states, the governor appoints the entire board. Because many parole board members are political appointments and because they vary so widely in their organizational structure and composition, it is no surprise that many boards have been criticized (Abadinsky, 2013). In many cases, this criticism focuses on members' lack of relevant background, training, or education. As a result of this criticism, more states have begun to pay closer attention to who is being recruited for these jobs and some states have even gone as far as specifying clear requirements for previous education, relevant work experience, and understanding of the field, as well as mandating specific representation by certain demographic groups and/or geographic areas. For example, the state of Maryland requires that candidates have at least a bachelor's degree in one of the social or behavioral sciences, as well as three years of relevant criminal or legal experience. Similarly, the governor of the state of Vermont has emphasized that those appointed to parole boards must have knowledge of and experience in correctional treatment and crime prevention strategies. Pennsylvania requires members of its parole board to have at least a bachelor's degree, as well as six years of professional experience in parole, probation, social work, or other related fields, with at least one year of supervisory experience (see Abadinsky, 2013). Such requirements are essential to increasing professionalism while also minimizing and preventing parolees from litigating parole board decisions.

While early release on parole is a common practice, not all prisoners become eligible for it. Eligibility for parole does not mean it will eventually be granted; it means only that a request will be considered. For prisoners to become eligible for parole release, they need to meet certain criteria, such as serving a required portion of their sentence, accumulating good-time credits, or having served time in jail before the imprisonment (see May et al., 2008). Prisoners can also earn eligibility by participating in or completing specific programs. They also need a positive review by an intelligence officer from the department of corrections, stating that the prisoner presents no imminent risk in his or her early release. In fact, regarding the decision to grant a prisoner a parole hearing, the Supreme Court ruled that such hearing may be less strict than a usual court case in terms of its due-process procedures, and that parole boards should enjoy wider discretion in their procedures. The result of this is that if prisoners are denied parole, they may be eligible to apply for a new consideration again in the future.

Parole Board Hearings

The most that can be generalized about parole hearings is that they are usually held in a state prison, and in many jurisdictions, members of the parole board are assigned a very heavy caseload (West-Smith, Pogrebin, & Poole, 2000). In addition, there is a great variation in the way in which such meetings are held. In some states, parole boards may open the hearings to the media, while others conduct their business behind closed doors. In some states, parole boards will entertain feedback from victims and/or their families, while others will not. Some will conduct interviews with the prisoners, while others will not and will base their decision only on available written reports (Abadinsky, 2013). These disparities in policy and process have led to accusations of bias, and the increase in cases that require individualized treatment can also introduce unwanted discretion into the parole system. To combat this, some jurisdictions have sought to bring greater structure, consistency, and objectivity to the decision-making process by using presumptive parole dates and parole guidelines. *Presumptive parole dates* are tentative dates for eligibility for parole, established when prisoners are admitted to prison, or shortly after. In this way, prisoners know when they can expect to receive parole if they comply with prison rules and regulations and participate in treatment programs as directed (see May et al., 2008). This approach draws heavily from a century-old policy used in the Irish correctional system, first developed by Alexander Maconochie and later adopted and further developed by Sir Walter Crofton. Setting a presumptive parole dates encourages a prisoner to take an active part in his or her own rehabilitation, while also attempting to reduce prisoner infractions. *Parole guidelines* are another way to unify, minimize and even eliminate bias and unwanted discretion in parole eligibility criteria. Parole guidelines are similar to sentencing guidelines in that risk and needs are assessed using scientific measures and instruments. These guidelines allow officials to objectively rate individual prisoners on variables believed to have high predictive validity for recidivism. Such variables include prior criminal history, age on set/at first offense, written infractions, and the type of offense. According to May and colleagues (2008: 454), "the idea is to reduce unfair disparity in decision making and to help promote community safety."

To achieve this goal, the U.S. Parole Commission, in the 1970s, developed the *Salient Factor Score (SFS)*, now a commonly used risk-assessment tool that enables parole board members to estimate an offender's prison sentence and likelihood of success or failure if released from prison to parole supervision (Bayens, & Smykla, 2013). The SFS has been revised and modified several times since the pilot stages. It now includes six static factors based on objective scales that were developed, examined, and validated using evidence-based research (see Ratansi & Cox, 2007). These six factors, mentioned above, are those that do not change over time and are known to be related to recidivism; again, they include age at first offense, number of previous convictions, and the type of offenses and convictions. The SFS ranges in score from zero to ten, and the score is then placed into one of four risk categories: Poor (0–3), Fair (4–5), Good (6–7), and Very Good (8–10). As a standardized instrument for risk assessment, the SFS helps parole boards make decisions. It also helps minimize litigation charging unfair process, and it eliminates potential accusations of discriminatory bias by members of the parole board.

In addition to calculating a SFS, other assessment measures may be taken during a parole board hearing. These may include interviewing prisoners to learn more about personal changes they may have made during the period of incarceration and any concrete plans the prisoner may have following her/his release into the community: who will they stay with, for example, or where they might seek employment. If parole is granted, a contract is drafted to define and detail the release plan, conditions, and an actual date of release. In cases when parole is denied, the prisoner is usually given a standard reason that reflects the shortcoming of their parole application. Reasons can vary to indicate things like: "poor disciplinary record," "lack of satisfactory parole program," "failure to complete treatment/educational program," or even simply "not enough time served." After prisoners are denied parole, there is a waiting period before they can have a new hearing. The length of time can vary from jurisdiction to jurisdiction, and it may also depend on the parole board's caseload, how many prisoners are confined in any given jurisdiction, and how many members sit on the parole board. After a parole denial, prisoners sometimes appeal the due process legality of their parole hearing in an attempt to achieve some relief and in some instances, possibly a reversal of a parole board's decision. As noted earlier; however, the U.S. Supreme Court has ruled in a number of cases that people sentenced to confinement cannot necessarily expect the same due-process rights during parole hearings as free members of the community would expect during criminal proceedings to determine guilt of an alleged crime.

Parole Revocation

The procedure around parole revocation—that is, the formal termination of an offender's freedom in the community and subsequent return to custody—is very similar to that practiced by probation officers. In fact, many community supervision agencies across the United State provide both probation and parole services, and it is not unheard-of for an officer to handle both probation and parole cases. While 58% of parolees completed their term of supervision in 2012, the reincarceration rate among parolees at risk for violating their conditions of supervision has continued to decline (Maruschak & Parks, 2012). A recent report by Kaeble, Maruschak, and Bonczar (2015) estimated 9.0% of all parolees who were at risk of violating their conditions of supervision during 2014 were reincarcerated for violations. Further, 2.8% of parolees who were at risk of violating their conditions of supervision due to a new crime and were incarcerated for a new sentence in 2014. The portion of parolees who were reincarcerated as a result of revocation was 5.2% in 2014, which indicates a minor decline from 2013, when that portion was 5.6%.

As with probation, parole can be revoked as a response to a new crime or on the basis of *technical violations*, which are violations of agreed-upon conditions of supervision. Yet, not all technical violations, nor even new crimes, will necessarily result in immediate revocation and incarceration. Often, parolees will be subjected to what is known as *graduated sanctions*, receiving increasingly harsher punishments and additional restrictions according to how often they violate the terms of their parole. If it is a first technical violation, for instance, a parolee might have their supervision tightened; repeat offenses may call for some jail time in lieu of being sent back to prison, or other additional restrictions. Note, however, that when parole is revoked, whether due to a new crime or a technical violation, the process is, unlike when parole is first granted, in fact governed by due process requirements.

Conclusion

Probation and parole are both forms of offender supervision in the community. However, the legal status of probationers is different from that of parolees. Community supervision in the form of either probation (in all its variations) and parole is designed to serve the goals of restorative justice, rehabilitation, and even retribution and deterrence. Although it is difficult for many people to understand how allowing convicted offenders to remain in general society can act as retribution or deterrence, evidence shows that the strict conditions of supervision, along with the infringement of many basic constitutional rights of people under probation and parole, do effectively limit the freedoms of convicted offenders while in the community, without the additional cost of imprisonment. Offenders under community supervision can be searched without a warrant, visited by their probation or parole officer without warning, and subjected to random urine tests. While on probation, convicted offenders are often required to make amends to their victims, via fines or other forms of restitution. With more than 7 million people under correctional supervision in the United States, community supervision, where feasible, seems to be a saner alternative to prison, as it can punish offenders while allowing them to rehabilitate and reintegrate as normative members of society. Unfortunately, this is not always as easy as one would expect, but if we can revise our policies in a way that redirects tax dollars to treat low-risk offenders in the community, we could significantly increase parole and probation's intensity, supervision, and services, and achieve better compliance and results. Changing probation and parole mode of operation with additional resources will result in enhancement of much needed services, and quality supervision and guidance. Such desirable changes would translate to less litigation by offenders and reduce unnecessary judicial intervention in the policies and practices of probation and parole agencies. Judicial intervention has come under scrutiny by the U.S. Supreme Court, which has debated and examined issues revolving around parole decisions. Later in the book, in Chapter 12, we examine the effects of community supervision and the law, looking at cases that focus on the rights and protections to which offenders under community supervision are entitled. As will be discussed in more detail, the United States Supreme Court ruled that the standards for due process in initial probation and parole hearings can be lower than when revocation decisions are made. This is particularly true in cases of parole release, which is considered an act of grace, where jurisdictions have the ultimate discretion to decide what constitutes acceptable due process at deciding if to grant a parole hearing or not.

Discussion Questions

1. Discuss the differences between probation and parole. Explain why such differences may invoke different judicial decisions.

2. Discuss the challenges faced by probation officers. How do these challenges lead to a lower quality of supervision?

3. Discuss the various conditions set for offenders under community supervision. Why would such seemingly easy conditions lead to revocation of parole or probation? In your opinion, when judges or boards decide whether to revoke parole or probation, should they take the supervised offender's life circumstances into consideration?

4. Discuss the importance of the presentencing investigation report (PSI). What are the main issues covered by this investigation? Should defense attorneys be allowed to review this report and object to its entirety or parts of it? Make sure to discuss relevant cases.

5. Discuss the difference between discretionary parole and mandatory parole. In your opinion, should there be any differences in parole boards' decision to grant or deny parole based on discretionary vs. mandatory parole? Discuss such differences in light of potential legal and constitutional violations.

6. Discuss the composition and structural variances of parole boards across the nation. How does this variation harbor potential for litigation?

List of Cases Cited

Bearden v. Georgia, 1983. 461 U.S. 660.

Booth v. Maryland, 1987. 482 U.S. 496.

Gagnon v. Scarpelli, 1973. 411 U.S. 778.

Gardner v. Florida, 1977. 430 U.S. 349.

Griffin v. Wisconsin, 1987. 483 U.S. 868.

Mempa v. Rhay, 1967. 389 U.S. 128.

Minnesota v. Murphy, 1984. 465 U.S. 420.

Miranda v. Arizona, 1966. 384 U. S. 436.

United States v. Knights, 2001. 534 U.S. 112.

Wiggins v. Smith, 2003. 539 U.S. 510.

Williams v. New York, 1949. 337 U.S. 241.

Chapter 4

Jail and Prison Administration

The decision to place individuals under correctional supervision and limit their movement and freedom is never taken lightly. It is an even weightier decision to confine individuals to correctional institutions, where they are stripped of most of their liberties. While the majority of the correctional population serves a sentence in the community (as discussed in the previous chapter), confinement in jails and prisons remains the most visible form of punishment. Confinement serves the penological goal of incapacitation, and of removing and separating individuals from the community. To understand this form of punishment, it is essential to first examine the structure and administration of jails and prisons. This will help us to, in turn, examine the judicial discourse around these institutions. We begin our discussion by looking at jails.

Jails

A *jail* is a facility that is authorized to hold pretrial detainees and sentenced misdemeanants for periods longer than 48 hours. Initially, jails were designed to detain suspected offenders before trial and for short periods of time before their sentences were decided. Perhaps because they occupy this unique short-term position in the overall criminal justice procedure, jails have not traditionally been considered places of punishment and their relationship to the entire criminal justice system has largely been neglected by criminological and penological research and discourse. Today, however, many jails are places of both detention and punishment, as they often hold convicted offenders who are sentenced for up to a year of incarceration. Some facilities hold offenders for even longer periods. This is a primarily a result of prison overcrowding, as many offenders with longer sentences must wait for space to open before they can be transferred. In fact, Ingraham (2015:1) notes that the United States operates more jails than degree-granting institutions (i.e., colleges and universities) and that "at any given time, hundreds of thousands [of] individuals are locked up in the nation's 3,200 local and county jails." Similarly, Lerman (2013) shows that the growth in spending on state corrections has outpaced increases in states' expenditures for educational programs and Medicaid. A report by Minton and Zeng (2015) estimates the number of inmates confined to county and city jails at about 750,000 at mid-year 2014. However, the actual impact of jails on individuals and communities is much larger. Each year, millions of people revolve in and out of local jails after staying there for short periods of time. In fact, according to the Bureau of Justice Statistics, from June 2013 to June 2014, local jails admitted about 11.4 million people. With numbers like these, jails affect the lives of more people than any other correctional or penal institution. The astronomical number of people who pass through these facilities places an enormous challenge on jail administrators and staff, who are required to manage an extremely diverse body of individuals: pretrial detainees who cannot afford bail to people accused of felonies as well as misdemeanors, mentally ill offenders, offenders who are chronically ill, and even extremely violent and dangerous offenders (Kosiak, 2011). This diverse population and the transient nature of jails—they tend to have more admissions and discharges than any other correctional facility—make for very complex and often punitive environments.

The highly diverse population in jails is echoed in highly diverse management styles, physical conditions, and rated capacity. *Rated capacity* refers to the number of beds placed or built inside a jail when it was first designed and constructed, but that number can change as a result of renovations or additions (Cornelius, 2008). Jails also differ in their *operational capacity*, which refers to the number of people that can be housed safely and with continued smooth day-to-day operations. Some facilities, such as Rikers Island in New York City and Chicago's Cook County jail, are outliers in terms of their size and capacity. These are large jail complexes. On the other hand, there are much smaller jails across the country, some of which have a capacity of no more than two dozen to three dozen beds. It is within this context of physical conditions, capacity, and architectural style that many jails across the country are characterized as overcrowded, dangerous, unhealthy, and inhumane. It is also within this context, in 1979, the U.S. Supreme Court ruled in the case of *Bell v. Wolfish* that inmates confined to jails who are not yet convicted and are in a pretrial state cannot be punished. We discuss this case in more detail throughout the chapters of this book; however, at this point, it is important to understand that this ruling was an important turning point in judicial intervention in jail practices, and in particular those pertaining to pretrial detainees. In that regard, the *Bell v. Wolfish* case was a clear warning to local jails to revise their policies and clean up substandard practices.

Diverse populations, varied structure, and high turnover all pose significant challenges for jail staff and administrators attempting to identify and responding to the various needs of jailed individuals, particularly those who suffer from mental illness. According to Fearn (2011), the transient nature of jail populations impedes the ability of jail staff and administrators to address the needs of mentally ill offenders, who are being pushed to the bottom of the to-do list, after more pressing concerns of safety and security. This is a considerable problem, because almost two-thirds of the nation's jail population has been identified as suffering from some form of mental illness. When compared with state or federal prison inmates, jail inmates tend to have markedly higher rates of mental illness or mental disorder symptoms, a fact that makes the management of jails very difficult and places its administrators in a higher risk of being litigated.

Overcrowding and deplorable confinement conditions have also inspired very aggressive judicial intervention. In the early 1980s, for example, a federal court took over the supervision of the Davidson County jail in Tennessee due to the unconstitutional conditions that resulted from overcrowding (Cornelius, 2008). One of the main contributors to jail overcrowding is prison overcrowding: many convicted offenders sentenced to state and federal facilities continue to be held in local jails, waiting for space to become available. Jails, however, have no other alternative for dealing with their own overcrowded facilities. While state and federal prisons can, and do, transfer inmates from one facility to another, jail administrators do not have the same privilege and the only way overcrowding can be alleviated is through the granting of bail, speedy trials, and judges' decisions to intervene. Overcrowding is particularly serious in large urban jails, such as the Cook County jail in Chicago, the Los Angeles County jail, and the jail on Rikers Island in New York City.

While jail overcrowding tends to be one of the main concerns in jail administration, their diverse population presents further challenges. Jails are not just diverse in the populations they hold, but also in their structure, administration, characteristics, and programs. Some jails offer an impressive array of programs, while others offer none. Inadequate programming—and the idleness and violence that can come from a lack of services—has also served as a catalyst for litigation.

The Political Context for Jail Administration

As a social institution, jails have failed to adapt to the enormous social changes that have shaped our society. Until recently, even officials most closely related to jails have had little or no interest in problems associated with jails, much less evolving or reforming them. American jails remain, in most instances, a local responsibility that is administered by local political authority, which reflects local prejudices that tend to be corrupt (Moynahan & Stewart, 1980). A majority of the jails in the United States are the responsibility of the sheriff, an elected official or one with very close ties to local political power, such as a mayor or governor. In this way, jails inevitably become highly politicized institutions (Siegel & Bartollas, 2016) that tend to draw negative attention and criticism that, while often valid (overcrowding, physical conditions, and inadequate space for holding offenders), can be politically motivated. Furthermore, most jail administrators are political appointees and do not necessarily possess the skills and training to manage jails. Such criticisms tend to be at the heart of litigation concerning the constitutionality of jails and the conditions of confinement that these facilities offer. Challenges to the conditions of jails are often associated with the fact that many jails are among the most poorly funded state-run facilities, a fact that often explains their conditions. Nonetheless, many jail administrators do maintain a high level of professionalism and are willing to follow standards developed by relevant national associations, such as the National Sheriffs' Association. Many jail administrators fight for increased budgets, improved conditions, and better staff. Yet, recent changes in jail administration can be seen as a direct outcome of judicial and legislative intervention. According to Moynahan and Stewart (1980), many efforts have been directed toward improving the physical conditions of jails and the treatment of inmates, while at the same time upgrading the qualifications, training, and conduct of jailers. Such changes resulted from a compliance with court mandated instructions.

The deplorable conditions in many jails around the country and the lack of sufficient funding have created an unprofessional work environment. Such conditions began to change with the formation of the National Sheriffs' Association in 1940, and later on with the establishment of the National Jailers Association and the Jail Managers Association. These professional associations provided a platform for discussion that addressed the many issues faced by jail administrators and staff. Specifically, a "*Jail Standards of the National Sheriffs' Association*" was developed. This pushed some states to develop their own standards, promoting a higher level of professionalism and minimizing political influence. During the 1960s and 1970s, the federal government began to support training programs for jailers, who previously had been simply trained on the job, without any systematic instruction. Needless to say, this attracted many individuals who were not suitable for this type of job. With federal support, training became more professional and systematic and covered various psychological, sociological, management and budgeting aspects of jail administration (Moynahan & Stewart, 1980). Today, jailer training is mandatory and requires completion of long academic training that touches on traditional security themes, as well as deviant behavior, psychology, sociology, law, security, addiction, mental illness, and many other issues that jailers are expected to deal with during their daily work.

Yet, even with all the advances in jail management and professionalism, jails continue to be used as pawns by local governments. According to Moynahan and Stewart (1980: 79), "some communities and localities take pride in being able to say that local authority controls the local jail. Consequently, regardless of the dilapidated condition of their facilities, some cities and counties fight to retain this dubious honor, while the harried administrators of these jails would eagerly shed their frustrating responsibilities of management and control." Hence it is not uncommon for localities to resist standardized control of jails, even where facilities remain in poor condition.

Overall, the public has shown little interest in jails, those who work in them, and the inmates held behind their walls. However, political attention occasionally emerges after highly publicized events, such as escapes, riots, or brutal deaths of guards or inmates. Jails also receive political attention during economic downturns, when local governments seek ways to trim expenses. In economically depressed periods, city and county jails have often been combined into one facility, to reduce administrative burdens and the number of jailers. Yet, despite the cost savings on personnel, equipment, time and effort, new challenges of course emerge, and these changes almost always affect the inmate population and the degree to which inmates are supervised.

Jail Conditions, Standards, and Management

As previously mentioned, many of the 3,200 jails in the U.S. have deplorable living conditions, with some facilities presenting serious health and safety concerns. In regard to health issues, Binswanger, Krueger and Steiner (2009) examined 419 jails and interviewed about 7,000 jail inmates, and found that the prevalence of chronic medical conditions of jail inmates is much higher than in the general population. This is likely due to the fact that many facilities are overcrowded, and house individuals in buildings more than a century old, with poor ventilation and/or heat (Kerle & Ford, 1982). Such evidence is alarming as it suggests a major public health risk is lurking behind these walls. Further, some jails have been found to have no functioning showers, and in some cases, inmates do not have running water in their cells. As a result, some inmates will use their toilet to wash their clothes and bed linens; many other facilities are infested with insects and vermin (Cornelius, 2008). Additionally, the destructive behavior by some desperate inmates will lead them to engage in behavior that endangers themselves and others, such as improvising makeshift cooking devices and cigarette lighters from live electric wires. This makes it more difficult to maintain facilities' structure and condition, and it can result in fires, injuries, and reduced usability of certain cells. Overcrowding only magnifies these problems. Overcrowded jails have resulted in a plethora of lawsuits and legal debates (Walker & Gordon, 1980) and even judicial intervention in jail administration. According to Kerle and Ford (1982), overcrowding, lack of recreation, and inadequate funding for local jails and detention centers across the country pose major problems. In such dreadful conditions, the daily tasks of jailers becomes extremely difficult, especially those that pertain to maintaining and ensuring the safety and well-being of inmates. Such conditions have even farther-reaching consequences, as they also affect the lives of those working in these facilities and the communities that surround them. Tuberculosis, hepatitis, HIV/AIDS, and other sexually contracted and transmitted diseases can be exported from jails to the community (Freudenberg, 2001). Further, the poor conditions also create situations in which violence is more likely and the safety of both jailers and inmates is jeopardized. Such conditions collide with the great diversity that characterize jail populations, as discussed earlier in this chapter, which exacerbates the inability of jail staff to effectively handle inmates, resulting in service deficiencies that increase the likelihood that inmates will suffer much greater harms as a result of their jailing (Briar, 1983).

The dire conditions in many jails have spawned a great deal of litigation that challenges alleged inhumane conditions and the low quality of supervision and treatment. In the past 25 years, some of the most significant changes have been made in the physical conditions of jails, particularly in living areas and the conditions inside cells and dormitories. Three distinct architectural styles of jails can now be found in America, reflecting the management philosophy that dominated at the time of their inception. Siegel and Bartollas (2016) identify these three styles and the management styles that corresponds with these architectural designs and reinforced by it:

1. *Linear design:* Cells are aligned in rows running down a central corridor. Jail officers have very limited interaction with inmates, mainly when feeding through a food slot in the cell door. The same slot is also used to deliver mail, commissary goods, medication, and other items. Officers cannot see from the hallway what the inmate is doing inside the cell and the only time they can see

and interact with the inmate is during scheduled check. When this linear-design jail is overcrowded or understaffed, it is especially difficult for the officers to supervise all inmates at all times. It is also extremely difficult for officers to address the needs of individual inmates in a timely manner.

2. *Podular design /remote surveillance design:* A central control booth is surrounded by living units called "pods." Compared with the linear model, officers can observe inmates fairly easily, yet officers are still limited in their communication with inmates, as most interaction is via an intercom. While this design enables better visibility of inmates in their cells, some blind spots do exist and there is evidence that inmate-on-inmate assaults occur in these blind spots (Cornelius, 2008). This design leans heavily on the *panopticon* design developed by Bentham to insure maximum control and supervision over incarcerated individuals. According to Cornelius (2008: 47), "if a problem occurs, the officer in the control booth has to call the squad for assistance, and the responding officers may have a limited or no idea what they are responding to. Inmates called the surveillance officer the 'puppet master' and the pods the 'fishbowl', which reduces the officer's authority." For this reason, officers in the control booth will often ignore minor infractions and violations to avoid the hassle of calling squad assistance and, even more discouraging, to avoid leaving their booth.

3. *Direct supervision:* Officers are placed inside a housing unit and do not have any barriers between them and the inmates. Under this model officers act as "behavior managers," gauging inmates' behavior and the overall atmosphere. Officers constantly interact with inmates in their unit, getting to know them and closely monitoring them. In this approach, officers can take a proactive stand, neutralizing incidents before or as they occur. Officers enjoy more authority and are treated as supervisors or managers of their cell block. Under the direct-supervision model, officers tend to exhibit a sense of pride as they are better able to counsel inmates, defuse tensions, and stop trouble before it escalates. Officers also tend to pay closer attention to details and develop a much better ability to sense risk and trouble.

While both the linear and podular designs offer a reactive type of management, the direct supervision design is highly proactive and has the ability to defuse potentially dangerous situations from escalating. This is important and relevant to our discussion of jail inmate litigation, as it provides a valuable insight into how different jail architecture and its associated management style generate environments that are conducive to civil and constitutional rights violations. Such designs and the associated managerial approaches tend to be the base of much litigation and later judicial intervention in jail management, discussed in more detail in Chapter 9.

Jail Personnel and Administration

Jail personnel have changed dramatically since the early days of jails. The traditional role of jailers as mere key keepers and guards who prevent inmates from escaping has been replaced by trained personnel. While a sheriff's office may be responsible for services, the primary responsibility for a majority of jails has shifted in recent years to local departments of corrections that assumed responsibility over the operation of local jails. This brought a higher level of professionalism to jails and current jail employees fall into two main categories: sworn staff and civilian staff. Sworn jail staff are uniformed personnel with specific law-enforcement training that meets state agency standard; civilian staff members have no law-enforcement training or authority, and they fulfill essential jail needs, such as food services, medical services, psychological and welfare support, substance-abuse counseling, and the like. Although they do not have specific law-enforcement training, civilian staff are nonetheless hired for their professional skills and qualifications. The hiring process involves for both sworn and civilian positions involves thorough screening.

Because jails vary in their structure, composition, and organizational subordination—some are directly under a sheriff's responsibility, while others are under the responsibility of a local correctional department—it is difficult to draw a clear hierarchical administrative sketch of jails. Whatever the larger organizational structure, however, there is always a single jail administrator—a warden or chief jailer—at the top of the organizational pyramid. As noted earlier in this chapter, this is almost always someone appointed by an elected sheriff, so the position has some political tone to it. Below this administrator is the jail command staff, those who ensure that all relevant policies are adhered to. In fact, the jail command staff is the one who carry out the day-to-day routine of the jail and ensure its smooth operation. Below the command staff are the jail officers who operate in a rank structure and serve specific roles such as leaders/commanders, assistant leader/commanders, line guards/officers, and floaters (i.e., correctional officers who are not assigned to any specific post but who assist with inmate transport, searches, post relief, escorts during visitation time, and other special tasks).

A portion of the civilian staff, while technically positioned below the jail administrator and command staff in organizational terms, operates in a parallel structure that advises and reports to the administration and command staff. These staff members are usually medical professionals, therapists, case managers (often trained in social work), drug counselors, psychologists, and the like. These employees are not entrusted with the security of the facility, instead, their primary concern is the welfare of the inmates. Jail employees who engage in such activities are often referred to as *diagnostic and treatment staff.* Identifying and understanding the varied relationships between sworn and civilian staff is critical to understanding constitutional responsibilities and upholding the many civil rights of the incarcerated. The organizational structure in a jail and the staffing levels can affect how they address inmates' rights and their motivations to act in one way or another. Sometimes conflicts emerge between these command staff and diagnostic staff, and such conflicts must be resolved by the jail administration, which is primarily concerned with security and the administration of punishment.

Other civilian staff work in jails, but they tend to fall at a lower level in the organizational structure. These are support teams who provide external services to the jail, such as sanitation, laundry, food services, and more. Additionally, administrative staff provide secretarial and clerical duties. Finally, there is the auxiliary staff, who are not considered jail employees, and are often volunteers who have been cleared to render assistance and services to inmates. There are also interns and other community members who volunteer their time to help operate jail facilities.

Prisons

At year-end 2014, United States prisons, both state and federal, held 1,561,500 people in 4,575 prisons across the nation. According to Lennard (2012) such grim statistics makes the U.S. a leading nation in prisons and incarcerated individuals. This is an imprisonment rate of 470 per 100,000. Although such a rate is considered very high compared to other industrialized and developed nations, such a rate was actually America's lowest imprisonment rate since 2004 (Kaeble et al., 2016). According to the Bureau of Justice Statistics, about half (48%) of all imprisoned individuals at year-end 2014 were serving time in only seven jurisdictions. Kaeble and her colleagues (2016) note that six states had correctional populations of 300,000 or more offenders: Texas (699,300), California (589,600), Georgia (579,600), Florida (382,600), Pennsylvania (360,800), and Ohio (326,300). The federal system held an additional 338,000 prisoners.

The scope and magnitude of American mass incarceration and the growth of prisons have introduced many administrative challenges to prison management, with a particularly detrimental effect on the interactions between correctional staff and incarcerated offenders, and the experiences of this latter group while serving their sentence. Such effects are central to any discussion of prison administration as they are rooted in different administrative experiences and penological ideologies. Carlson and Dilulio (2015) explain that almost all of today's penal leaders began their correctional career at the bottom; they came into the field of corrections as entry-level staff and worked their way up to top managerial roles. In the process, many of these administrators, while devoted correctional professionals, never received any specific training in administration to prepare them for the position of prison warden, except for their "on the job" training. Dufee (1986) points out that although controlling and supervising inmates, along with providing them with counseling, may be referred to as "management" of offenders, this is not the same as managing the correctional institution, from an organizational perspective. Correctional management and administration, Dufee argues, should focus on how correctional activities are organized, instead of on managing a single person, group, or activity within the organization. In fact, he goes on, the concept of management does not deal with one or several sets of people, but with wider systematic and organizational oversight. Carlson and Dilulio (2015) highlight how managing correctional institutions is very different from other types of organizational management, as corrections is a highly demanding environment in which leaders and managers of institutions must have the ability to effectively govern thousands of staff and inmates. The challenge of managing a correctional facility, such as a prison, has become even more complex in an era of mass incarceration that is associated with changes in sentencing polices and prison populations; populations that have become more aggressive and dangerous. Even more difficult is the task of managing prisons in times when the expanding inmate population, along with reduced budgets and other vital resources, results in prisoner litigation and legal complications, which draw the attention of politicians who want to micromanage institutions and staff. We discuss these issues in greater length in Chapters 14 and 15. For now, it is important that we understand the multifaceted task of managing prisons, which has never been more difficult than it has been in the past four decades.

The Prison as a Total Institution

Prison life is mundane, and its operations are dictated by clear and rigid rules aimed to depersonalize the relationship between the staff and those sentenced to serve their punishment. Prisons are characterized by an extremely bureaucratic management style that eliminates privacy and personal interests. Its entire operations are predetermined and aimed to serve the security and safety of both inmates and correctional staff. Inmates are limited in their movement, possessions, and clothing, and are identified by assigned numbers, sometimes even via technology such as electronic ankle bracelets or radio-frequency identification (RFID) tags.

The dominant administrative approach in prison is separation between staff and inmates, achieved by strict rules, uniforms, and demonstration of power. Sworn prison staff are legally authorized to use force to achieve compliance and enjoy additional rights that diminish the civil rights of the incarcerated individual. For example, prison guards are authorized to conduct searches of inmates' belongings and body, and they are entitled and backed by rules and regulations to seize inmates' property and personal items that are deemed contraband or otherwise unauthorized. All of these activities are aimed at achieving maximum compliance and domination over the incarcerated individuals.

Prisons operate on two levels, formal and informal. According to Goffman (1968), the formal level is the one that emphasizes clear rules and regulations, demanding an uncompromising discipline and order, whereas the informal level is the latent activities driven by personal and group motives and interests that shape institutional adjustment scenarios beneficial to those confined within the institution. These two levels are in opposition, as they compete for institutional control. These conflicts eventually promote change in the organizational structure and force changes to the way in which inmates are managed. We discuss Goffman's theory and the bureaucratic approach to correctional management in more detail in Chapter 14. At this early point, it is important for us to establish the notion that these competing levels of operations have a significant impact on the administration and management of prisons and the way in which competing cultures within prisons enable and foster prisoner litigation, and later invite judicial intervention that can change the administrative approach. Specifically, it is crucial to understand that when we aim to examine organizations, and prisons are no different, we must examine them in a holistic manner, in which all involved individuals are viewed as equal players. This means that, although the official rules say otherwise, prison is not run solely by correctional administrators and officers, but also by the individual inmates residing within its walls.

Administrative Models for Prison Management

As mentioned earlier, managing a prison is not an easy task. In many aspects, contemporary prison administration is a direct descendant of early punitive philosophies and views of offenders and the reasons why people commit crimes. Over time, prisons and their administration developed in a way that reflected the harsh ideals of uncompromising discipline to gain full control and obedience. This is called the *authoritarian model* of prison administration, and it governed prison management from the early days of penitentiaries until the mid-20th century (Barak-Glantz, 1986). The authoritarian model is marked by a centralized administration style, with a strong leader and firm control of the prison environment. Both inmates and correctional staff are subject to harsh discipline. This management style is characterized by a highly disciplined workplace, with consistent application of rules and all decisions usually made by one leader who is the center of power in the organization. There is no room for anyone but the leader to make decisions and all corrections officers are expected to follow all rules and instructions, even if this may not be conducive to the prison and its organizational environment. Prisons operating under this type of administrative model tend to have high levels of corruption, low levels of motivation and morale, and very little respect for human rights and constitutional guarantees.

This authoritarian management system frequently violated civil rights and eventually, litigation emerged and exposed the harsh treatment of inmates as well as the brutal conditions common in prison facilities. In response, prisons adapted a more *bureaucratic model* of management, maintaining a strict hierarchical system, but no longer focused on one dominating personality. Instead, the bureaucratic model of prison management advocates for control to be set in a system of rank that is almost paramilitary in nature. There is a clear chain of command and a rigid form of communication. Rules and regulations for the operation of the prison are set down in manuals and are otherwise well documented. All members of the staff are trained in the operation standards and manuals, which are made clear to all prison employees at all ranks. Absolute compliance is expected and staff members can be held accountable if they do not comply with written expectations. This was an important development that followed judicial intervention in correctional management. The bureaucratic model typically produces professionalism, but it can be slow to adjust to change, and it discourages institutional innovation.

A third form of prison management is more liberal in its approach. The *participatory model* of prison management tends to be more open and democratic. It encourages all members of the prison to participate in administrative decisions, requesting staff feedback and input into how things are done and operate. At times, inmates may be invited to take part in discussions as well. While this approach increases prison staff motivation and even promotes a dialogue with inmates, it is not effective in highly dynamic prison environments with fast-moving crisis situations.

This is because the participatory model tends to be time-consuming and may lose decision-making momentum in convoluted discussions.

Comparing these three models of prison management, it is easy to guess which is most prevalent. While the participatory model seems ideal, it is the least effective of the three and does not enjoy much support in the correctional arena. Both the authoritarian and bureaucratic administrative models provide the necessary organizational platform to achieve the correctional goals discussed earlier in this book. Indeed, the most prevalent management model in prisons in the United States is the bureaucratic one, with a hierarchical, centralized, and paramilitary structure. This system is very controlling and lacks flexibility, but it nonetheless provides an efficient and functional structure that enables the management of thousands of inmates, staff, and support personnel. Due to its uniformity and clear chain of command, this model can effectively react to incidents of violence, while at the same time provide a proactive plan to minimize inmate infractions and defuse dangerous situations before they escalate. Under the bureaucratic hierarchical model, a warden, who is subordinate to the general commissioner of corrections (a political appointee), is at the helm of a specific prison organization. The warden normally has the direct assistance of an executive assistant and an administrative assistant, as well as a team of associate wardens, each of whom oversees various programs and/or the daily running of the facility. Through this team, the warden can instruct, control and direct the operations of the prison. This hierarchy not only conveys clear standards and communication channels, but it also develops and maintains a system of accountability, in which each employee and correctional staff members is accountable to the commanding officer or associate warden, and in turn to the warden, who is in turn accountable to the commissioner. The commissioner is also accountable to the political allies who supported him or her and as such, has loyalties to the political elite. It is within this context that many prisoners' lawsuits and their judicial outcomes must be examined for us to better understand the political context and the penological ideology it serves.

Conclusion

Even though jails are not technically supposed to be a place of punishment, they often function this way, alongside prisons. The governing understanding is that these are institutions tasked to incapacitate, deter, rehabilitate, and maintain public safety. Yet, the complex dynamics and variations in jails and prisons place them in a very difficult and often conflicted position. These complex dynamics come to the forefront because the organization and structure of a jail or prison is significantly affected by the goals it strives to achieve. Specifically, many believe that the conditions necessary to reform or rehabilitate an offender conflict with the conditions that are so essential to the punishment of the offender. On one hand, there is the false perception that the public demands tough-on-crime stance and accordingly support harsh confinement conditions that will make offenders suffer. On the other hand, the public acknowledges the importance of treating offenders in an attempt to rehabilitate them.

Those who engage in the study of penology and corrections usually advocate for more humane conditions of confinement and treatment of offenders while incarcerated, remembering that almost all offenders will eventually be released into the community and will need to reintegrate. Confronted by these contradictory pressures, correctional administrators often try to walk a fine line between these two missions, attempting to achieve both custodial and rehabilitation goals that will lead to successful reintegration. The task is not easy, and as will be discussed later in this book, the difficulty is manifest in litigation and judicial intervention in correctional management.

Jails and prisons, as discussed in this chapter, tend to be characterized by great diversity in terms of their organizational structure, affiliation, and administration philosophies and strategies. Regardless of their management style, jails and prisons work to achieve the social goals of confining offenders and preparing them for reentry and reintegration in the community. Along the way, these institutions struggle with many conflicting demands, and at times such demands rise to the surface in the form of litigations. Successful prisoners' litigation is a clear indication that administration and management styles and philosophies must adapt to the changing and growing prison population. Without proper adaptation, jails and prisons risk becoming disorganized institutions, and their disorganization becomes their Achilles' heel in a system aimed at justice. We return to discuss these issues in Chapters 14 and 15, after gaining deeper understanding of the issues that invoke litigation and judicial intervention.

Discussion Questions

1. Discuss the problematic jail environment. How does the diverse human environment of jails make them highly susceptible to prisoners' litigation?

2. Discuss the importance of the *Bell v. Wolfish* U.S. Supreme Court case and how it is relevant to the dire conditions of many American jails.

3. How does the rapid turn of jail inmates affect the ability of jail administrators to address the needs of individuals placed in jail?

4. Discuss the connection between politics and jail administration. How does local politics can affect jail administration?

5. Discuss the far reaching effect of the National Sheriffs' Association. How did this organization affected the thinking of jailers as a profession? And what potential effect did it have on reduction of prisoners' litigation?

6. How does jail architecture complement and correspond with the management style of the facility?

7. Carlson and Dilulio explain that almost all of today's penal leaders began their career at the bottom. Discuss the potential difficulties such correctional leaders are facing in today's rapidly changing prison environment, and the consequences that such difficulties may have on prisoner's litigation.

8. Discuss the prison characteristics as a total institution and how such characteristics translate into daily management of the prison. In your opinion, how likely is it that the characteristics of the prison as a total institution will result in prisoners' litigation? Explain.

9. According to Goffman, prisons operate on two levels: formal and informal. Discuss the effects of these two competing levels of institutional operation in regard to potential prisoners' litigation.

10. Discuss the different administrative models for prison management and how each promote/prevent prisoners' litigation.

Chapter 5

First Amendment: Freedom of Speech

The First Amendment states that the government shall make no law "abridging the freedom of speech, or the press." Freedom of speech is considered a fundamental right in America, and the right has been interpreted to encompass more than just spoken and written words, but also to include symbolic acts and gestures. A detailed analysis of how the courts have interpreted and applied the First Amendment to the non-incarcerated is well beyond the scope of this text. Nevertheless, it is important to provide a brief overview so as to better understand precisely what rights the incarcerated have when it comes to freedom of speech.

A General Overview of Free Speech Rights

An initial reading of the First Amendment may lead one to think that the First Amendment prohibits the government from making any law that restricts or curtails speech in any way. In fact, this has proven not to be the case. Under certain circumstances, judicial precedent has been set so that the government may sometimes limit this right, according to when or where the "speech" is performed. These limitations can be either content-based—that is, they depend on what is being said, the message—or non-content-based, connected not to what is said, but rather to when or where it is said.

In order for the government to limit an individual's speech based on the content of the speech itself, the restriction must pass the same *strict scrutiny test* required by all laws pertaining to constitutional rights: the restriction must be necessary to serve a "compelling interest" and be the "least restrictive means to further the articulated interest." (*Sable Communications of California, Inc. v. Federal Communications Commission*, 1989) In other words, in order for government to limit one's right to express a message, the restriction must serve an extremely important objective being served (compelling interest), and it must not be too broad or burdensome—that is, in the case of freedom of speech, it cannot restrict other speech that does not implicate government interest. The most common example of an acceptable content-based restriction is the prohibition against falsely yelling "fire" in a crowded theater. The compelling interest is to prevent a stampede that could cause serious injuries. It is the least restrictive means because it is narrowly tailored to prohibit only the false yelling of "fire" and does not unnecessarily prevent people from yelling other things. Furthermore, there was most likely no political message behind yelling "fire." Instead, the person who uttered this phrase was most likely intending to cause some degree of chaos or harm. It is important to note that while most content-based speech must pass the strict scrutiny test in order to be enforceable, certain content-based speech (e.g., commercial speech, nude dancing) need only pass intermediate scrutiny. This is allowed because there is no inherent political message behind the speech. The framers of the Constitution wanted to make sure that political ideas were not limited and their gist was brought forward with the establishment of judicial scrutiny during the end of the 1930s.

As previously stated, non-content-based restrictions are those that seek to limit not the speaker's message, but the time, place, or manner of in which it is delivered. To be considered constitutional, non-content-based restrictions need not pass strict scrutiny, but rather must pass the lower standard of "intermediate scrutiny." This means that the Supreme Court will not uphold a non-content-based restriction if it does not meet a "significant" or "substantial" or "important" interest of the government. Further, the restriction must be narrowly tailored but not necessarily the least restrictive means. An example of a valid non-content-based restriction is a common city ordinance, in many U.S. cities, that prohibits adult theaters from being located within 1,000 feet of "any residential zone, single- or multiple-family dwelling, church, park, or school." The ordinance was held to be constitutional in that it was in furtherance of a substantial government interest and content-neutral since the ordinance was for the purpose of limiting the secondary effects of crime and noise associated with adult theaters (*Renton v. Playtime Theaters*, 1986).

As you may have guessed, if there is strict scrutiny and intermediate scrutiny, then there must be a lower level of scrutiny. The lowest (weakest) level of scrutiny is known as the "rationally-related test." Generally, speech is considered to be a fundamental right and as such receives heightened levels of protection. However, certain speech is considered "unprotected speech," which means that one does not have a fundamental right to engage in this form of speech. Obscenity, child pornography, and fighting words are a few common examples of unprotected speech. These categories of speech are considered unprotected because "such utterances are no essential part of any exposition of ideas, and are of such slight social value as a step to truth that any benefit that may be derived from them is clearly outweighed by the social interest in order and morality" (*Chaplinsky v. New Hampshire*). The government may enact legislation designed to prohibit unprotected speech (e.g., expressions considered obscene or speech constituting fighting words) so long as the law serves a legitimate governmental interest and the law is rationally related to the achievement of that interest.

Free Speech Rights of the Incarcerated

We now know that free citizens have a constitutionally protected right to freedom of speech and that speech has been interpreted to include not only the spoken word but also writings, pictures, expressive conduct, and symbolic acts and gestures. We also know that if the government would like to infringe on that right, it must possess either a compelling interest (in the case of content-based communication) or a substantial interest (regarding non-content-based communication) in the objective being served, or, in the case of speech categorized as unprotected, demonstrate that the law is rationally related to a desired objective. But what about incarcerated individuals? As previously noted, prisoners are not without constitutional protections. The 1974 case of *Wolf v. McDonnell* established this clearly when the Supreme Court ruled that prisoners' First Amendment rights are not violated by inspection of their mail for contraband, so long as the mail is not read and the inspection is done in the prisoner's presence so that he can be assured that the privacy of his communications is not breached. But is the free speech provision of the First Amendment one of them? If so, is it the same level of protection as free citizens receive? If the incarcerated have less protection, then how do we assess what is and is not a violation of an inmate's free speech rights? Another question that should be asked is, Should convicted offenders' right to free speech be limited as part of their punishment and as a means of incapacitation?

Communication between Inmates and Non-Inmates

a. Family and Friends

In the early 1970s, a rule in the California Department of Corrections stated, "The sending and receiving of mail is a privilege, not a right, and any violation of the rules governing mail privileges either by you or by your correspondents may cause suspension of the mail privileges" (Hardwick, 1985: 275). This rule was known as Director's Rule 2401. An inmate could be determined to have violated a mail privilege by violating Director's Rules 1201 and 1205. Rule 1201 provided that inmates are not to "agitate, unduly complain, magnify grievances, or behave in any way which might lead to violence." Rule 1205 provided that contraband includes "any writings or voice recordings expressing inflammatory political, racial, religious, or other views or beliefs when not in the immediate possession of the originator, or when the originator's possession is used to subvert prison discipline by display or circulation." Rule 1205 also includes writings not defined as contraband but "in the judgment of the warden or superintendent tend to subvert prison order or discipline." Lastly, rule 2402 (B) provided that inmates "may not send or receive letters that pertain to criminal activity; are lewd, obscene, or defamatory; contain foreign matter, or are otherwise inappropriate." In sum, an inmate's mail privileges could be suspended if, in the eyes of prison officials, either the inmate or one corresponding with the inmate engaged in correspondence likely to subvert discipline. What was considered undue complaining or inflammatory was left to the discretion of prison officials. If correspondence was considered to violate the relevant rules, the prison official could: (1) refuse to deliver and return letter to the author; (2) submit a disciplinary report that could lead to suspension of mail privileges; and/or (3) place a copy of the letter in the inmate's file, which could impact the inmate's work and housing assignments or parole eligibility. These rules were challenged in the case now known as *Procunier v. Martinez*. In *Martinez*, inmates brought a class action suit against the director of the California Department of Corrections challenging the constitutionality of the mail censorship rules. Specifically, the inmates argued that the rules violated their First Amendment rights.

Lower-level federal courts had previously adjudicated similar cases involving censorship of prisoner mail and free speech, but not in a consistent manner (some maintained a hands-off approach, while others required prison officials demonstrate a compelling interest). Such inconsistency in the law made it difficult for prison officials to anticipate the constitutionality of proposed prison restrictions. In order to determine the appropriate standard of review for prison regulations that restrict freedom of speech, the Supreme Court decided to hear this case.

According to the Court, the California Department of Correction's rules involved more than just the rights of inmates, but also included the rights of non-inmates. The Court stated, "The wife of a prison inmate who is not permitted to read all that her husband wanted to say to her has suffered an abridgement of her interest in communicating with him as plain as that which results from censorship of her letter to him." Whether the non-inmate is the author of the correspondence or the recipient, censorship of prisoner mail causes an incidental restriction on the First and Fourteenth Amendment rights of free citizens. Consequently, the Court looked not to "prisoner rights" cases but to cases dealing with incidental restrictions on First Amendment freedoms. Relying on the rationale of these cases, the Court formulated a standard of review for cases involving censorship of prisoner mail. The Court held that censorship of prisoner mail is justified if the following criteria are met:

1) The prison regulation "must further an important or substantial governmental interest unrelated to the suppression of expression"; and

2) "limitation of First Amendment freedoms must be no greater than is necessary or essential to the protection of the particular governmental interest involved."

An "important or substantial governmental interest" in a prison setting is the interest in maintaining order and security, preventing escape, and promoting rehabilitation. A limitation that is "no greater than is necessary or essential" is one that is not overly broad. In sum, the Court applied a medium, or intermediate, level of scrutiny.

Having created the standard of review, the Court applied the facts to this standard. Procunier had argued, on behalf of the prison, that the governmental interest served by the censoring rules is the prevention of flash riots and promotion of inmate rehabilitation (*Procunier v. Martinez*). The Court, however, held that the prison rules were overly broad, as they also censored statements beyond those thought to encourage violence, including unflattering and critical remarks about prison officials and conditions. Additionally, the rules were not limited to incoming mail but also applied to letters sent to friends and family. The Court did not see how censoring this speech could achieve prison objectives. In sum, the Court attempted to develop a standard of review for analyzing the free speech rights of inmates, and applied this standard to find the California Department of Corrections' censorship rules unconstitutional.

b. Representatives of the Media

In the same year as *Martinez*, the Supreme Court heard *Pell v. Procunier,* another case involving the First Amendment rights of prisoners. *Pell* involved prison rules that prohibited face-to-face communications between inmates and members of the media.

Seeking injunctive and declaratory relief, four inmates and three journalists brought suit under Section 1983 (as recalled from earlier chapters, Section 1983 refer to the assumed direct liability of prison officials and staff for the conditions of confinement and for what inmates perceive as inadequate treatment and violations of their civil rights) against the director of the California Department of Corrections, alleging that a prison regulation prohibiting face-to-face interviews between inmates and the media was unconstitutional. The prison regulation in question was § 415.071 of the California Department of Corrections Manual, which stated that "press and other media interviews with specific individual inmates will not be permitted." Prior to the promulgation of this rule, members of the media had had fairly free access to any inmate they wished to interview, but they tended to concentrate their attention on a relatively small number of inmates. Due to the increased attention, certain inmates gained notoriety and influence within the prison. This became a source of disruption and disciplinary problems and, as a consequence, the regulation was enacted.

Inmates asserted that § 415.071 violated their First Amendment right to freedom of speech. The journalists claimed that the rule limited their ability to gather news and thus unconstitutionally infringed upon their First Amendment guarantee of freedom of the press. The case ultimately made its way to the Supreme Court. The Supreme Court began its analysis by noting that prisoners retain the right to freedom of speech so long as the right is not inconsistent with the legitimate needs of the prison. The purpose of prison is to isolate criminal offenders from society. The belief is that the condition of being in prison and isolated from society will serve as a deterrent to crime. Moreover, prisons help protect society from criminals, while at the same time, "the rehabilitative processes of the corrections system work to correct the offender's demonstrated criminal proclivity" (Klein, 1978: 3). Correctional institutions also need to provide internal security for prison officials and inmates alike.

According to the Court, First Amendment challenges to prison rules must be reviewed in terms of the legitimate objectives of the prison. In *Pell*, the policy of the California Corrections Department was that family, clergy, attorneys, and friends were allowed to visit inmates because such visits aided in rehabilitation and did not compromise the legitimate security objectives of the prison. However, face-to-face communications with inmates raised potential administrative and security concerns and thus required some limitations. The Court found this to be a legitimate interest of the government and asserted that, absent evidence of an exaggerated response, courts "should ordinarily defer" to the expert judgment of prison officials when dealing with the administration of correctional facilities.

In addition to finding the security objective legitimate, the Court determined that § 415.071 was not overly broad. Inmates could still communicate with members of the media via mail or through other visitors (e.g., friends, family). The Court again engaged in medium-level scrutiny. With regard to the journalists, the Court held that the rule did not violate their right of freedom of the press. The journalists possessed the same access to information as was available to the public, meaning that they were allowed to interview prisoners but could not request specific individuals.

Communication among Inmates

During the 1970s, inmates were attempting to form prisoner labor unions for the purpose of improving work conditions through collective bargaining power. In 1974, the North Carolina Prisoners' Labor Union (NCPLU) was incorporated. One of its stated goals was to form a prisoner labor union at every prison and jail in North Carolina. The NCPLU also sought to alter or eliminate certain Department of Corrections practices and policies of which the inmates did not approve. By 1975, the union grew to approximately 2,000 members located in 40 different prison units throughout the state of North Carolina. The North Carolina Department of Corrections became concerned about the NCPLU, believing that it posed a threat to the maintenance of discipline and control. As stated by the commissioner of the Department of Corrections: "The creation of an inmate union will naturally result in increasing the existing friction between inmates and prison personnel. It can also create friction between union inmates and non-union inmates." In response, corrections officials promulgated a regulation that forbade prisoners from soliciting others to join the union, banned union meetings, and refused to deliver bulk mailings sent to the prison for distribution. In the case now known as *Jones v. North Carolina Prisoners' Labor Union*, the union initiated a lawsuit based on 42 U.S.C.S. § 1983. The NCPLU asserted, among other things, that the regulations violated their free speech rights under the First Amendment. The District Court agreed with the NCPLU and granted injunctive relief, prohibiting the enforcement of the regulations at issue. The Department of Corrections appealed to the United States Supreme Court.

As in *Pell*, the Court noted that with incarceration comes the necessary limitation or withdrawal of many rights or privileges, and courts should show deference to the administrative decisions of prison administrators. The Court found that the administrators' concerns were reasonable and held that the regulations were consistent with the legitimate operational considerations of the institution. This, in a way, achieves the goal of incapacitation, as it limits the inmates' ability to organize, which could become hazardous to the operation of the facility and potentially to public safety. Further, the regulations did not hamper the ability of inmates to communicate their grievances to prison officials, but merely affected one way in which they could do so. So long as the regulations are designed to address a legitimate concern (activity that could lead to violence and disorder) and are no broader than necessary to address that concern (the inmates in this case have alternative channels to exercise the right to free speech), the institutional need outweighs the First Amendment rights of the inmates.

Another case involving communications between inmates (in part) is *Turner v. Safley* (1987). The Missouri Division of Corrections was enforcing a rule that involved correspondence between inmates. The rule allowed inmates to correspond with inmates located in other facilities if those inmates were immediate family members or if communication concerned legal matters. However, all other forms of correspondence with other inmates were prohibited unless the classification/treatment team of each inmate deemed it in the best interest of the parties involved (Miller, 2003). A prisoner-initiated class action lawsuit alleged that the Missouri correctional rule violated their First Amendment free speech rights. The determination of whether to permit inmate correspondence was not based on a review of the content of the letters, but rather on a correctional officer's familiarity with the particular inmate's progress reports, conduct violation history, and psychological reports. The District Court relied on the *Procunier v. Martinez* ruling of 1974 and thus applied a medium-level substantial interest test and found the rule unconstitutional in that it was overly broad and applied in an arbitrary and capricious manner. The appellate court affirmed.

For *Procunier v. Martinez*, the Supreme Court had granted certiorari with the intent of formulating a standard of review for prisoners' constitutional claims. But because that case involved content-based censorship of correspondence with the general public, the Court failed to complete this task. It did not address "questions of prisoners' rights," so in the case of *Turner*, it granted certiorari once again. Certiorari comes from Latin, and means to be "more fully informed." Accordingly, in the American legal system granting certiorari means that there is a consensus by four Justices that the circumstances described in certain petition is sufficient to warrant review by the Court (other colloquially refer to this as "the rule of four").

The Supreme Court began its analysis by reviewing four prisoner freedom of speech cases decided after *Martinez* (*Pell* and *NCPLU* described above, as well as *Bell v. Wolfish* and *Block v. Rutherford*) and determined that the heightened scrutiny standard is not the appropriate standard. In the Court's estimation, such a standard would hamper prison officials and overly involve courts in the running of prisons. Consequently, in the *Turner* ruling, the Court fashioned a new standard, by which the prison rule need only be rationally related to "legitimate penological objectives," and not an "exaggerated response" to prison administration concerns (Oei, 1988). The Court provided four factors that must be considered when assessing the reasonableness of a prison regulation:

1. "[T]here must be a 'valid, rational connection' between the prison regulation and the legitimate governmental interest put forward to justify it";

2. "whether there are alternative means of exercising the right that remain open to prison inmates";

3. "the impact accommodation of the asserted constitutional right will have on guards and other inmates, and on the allocation of prison resources generally"; and

4. "absence of ready alternatives."

Applying the rationally related standard of review, the Court concluded that Missouri's prohibition on inmate-to-inmate correspondence was not unconstitutional. The prison regulation was promulgated because communications between inmates of different institutions could be used to hatch escape plans or coordinate violent attacks such as gang violence. This limitation is rationally connected to legitimate security concerns of the prison. Further, the regulation does not deprive inmates of all forms of expression (alternative means remain available), but rather is limited to just a small class of inmates who present security concerns. Also, accommodation is not reasonable, as monitoring inmate correspondence would be too burdensome and thus present the risk that prison officials would miss dangerous messages. Last, there are no clear alternatives to achieving the policy objectives. Since the regulation is rationally related to valid penological objectives and content neutral, and accommodation would be considered overly burdensome, the Court held that the Missouri Department of Corrections' rule regarding inmate-to-inmate correspondence did not infringe on the First Amendment rights of inmates.

In sum, the Court in *Turner* made clear that when analyzing prisoner First Amendment free speech rights in cases that do not involve non-inmates, the appropriate standard of review is the lowest (weakest) level of scrutiny, known as the "rationally related" test.

Receipt of Publications

From the preceding cases, we get a sense of First Amendment rights as they pertain to inmate communications with other inmates, with non-inmates, and with members of the media. But what about the receipt of items such as newspapers, magazines, and books? Do inmates have a constitutional right to receive publications? Is it an unlimited right? If not an unlimited right, then to what extent can corrections officials regulate receipt of such items? How do we determine the constitutionality of these regulations?

In *Thornbaugh v. Abbott*, 490 U.S. 401 (1989), the Supreme Court of the United States decided a case that involved issues related to the constitutionality of limitations on receipt of publications. The lawsuit was initially filed in 1973 and certified as a class action suit in 1974. In 1978, three publishers were added as party plaintiffs. The three publishers were the Prisoners' Union, Weekly Guardian Associates, and the Revolutionary Socialist League. The inmates and publishers challenged the constitutionality of Sections 540.70 and 540.71(b) of regulations promulgated by the Federal Bureau of Prisons. The plaintiffs argued that under the standard of review provided by *Procunier v. Martinez*, these regulations violated their First Amendment rights. Section 540.70 permitted federal prisoners to receive outside publications but reserved the right for prison officials to reject publications determined to be detrimental to institutional security. Section 540.71(b) provided the criteria for rejection and read as follows:

(1) It depicts or describes procedures for the construction or use of weapons, ammunition, bombs or incendiary devices;

(2) It depicts, encourages, or describes methods of escape from correctional facilities, or contains blueprints, drawings or similar descriptions of Bureau of Prisons institutions;

(3) It depicts or describes procedures for the brewing of alcoholic beverages, or the manufacture of drugs;

(4) It is written in code;

(5) It depicts, describes or encourages activities which may lead to the use of physical violence or group disruption;

(6) It encourages or instructs in the commission of criminal activity;

(7) It is sexually explicit material which by its nature or content poses a threat to the security, good order, or discipline of the institution, or facilitates criminal activity.

Program Statement No. 5266.5 provided guidance as to what type of sexually explicit material was prohibited under 540.71(b)(7):

(1) Homosexual (of the same sex as the institution population).

(2) Sado-masochistic.

(3) Bestiality.

(4) Involving children.

According to the regulations, only the warden may reject a publication, and only if it is deemed detrimental to security, order, or discipline within the prison or if it could facilitate criminal activity. The warden may not prohibit specific publications but rather specific issues of a publication. Thus, each issue must be reviewed separately [§ 540.71(c)]. The rules also allow for certain procedural safeguards. For instance, if a publication is rejected, the warden must notify the inmate promptly and provide the reasons for the rejection and identify the specific material deemed objectionable [§ 540.71(d)]. Further, the warden must send a copy of the rejection letter to the sender of the publication [§ 540.71(e)].

The District Court did not apply the *Martinez* standard, but the Court of Appeals did. The United States Supreme Court granted a writ of certiorari for the purpose of determining the appropriate standard of review when determining the constitutionality of regulations limiting what publications may be received by inmates.

In *Thornburgh*, the Court addressed the subject of incoming publications, produced for a broad audience but specifically requested by individual inmates. Certain publications may create danger or disorder in the information they provide or because prisoners may see particular material in the hands of one prisoner and draw inferences about that inmate's beliefs, sexual orientation, or gang affiliation.

Because *Martinez* involved outgoing correspondence with non-inmates, the Court did not believe it posed the same risks as incoming publications and thus applied the *Turner* reasonableness standard of review. The first factor in the reasonableness test is whether the regulations are legitimate, neutral, and rationally related to the government's stated objective. The objective of the regulations in this case is to protect prison security, which is clearly legitimate. The question of neutrality is less obvious but the Court held that the regulations are neutral, even though they do, to some extent, restrict based on content (e.g., procedures for constructing weapons or manufacturing alcohol) due to the potential implications of that content. Nevertheless, the Court found the regulations further an important or substantial governmental interest while being unrelated to the suppression of expression.

According to the Court, the second factor in the reasonable test was also satisfied, in that alternative means of exercising the right of receiving publications remained open. Inmates could still receive a broad range of publications. Regarding the third factor of the *Turner* requirements, the Court held that accommodation of the asserted constitutional right would have a significant impact on guards and inmates in terms of safety. The fourth and final factor of reasonableness is whether easy alternatives to the rules exist. The Court determined that prison officials rejected less restrictive alternatives because they would result in discontent, or no greater security, and thus the promulgated regulations are not an exaggerated response to their security concerns.

Relying on the requirements set out by *Turner*, the United States Supreme Court in *Thornburgh* upheld regulations that censored publications were deemed to pose a risk of violence and disorder. One of the criteria for censorship in *Thornburgh* was receipt of publications containing "sexually explicit material which by its nature or content poses a threat to the security, good order, or discipline of the institution, or facilitates criminal activity" (e.g., homosexuality, sado-masochistic, etc.). But what about the receipt of nude or seminude photos from wives or girlfriends? Does it matter that the pictures were part of a private letter as opposed to a mass-produced publication? In *Giano v. Senkowski* (1995), the United States Court of Appeals (Second Circuit) addressed this very question. In 1991, an inmate by the name of Julio Giano received two seminude photos of his girlfriend that she had personally mailed to Giano. According to prison rules, inmates were prohibited from receiving sexually explicit photos of their wives and girlfriends. However, according to those same rules, inmates could receive commercially produced seminude and nude photos. The pictures sent to Giano were confiscated and Giano brought a Section 1983 suit claiming the prison policy violated his First Amendment right to free speech and the Fourteenth Amendment's right to equal protection.

Prison officials asserted that allowing inmates to possess nude or seminude pictures of their wives and girlfriends could cause violence between inmates or with guards. The court applied the four requirements set forth by *Turner* and found that there was a rational connection between the rule and the stated objective. The court also determined that inmates had alternative ways of exercising their rights. They could receive commercially produced erotica and non-nude photos of wives and girlfriends. Accommodating the prisoners' request would have a negative impact on guards and prisoners alike, and there was no existing reasonable alternative to the rule. Regarding the Fourteenth Amendment claim, the court found that the rule applied to all inmates.

In *Thornbaugh* and *Giano*, the courts addressed the constitutionality of prison regulations that prohibit certain types of publications and pictures for security purposes. However, in *Jerry Rice v. State of Kansas*, the contested regulations were created with the objective of promoting good behavior and rehabilitation. In *Rice*, inmates challenged the constitutionality of two regulations of the Kansas Department of Corrections. The first regulation stated: "All books, newspapers, or periodicals shall be purchased through special purchase orders. Only books, newspapers, or periodicals received directly from a publisher or a vendor shall be accepted" (Kansas Department of Corrections: Policies and Procedures). The second rule limited the amount of money inmates could spend from their commissary account in a month. The combined effect of these two rules limited what inmates could purchase. Further, the requirement that all purchases be made through the inmate's account prevented inmates from receiving gift subscriptions (publications purchased by friends or family outside of the correctional facility). Gift subscriptions, it was believed, would undermine the privilege and negate the incentive to behave well.

The stated purpose for these regulations was that they promote rehabilitation by encouraging good behavior and facilitating better decisions. The rules were intended to create behavior incentives by allowing deserving inmates the opportunity to use a certain portion of their money in a discretionary way. An inmate could earn this privilege by remaining free of disciplinary convictions and demonstrating a willingness to participate in work assignments and certain programs.

In its analysis, the Supreme Court of Kansas applied the *rational basis test* provided by *Turner v. Safley* and determined that there was substantial evidence to support the finding that the regulations are rationally related to the rehabilitation of the inmates. Inmates had alternative means to exercise their rights, as they could purchase publications themselves (up to $30 worth) via their inmate accounts, they could access publications kept in the prison library, or they could petition the warden for a waiver of the $30 limit, thereby allowing them to purchase publications exceeding $30. Accommodation in terms of allowing gift subscriptions would undermine the system of incentive and rewards that aids in the rehabilitation of inmates. It would also substantially increase the number of publications coming into the prison, thereby burdening prison officials with the extra work of screening and delivering these publications. Last, it was suggested that one alternative to the prison regulation would be to have friends or family members wishing to provide a gift subscription complete paperwork that would provide sufficient data to enable officials to monitor incoming publications. The Court determined that although this was an alternative, it would undermine the incentive-based system and would burden the correctional facility with the task of verifying accuracy of information provided by family and friends.

In sum, the Court determined that although the regulations may not be the best method of fostering inmate rehabilitation, they are not an unreasonable response and are rationally related to a legitimate government interest.

Correspondence in Languages Other than English

In 1994, a federal court of appeals heard *Thongvanh v. Thalacker*. In this case, Iowa prison officials prohibited Thongvanh from corresponding in Lao, his native tongue, with anyone other than his parents and grandparents, who spoke no English. Thongvanh asserted that this rule was unconstitutional in that it violated his right to free speech under the First Amendment. Iowa prison officials claimed that the rule was necessary for security reasons because the prison had no Lao translator. The court again relied on the four factors provided in *Turner* to determine the constitutionality of the regulation, and in this case they found it unconstitutional. Although the prison had a legitimate security interest in monitoring mail, accommodating Thongvanh's right was not difficult and there was not an absence of a ready alternatives to the regulation. A local refugee center could provide Lao translators at no cost. It was not clear from the court's decision, however, whether inmates have a constitutional right to correspond in their native tongue. Would the result have been different if there had been no local refugee center?

Conclusion

For a long time, the Supreme Court was reluctant to get involved in the question of constitutional rights of inmates, such as free speech. This attitude changed during the 1970s, as awareness of civil rights began to increase, as discussed in Chapter 2. In *Martinez*, the Court stated it would address the question of constitutional rights of prisoners but instead focused on the incidental intrusion on the rights of non-inmates and applied an intermediate level of scrutiny. Although *Pell* also involved communications with non-inmates, the Court focused on balancing the policy objectives of the regulations and the intrusion on the inmate's free speech rights. The Court's emphasis on deference to administrative decisions of prison officials and finding alternative means of communication available tipped the balance in favor of the prison.

When the Court considered cases involving communications between inmates or receipt of correspondence or publications, then the Court has been even more deferential to policy objectives (rehabilitation, security) and the administrative decisions of prison officials. *Turner* finally addressed the question that *Martinez* failed to answer, providing a four-factor test to analyze the constitutionality of a rule purported to infringe on a constitutional right. The new, more flexible and deferential standard required only that the prison regulation be rationally related to the policy objective. This is the lowest level of scrutiny. After *Turner*, the Supreme Court and lower federal courts have all relied on the *Turner* rationally related test to decide the constitutionality of a variety of prison regulations.

Convicted offenders, it seems, are limited in their ability to exercise the freedom of speech right when this right contradicts prison management. Specifically, and as noted before, the ultimate priority, as seen by the Supreme Court, is to help correctional administrators maintain safety and order in their facilities. Such a goal may at times be viewed as a violation of basic rights guaranteed by the First Amendment; however, one must not forget that non-content-based restrictions are those that seek to limit the time, place, or manner of speech, and not the message of the speaker. That an individual was convicted of a crime and has been sentenced to incarceration poses a limit on time, place, and manner — limitations that become an essential part of the punishment and the pains of incarceration.

Discussion Questions

1. Should convicted offenders sentenced to incarceration receive the same level of protection of their freedom of speech as that possessed by free citizens?

2. If the incarcerated offenders have less protection, how do we assess what is and is not a violation of an inmate's free speech rights?

3. Should the right to free speech be limited to convicted offenders as part of their punishment, and as a mean of incapacitation?

4. Discuss the rationale behind the cases that impose limits on prisoners' freedom of speech? What is the justification for such rulings, and how does it serve the goals of incapacitation?

5. What is the concern that correctional officials have with inmates' written communications? Why isn't restriction of this communication viewed as a violation of the First Amendment freedom of speech clause?

6. Discuss the problem that correctional officials face when prisoners wish to communicate in a language other than English. What are the cases associated with this issue, and how did the court reason in their decision?

7. Why is it problematic for incarcerated individuals to receive printed material from their friends and families? What are the standards used by correctional administrators and justified by the courts to allow or disallow such material to enter prison?

List of Cases Cited

Bell v. Wolfish, 1976. 441 U.S. 520.

Block v. Rutherford, 1984. 468 US 576.

Chaplinsky v. New Hampshire, 1942. 315 U.S. 568.

Giano v. Senkowski, 1995. 54 F.3d 1050.

Jerry Rice v. State of Kansas, 2004. 95 P.3d 994.

Jones v. North Carolina Prisoners' Labor Union, Inc., 1977. 433 U.S. 119.

Pell v. Procunier, 1974. 417 US 817.

Procunier v. Martinez, 1974. 416 US 396.

Renton v. Playtime Theaters, 1986. 475 U.S. 41.

Sable Communications of California, Inc. v. Federal Communications Commission, 1989. 492 U.S. 115.

Turner et al. v. Safley, 1987. 482 US 78.

Thornbaugh v. Abbott, 1989. 490 U.S. 401.

Thongvagnh v. Thalacker, 1994. 17 F.3d 256.

Wolf v. McDonnell, 1974. 418 U.S. 539.

Chapter 6

First Amendment:
Freedom of Religion

Congress shall make no law respecting an establishment of religion, or prohibiting the free exercise thereof; or abridging the freedom of speech, or of the press; or the right of the people peaceably to assemble, and to petition the Government for a redress of grievances.

Religion has always played an important role in correctional practices in America, from the early days of penitentiaries, when Quakers introduced their faith as a guide for repentance and rehabilitation of offenders. Today, various religious groups have the power to affect legislation that protects the right to practice faith in accordance with the First Amendment, and thus enable correctional facilities to be more conducive to practices reflecting religious diversity. This fits in with recent trends in criminological and penological discourse that promote restorative justice, which stems from strong biblical notions of justice. Under President George W. Bush, faith-based prison programs and prison units aimed at rehabilitating offenders received a great deal of governmental support.

In addition to protecting an individual's right to freedom of speech, as discussed in the previous chapter, the First Amendment also protects religious freedom. The guarantee of this freedom consists of two complementary clauses: the *establishment clause* and the *free exercise* clause. The establishment clause generally prohibits the government from establishing a religion or preferring (promoting) one religion above others. While the latter, the free exercise clause, protects individual religious beliefs, practices, or expression from government intrusion in the form of proscriptions or discrimination.

In the 19th and early 20th centuries, with regard to freedom of religion, federal courts applied the United States Constitution when hearing cases challenging federal laws, while state courts analyzed cases based on their respective state constitutions. States typically recognized the right to free exercise of religion, but with broad authority to regulate. For example, in *Reynolds v. United States*: The Court held that while laws "cannot interfere with mere religious belief and opinions, they may with practices." The Court felt that allowing a religious belief to be used as a justification for a criminal act (in this case, polygamy) would result in citizens becoming laws unto themselves. States tended to support the establishment of religion, as indicated by their support for religious-based institutions such as religious schools and hospitals, though this tended to favor only one religion, Christianity, and more specifically, Protestantism. As varying strains of Christianity became more popular, however, and immigration brought an influx of other religions (Jews, Muslims, Buddhists, Hindus, etc.), there was a corresponding increase in challenges to existing laws. Frustrated with the response of state courts, individuals increasingly turned to federal courts to address their grievances. In the year 1940, things started to change.

Although the establishment and free-exercise clauses work together, they have been considered separately, spawning two distinct lines of analysis. In *Cantwell v. Connecticut*, the Supreme Court ruled in favor of Cantwell, a Jehovah's Witness family, in a suit challenging a Connecticut statute that required a license to solicit for religious purposes. In this case the Court held that the First Amendment "embraces two concepts—freedom to believe and freedom to act. The first is absolute but, in the nature of things, the second cannot be. Conduct remains subject to regulation for the protection of society." Absent clear and present danger, however, the government may not engage in prior restraint when it would determine what was a religious cause and thus permissible. This would be a deprivation of a liberty without due process of law, in violation of the Fourteenth Amendment. In the process, the Court's ruling established the free-exercise clause as a fundamental right that therefore applies in all states via the Fourteenth Amendment. Accordingly, in order to be constitutional, any law infringing on this right must be shown to be nondiscriminatory and related to an important or significant governmental interest. As for the establishment clause's application to the states, the Supreme Court decided on the issue in 1947, in *Everson v. Board of Education*, a case about busing for private and public schoolchildren. Citing *Reynolds v. United States*, Justice Hugo Black stated:

> The 'establishment of religion' clause of the First Amendment means at least this: Neither a state nor the Federal Government can set up a church. Neither can pass laws which aid one religion, aid all religions, or prefer one religion over another. Neither can force nor influence a person to go or to remain away from church against his will or force him to profess a belief or disbelief in any religion. No person can be punished for entertaining or professing religious beliefs or disbeliefs, for church attendance or non-attendance. No tax in any amount, large or small, can be levied to support any religious activities or institutions, whatever they may be called, or whatever form they may adopt to teach or practice religion. Neither a state nor the Federal Government can, openly or secretly, participate in the affairs of any religious organizations or groups, or vice versa. In the words of Jefferson, the clause against establishment of religion by law was intended to erect 'a wall of separation between church and state.' (as cited in Berman, 1986: 784)

Standards of Review Today

Establishment Clause

In *Everson v. Board of Education*, the Court attempted to create a clear line of separation between church and state. Since that decision, the Supreme Court has fashioned a number of tests for evaluating whether government actions or laws have violated the establishment clause. The first test was developed 27 years after *Everson*, when the Supreme Court crafted a strict doctrinal framework for separation in the case *Lemon v. Kurtzman*. This doctrinal framework came to be known as the *Lemon test*. According to the Court, when a law is challenged under the establishment clause, constitutionality is determined by whether the law:

1. has a secular purpose;

2. has a primary effect that neither advances nor inhibits religion; and

3. fosters no excessive entanglement between church and state.

The *Lemon* test was developed to analyze the case of state funding for "church-related educational institutions." The Court held that government funding for parochial schools advanced religion, and the need to enforce the laws would result in excessive entanglement between church and state.

The *Lemon* test is likely the most frequently applied test, but critics complain it is unworkable. Over time, the Supreme Court itself moved away from the *Lemon* test. In *Marsh v. Chambers*, the Court upheld the Nebraska legislature's practice of starting each day with a prayer led by a state-funded chaplain, based on the fact that such a prayer is a long-established tradition that "has become part of the fabric of our society." A year later, in *Lynch v. Donnelly*, the Supreme Court ruled that a Nativity scene in a Rhode Island city Christmas decoration was permissible, on the grounds that a reasonable person would not perceive the scene as endorsing religion. The decision clarified the establishment clause, however, to specify that the government should be neutral so as not to endorse or disapprove of any specific religion. For instance, one of the reasons that the authors of the Bill of Rights included the so-called establishment clause was so that one religion would not be favored, nor would the United States have an official religion, as the United Kingdom has the Church of England. The language put forward in *Lynch v. Donnelly* has come to be known as the *endorsement test*. The endorsement test has been applied primarily to cases involving expression of religion, as in the cases above, involving religious symbols on government property or religious prayers during public events.

A third significant test is known as the *coercion test*. In *Lee v. Weisman*, a public school invited a Jewish rabbi to speak at a graduation ceremony. Mr. Weisman, a parent of one of the graduating students, filed for a temporary injunction to stop the rabbi from speaking but lost and the rabbi gave the benediction as planned. After the graduation ceremony, Mr. Weisman sought a permanent injunction and won. The case was appealed by the school district to the United States Supreme Court, which held that having a religious figure speaking at a public school creates a coercive atmosphere that is sponsored by the state. Justice Kennedy stated: "As we have observed before, there are heightened concerns with protecting freedom of conscience from subtle coercive pressure in the elementary and secondary public schools. Our decisions in *Engle v. Vitalie*, and *Abington School District v. Schempp*, recognize, among other things, that prayer exercises in public schools carry a particular risk of indirect coercion. The concern may not be limited to the context of schools, but it is most pronounced there. What to most believers may seem nothing more than a reasonable request that the nonbeliever respect their religious practices, in a school context may appear to the nonbeliever or dissenter to be an attempt to employ the machinery of the State to enforce a religious orthodoxy."

Essentially, the Court feared that a student would become ostracized by their peers for refraining from engaging in the practices of other religions, or conversely, for practicing their own religious beliefs. The manner in which to analyze and interpret cases involving the establishment clause has yet to be fully settled. There is no single test or approach that is, or has been, consistently applied. The test applied appears to be dependent on the nature of the legal issue, whether it involves religious expression or government funding of religion.

The Establishment Clause and Prison

The vast majority of prison-related cases addressing First Amendment rights to freedom of religion have involved questions of infringement on free exercise, not on establishment of religion. However, in the latter category, there are a few cases worth noting.

As previously noted, in *Everson v. Board of Education*, the Court asserted that neither federal nor state governments may engage in activity that aids religion. However, state and federal prisons regularly employ chaplains and purchase religious materials such as Bibles for distribution. Is this not a clear violation of the establishment clause of the First Amendment as interpreted by the Court in *Everson*? Although there is no case that speaks to this point directly, this question has been discussed in other establishment cases. In *Abington School District v. Schempp*, the Court held unconstitutional a rule that required public school students to read passages from the Bible and recite the Lord's prayer. In his concurring statement, however, Justice Brennan makes a distinction between the circumstances in Abington School District and those in military or prison settings. Justice Brennan stated:

> There are certain practices, conceivably violative of the Establishment Clause, the striking down of which might seriously interfere with certain religious liberties also protected by the First Amendment. Provisions for churches and chaplains at military establishments for those in the armed services may afford one such example. The like provision by state and federal governments for chaplains in penal institutions may afford another example. It is argued that such provisions may be assumed to contravene the Establishment Clause, yet be sustained on constitutional grounds as necessary to secure to the members of the Armed Forces and prisoners those rights of worship guaranteed under the Free Exercise Clause. Since government has deprived such persons of the opportunity to practice their faith at places of their choice, the argument runs, government may, in order to avoid infringing the free exercise guarantees, provide substitutes where it requires such persons to be (as cited in Berman, 1986: 296–98).

Although only dicta without the force of law, the Court's statements strongly suggest that under unique circumstances, enforcing the Establishment Clause in prison settings in a similar manner to how it is enforced in public schools could deny an inmate of free exercise rights (see also *Katcoff v. O'Marsh,* in which military chaplains were deemed not unconstitutional because chaplains provide religious services to those who want them; they are not employed to proselytize. Moreover, they are often located in places where such services are not readily accessible).

In *Muhammad v. City of New York Dept. of Corrections,* the Nation of Islam (NOI) brought a suit alleging violations of the First Amendment when the *City of New York Department of Correction (DOC)* refused to hire a NOI minister or provide NOI specific religious services or religious texts. Applying the *Lemon* test, the court determined that the establishment clause was not violated because the DOC accommodated, evenly and fairly, a variety of religious denominations, including Muslims. The court, citing *United States v. Kahane,* made the point that in the prison context, there is a special exception through which the establishment clause must be balanced with the demands of the free exercise clause. In light of prison administration demands, prisons are not required to provide a chaplain of every faith or sect, as long as the refusal is not for the purpose of discriminating against the minority faith.

In *Kerr v. Farrey,* a federal court addressed the question of whether it is a violation of the establishment clause to force an inmate to participate in a religious substance abuse program, or otherwise be classified as a higher-risk inmate and thus lose parole eligibility. The district court applied the *Lemon* test and determined that the prison's policy did not violate the establishment clause. The Court of Appeals then reversed the decision, ruling that when an inmate claims he or she has been coerced to "subscribe to religions generally, or to a particular religion," then the court must consider three points:

1. whether the state has acted;
2. whether the action amounts to coercion; and
3. whether the object of the coercion was religious or secular.

Obtaining guidance from cases addressing the same, or similar, issue (see *David Griffin v. Coughlin, Warner v. Orange County Dept. of Probation, O'Connor v. California*), the Court of Appeals found that the state had acted through the program, the lack of choice was coercion, and the substance abuse program was in fact religious.

While *Kerr* found that the *Lemon* test was the incorrect test to apply in cases when an inmate claims coercion, *Alexander v. Schenk* held that the *Lemon* test is required to assess a violation of an inmate's constitutional rights when there is no claim of coercion. Additionally, the court in *Schenk* noted that if an inmate claim involves a challenge to a regulation or order of the correctional facility, then the requirements of *Turner v. Safley* should apply, and the prison's action will be upheld only if "reasonably related to legitimate penological interests."

In sum, when reviewing establishment clause actions brought by inmates, the standard of review depends on whether the alleged violation involves coercion. If so, then the court must consider the three factors provided in *Kerr v. Farrey*. If not, then courts should apply the *Lemon* test — (1) law has secular purpose; (2) primary effect neither advances nor inhibits religion; and (3) does not foster entanglement between church and state — in conjunction with the *Turner* requirements (i.e., that there is substantial evidence to support the finding that the regulations are rationally related to the rehabilitation of the inmates), considering (1) rational connection between regulation and legitimate governmental interest; (2) availability of alternative means of exercising the asserted constitutional right; (3) extent to which accommodation will impact prison staff and prison resources; and (4) whether regulation is an exaggerated response to prison concerns.

Free-Exercise Clause

As previously mentioned, the Court in *Reynolds v. United States* provided the government with broad authority to regulate religious practices, which was later narrowed by the decision of *Cantwell v. Connecticut*. *Cantwell* held the free exercise of religion to be a fundamental right, and as such, applicable to the states. Thus, any state regulation infringing on this fundamental right must be related to an important or significant governmental interest, or the regulation must be addressing a "clear and present danger."

The standard of review for free-exercise cases was modified again in 1963 with *Sherbert v. Verner*. Sherbert, a Seventh-day Adventist, was fired after refusing to work on Saturday, the Church's day of Sabbath. Sherbert was then denied unemployment compensation because the state did not accept the justification for the refusal to work on a Saturday. The Supreme Court ultimately heard the issue presented in *Sherbert v. Verner* and held that the denial of Sherbert's unemployment claim was unconstitutional. In order for the government to burden the practice of one's religion, the government must show that it has a "compelling state interest" that justifies the action. This balancing test between government interests and religious behavior came to be known as the *Sherbert test*.

The *Sherbert* test was considered authoritative until the Supreme Court heard *Employment Division v. Smith*, another unemployment case but with a different outcome. In this case, two Native Americans were fired from their jobs as substance abuse counselors and subsequently denied unemployment compensation due to their use of peyote, an illegal drug. The Native Americans argued that their religion involves the ingestion of peyote during religious ceremonies. Unlike in *Sherbert,* the Court in *Smith* held that the government could deny unemployment compensation when the religious conduct is in violation of a legitimate law. The Court stated that a law that is "neutral" and "generally applicable" is constitutional, even if it "burdens, harms or jeopardizes" an individual's religion. The Court determined that the purpose of the peyote prohibition was not to prevent a religious act but to prevent its use by everyone (neutral and generally applicable). The Court further stated, however, that if the law is not neutral or generally applicable, then it must be related to a compelling government interest and narrowly tailored to be considered constitutional. By not requiring neutral, generally applicable laws to be related to a compelling government interest, the Supreme Court weakened the free-exercise clause.

The new standard fashioned by the Court in *Smith* did not sit well with many in Congress or the general population. In response, Congress passed the *Religious Freedom Restoration Act (RFRA)* in 1993. The RFRA was created to reinstitute the "compelling interest" requirement, even for laws that are neutral and generally applicable, on the premise that a religiously neutral law could interfere with the exercise of religion as much as a non-neutral law could. In *City of Boerne v. Flores*, the Catholic Church was denied a permit to expand because a specific church was located in an area zoned for historic preservation. The Church sued under RFRA, claiming the zoning ordinance violated their fundamental right to free exercise of their religion. The city of Boerne argued that RFRA was unconstitutional because it dictated to state and local governments the manner in which to determine what constitutes a constitutional violation. In this case, the Supreme Court held that the RFRA is not a proper exercise of Congress' enforcement power and thus is unconstitutional as applied to the states. Thus, the standard of review for claims of free exercise violations by state governments continued to be the *Smith* test, whereas for claims involving federal laws, the RFRA continued to apply. As a result, Congress passed the *Religious Land Use and Institutionalized Persons Act (RLUIPA)* in 2000. This law asserted that no government could implement a land use regulation that would burden one's right to free exercise of their religion, unless the government could demonstrate it had a compelling interest to do so. The RLUIPA also applies to prisoners, as it requires federal and state governments to demonstrate a compelling interest to burden their religious practices.

The Free Exercise Clause and Prison

A review of the history of the free exercise clause and the Supreme Court indicates a state of flux, in which the standard of review was reformulated numerous times over more than a century. Similarly, the determination of the proper standard of review for prisoner free exercise claims remains to be settled. Typically, the courts will seek to balance the constitutional right with the penological needs and objectives of the prison, as well as the financial burden imposed by accommodating the prisoner's desired practice. Because prisoners may claim religious practice in order to obtain certain privileges (e.g., certain foods) or to create difficulties for prison officials, the analysis of inmate claims often necessitates determining whether the religion is real and the beliefs are sincerely held.

Real Religion

In the early 1970s, a federal inmate by the name of Harry Theriault created a religion known as Church of the New Song (CONS). The religion was based on Eclatarianism, the belief in Eclat as the supreme power. Theriault filed a class action lawsuit after prison officials denied him and other believers the right to conduct religious practices. In *The-riault v. Carlson*, a district court held that it could not rule that CONS was not a legitimate religion because the establishment clause requires the government to remain neutral on matters of religion. Accepting CONS as a religion, the court held that the free exercise clause requires that prison authorities allow for similar privileges as other, more main-stream faiths. This holding was overturned in *Theriault v. Silber*, when the Fifth Circuit Court of Appeals abandoned the policy of neutrality and created guidelines for deter-mining the legitimacy of prison religions. The court found CONS not to be a legitimate religion, but rather a creation, disguised as a faith, manufactured for the purpose of in-terfering with prison administration and obtaining certain privileges. Compare *Silber* to *Lipp v. Procunier*, in which the court, citing *Cantwell v. Connecticut*, held that the Met-ropolitan Community Churches, catering to the spiritual needs of homosexuals or those with a homosexual orientation, was a legitimate religion. By citing *Cantwell*, the court reaffirmed that government may not restrict one's freedom to subscribe to a particular religion, or the form of worship, for the First Amendment right is absolute. However, the manner in which one chooses to practice his or her religion is not an absolute, and thus subject to regulation for the protection of society. The court in *Lipp* held that the Metropolitan Community Church did not promote illegal practices and that the inmates sincerely believed in the espoused tenets of the religion.

Sincerely Held Beliefs

It is not sufficient in and of itself that the religion be considered a legitimate religion in order to garner constitutional protection. An inmate must also be a sincere believer in the religion. The concern is that prisoners will assert religious adherence for the pur-pose of obtaining certain secular desires. Per the decision in *Dehart v. Horn*, "The mere assertion of a religious belief does not automatically trigger First Amendment protections, however. To the contrary, only those beliefs which are both sincerely held and religious in nature are entitled to constitutional protection." If a prisoner's request for a particular accommodation (e.g., diet) is not a function of a sincerely held belief, then the First Amendment does not impose on prison officials a requirement to accommodate. Once determined that an inmate is a sincere believer in a legitimate religion, the ruling con-tinued, courts can apply the *Turner* analysis to assess whether a prison policy is infringing on a constitutional right. In other words, the courts must decide whether there is a ra-tional connection between prison policy and a legitimate penological interest.

Prayers

One area in which the courts have often had to balance the free exercise clause with prison interests and needs involves the right to pray. While prisons are not re-quired to accommodate every request for time or space to pray, they must provide opportunities to do so when reasonable, even if for minority religions. The Supreme Court in *Cruz v. Beto*, "We do not suggest, of course, that every religious sect or group within a prison—however few in number—must have identical facilities or personnel. A special chapel or place of worship need not be provided for every faith regardless of size; nor must a chaplain, priest, or minister be provided without regard to the extent of the demand. But reasonable opportunities must be afforded to all prisoners to exercise the religious freedom guaranteed by the First and Fourteenth Amendments without fear of penalty." Thus, the Court protects an inmate's fundamental right to practice a religion but acknowledges that prisons are not necessarily required to provide equal facilities for each religion.

The issue of what is considered a reasonable opportunity to practice religion was addressed in *O'Lone v. Estate of Shabazz*. In *O'Lone* prison regulations required inmates to work away from the prison. Muslim inmates argued that the regulation prevented them from returning to the prison to participate in Jumu'ah (i.e., Friday-afternoon congregational prayer), thus violating their First Amendment rights. Applying the *Turner* standard, the Court noted that prison regulations alleged to violate constitutional rights are appropriately reviewed under the reasonableness standard, meaning that the regulation is valid if it is reasonably related (logically connected) to legitimate penological interests. The Court reasserts the need for deference to institutional administrators on how best to run prisons. In *O'Lone*, the Court held there was a logical connection between the prison policy and its objectives. Accommodating the request of the Muslim inmates would have been very burdensome and reduced security. Further, the prison regulation did not prevent Muslim inmates from practicing their religion entirely and left open other means of exercising the right.

As previously noted, Congress enacted the Religious Freedom Restoration Act in 1993. This act stipulated, "Government may substantially burden a person's exercise of religion only if it demonstrates that application of the burden to the person

(1) is in furtherance of a compelling government interest; and

(2) is the least restrictive means of furthering that compelling governmental interest" (42 U.S.C. § 2000).

In *Mack v. O'Leary*, the Court, for the first time, specified the meaning of the phrase "substantially burden a person's exercise of religion." According to the Court, a substantial burden on one's freedom to exercise his or her religion is a government regulation "that forces adherents of a religion to refrain from religiously motivated conduct, inhibits or constrains conduct or expression that manifests a central tenant of a person's religious beliefs, or compels conduct or expression that is contrary to those beliefs." As applied to the incarcerated, if it is demonstrated that a prison policy does constitute a substantial burden on the exercise of religion, then the burden of proof shifts to the defendant (the correctional facility and prison officials) to show that it had a compelling interest in imposing the burden and that there were no less restrictive means of doing so. However, as the Court noted in *Mack v. O'Leary*, maintaining order and security in prisons is considered a compelling interest, and courts are to continue to defer to prison officials on how best to achieve these objectives. Further, the Court noted that prison officials "do not have to do handsprings to accommodate the religious needs of inmates, and the less central an observance is to the religion in question the less the officials must do."

Religious Diets and Other Practices

Claims that prison policy interferes with religious dietary laws must also be considered in light of prison security needs and availability of resources. Courts have held that the Constitution prohibits prison officials from enacting polices preventing inmates from observing religious dietary obligations where accommodation would not be burdensome for the prison; one example is *Kahane v. Carlson*, in which the incarcerated plaintiff sued for provision of a kosher diet. Accommodation is considered to be burdensome when it would require extra work and man hours of prison staff and when it would compromise orderliness. Compare *Kahane* with *Uday v. Kastner*, in which an inmate claimed that his religion dictated that he eat only organic food washed in distilled water; the appellate court found that accommodating this claim would disrupt prison order by encouraging the proliferation of similar claims for specific religious diets. Generally speaking, the courts apply the *Turner* standard when reviewing these cases. Thus, the court must assess whether the regulation is rationally connected to a legitimate prison objective, whether there are alternative ways for the inmate to exercise the right, how it will affect prison guards and other inmates, and whether there are "ready alternatives" available to accommodate the inmate that would do little to interfere with penological interests. However, "ready alternatives" does not mean "least restrictive" alternative, as was concluded in *Spies v. Voinovich*, a case regarding the provision of a vegan diet for a practicing Buddhist inmate.

It seems clear that the Constitution requires that prison officials accommodate religious diets when these diets are not overly burdensome or a threat to order and security. However, what do prison officials do when there is a question as to whether the inmate is truly a member of a particular faith? For instance, by religious law, for one to be considered Jewish, a person must be born to a Jewish mother or have participated in a formal conversion; for one to be considered Muslim, the common convention requires one to have a Muslim father; however, different schools and sects of Islam may not have this requirement and simply acknowledge one as being Muslim if he or she has a Muslim parent or undergoes a formal conversion. How do courts analyze a free exercise claim when an inmate requests special religious dietary needs such as kosher or halal food but, from an ecclesiastical standpoint, religious leaders do not consider the inmate a member of that faith? The courts are not to consider ecclesiastical questions. Rather, the courts need only assess whether an inmate's religious beliefs are sincere. Thus, as was discussed in the case of *Jackson v. Mann*, if a person claims to be Jewish but is not recognized as Jewish by a rabbi, prison officials may still have to accommodate his dietary needs, so long as it is determined that the inmate's Jewish beliefs are sincerely held.

What if an inmate is a practicing member of a particular faith, but a prison regulation impinges on his right to engage in a dietary practice that is not mandated by his religion? In *Levitan v. Ashcroft*, federal prisoners objected to prison regulations that prevented Catholic inmates from imbibing a small amount of wine during Communion. The prison officials argued that drinking of the wine was not a mandated practice for communion. The United States Court of Appeals, District of Columbia Circuit, disagreed and ruled that the ban on prisoners consuming wine during service was unconstitutional: "The fact that the First Amendment does not protect only compelled religious conduct does not mean that the Constitution forbids all constraints on religiously motivated conduct, however trivial. Instead, the First Amendment is implicated when a law or regulation imposes a substantial, as opposed to inconsequential, burden on the litigant's religious practice." The court further explained that the religious practice may be a central tenet or simply important to the practice of the religion and a sincerely held religious belief.

In addition to prayer and diet, freedom of religion cases involving inmates have covered other religious requirements. For instance, courts have heard cases about rights to have long hair, in *Goings v. Aaron*, and rights to maintain facial hair, in *Moskowitz. v. Wilkinson*. In general, courts have upheld grooming restrictions, considering them reasonably related to legitimate penological interests. Hair can interfere with the ability of prison staff to capably identify inmates and to stop (or limit) the transporting of drugs, weapons, or any other prohibited items. Such issues are obviously of serious concern to prison administrators. For additional cases on this issue, you may wish to read *Diaz v. Collins*, *Hines v. South Carolina Department of Corrections*, and *Flagner v. Wilkinson*.

Conclusion: Religion, Penology, and Correctional Practices

Historically, religion in the United States has played a significant role in efforts to rehabilitate criminals, largely because the deeply embedded Judeo-Christian concepts of repentance and redemption suggest that people are capable of moral regeneration. The first to introduce religion to the prison setting were the Quakers, who sought to rehabilitate incarcerated offenders by introducing them to religious scripts and preaching their gospel. Under Quaker philosophy, a major goal of confinement was penance through required Bible study and reflection on one's sins (Sumter & Clear, 2005). Since that time, rehabilitation through religion has become a major characteristic of the correctional landscape; however, it has presented its own problems along the way. Prison administrators often perceive inmates as adopting religion in order to manipulate the system and obtain leniency. Nonetheless, correctional administrators can encounter many legitimate challenges when asked to accommodate different religions. The challenges of accommodating religion in prison often have little to do with the belief system itself, but more with the special security interests of prisons, and the limited resources available. Consider the simple act of congregation, which might cause conflict between different groups of inmates. Giving congregation space to one group, for instance, may then cause resentment in another group, leading to a fight over the same limited space.

Discussion Questions

1. Discuss the potential difficulty for correctional administrators to fully maintain freedom of religion inside correctional institutions. What are some of the challenges that emerge in this context?

2. How do the *establishment clause* and the *free exercise clause* serve the First Amendment protection of freedom of religion? How do they apply to correctional institutions? Discuss the relevant cases.

3. What are the various tests fashioned by the Supreme Court to evaluate whether governmental actions violate the establishment clause?

4. What is the *Lemon test*? How does it relate to the establishment clause, and what are some of the critiques directed at it?

5. What is the *coercion test*? How is it different from the *endorsement test*? Discuss these two tests in the context of judicial rulings.

6. How did the Religious Freedom Restoration Act of 1993 change the courts' approach to prisoner litigation with regard to their right to freedom of religion?

7. How do courts deal with an inmate's claims to freedom of religion while maintaining the penological needs and objectives of the prison?

8. Discuss the main issues surrounding the establishment of the Church of the New Song (CONS). How does this case demonstrate the court's point of view when it comes to freedom of religion?

9. What are the main issues that occupy the courts in their consideration of the free exercise clause? How do such considerations aim to serve correctional security needs?

10. What are the penological aspects considered by the courts in deciding cases pertaining to freedom of religion?

11. Are correctional institutions mandated to provide equal facilities to all religions? Discuss this issue in the context of the correctional need for security, and religion's relevance to penological ideologies.

12. How do courts analyze a free exercise claim when an inmate requests a special religious diet but is not considered a member of that faith by religious leaders?

List of Cases Cited

Abington School District v. Schempp, 1963. 374 U.S. 203.

Alexander v. Schenk, 2000. 118 F. Supp.2d 298.

Cantwell v. Connecticut, 1940. 310 U.S. 296.

City of Boerne v. Flores, 1997. 521 U.S. 507.

Cruz v. Beto, 1972. 405 U.S. 319.

David Griffin v. Coughlin, 1996. 88 N.Y.2d 674.

Dehart v. Horn, 2000. 227 F.3d 47.

Diaz v. Collins, 1997. 114 F.3d 69.

Employment Division v. Smith, 1990. 494 U.S. 872.

Engle v. Vitalie, 1962. 370 U.S. 421.

Everson v. Board of Education, 1947. 330 U.S. 1.

Flagner v. Wilkinson, 2001. 241 F.3d 475.

Goings v. Aaron, 1972. 350 F. Supp 1.

Hines v. South Carolina's Department of Corrections, 1998. 148 F.3d 353.

Jackson v. Mann, 1999. 196 F.3d 316.

Kahane v. Carlson, 1975. 527 F.2d 492.

Katcoff v. O'Marsh, 1985. 755 F.2d 223.

Kerr v. Farrey, 1996. 95 F.3d 472.

Lee v. Weisman, 1992. 505 U.S. 577.

Lemon v. Kurtzman, 1971. 403 U.S. 602.

Levitan v. Ashcroft, 2002. 281 F.3d 1313.

Lipp v. Procunier, 1975. 395 F. Supp 871.

Lynch v. Donnelly, 1984. 465 U.S. 688.

Mack v. O'Leary, 1996. 80 F.3d 1175.

Marsh v. Chambers, 1983. 463 U.S. 783.

Moskowitz v. Wilinson, 1977. 432 F. Supp 947.

Muhammad v. City of New York Department of Corrections, 1995. 904 F. Supp 161.

O'Connor v. California, 1994. 855 F. Supp. 303.

O'Lone v. Estate of Shabazz, 1987. 482 U.S. 342.

Reynolds v. United States, 1878. 98 U.S. 145.

Sherbert v. Verner, 1963. 374 U.S. 398.

Spies v. Voinich, 1999.173 F.3d 398.

Theriault v. Carlson, 1973. 353 F. Supp 1061.

Theriault v. Silber, 1978. 391 F. Supp 578.

Turner v. Safley, 1987. 482 U.S. 78.

Uday v. Kastner, 1986. 805 F.2d 1218.

United States v. Kahane, 1975. 396 F. Supp 687.

Warner v. Orange County Dept. of Probation, 1994. 870F. Supp. 69.

Chapter 7

Fourth Amendment: Search and Seizure

It is commonly held that the ten amendments that make up the Bill of Rights were enacted in response to the perceived abuses of American colonists by British colonial rule. The exact language of the Fourth Amendment is:

The right of the people to be secure in their houses, persons, papers, and effects against unreasonable searches and seizure, shall not be violated; and no warrants shall be issued but upon probable cause, supported by oath or affirmation, and particularly describing the place to be searched, and the persons or things to be seized.

The inspiration for the Fourth Amendment was most likely the fact that American colonists had no safeguards against search and seizure of property by the British colonial authorities. These authorities had what were called "writs of assistance," which allowed them to search anyone or their property at any time. This general warrant that could allow authorities unfettered powers to search and seize evidence did not strike Americans as especially fair (Samaha, 2012).

The language of the Fourth Amendment seems somewhat jumbled and wordy, and unfortunately, jurisprudence regarding the amendment has been just as chaotic. As Amar (1994) notes, the Supreme Court, in some cases, holds that the words of the amendment should be strictly construed, while in other instances, the Supreme Court seems to have provided a near limitless number of exceptions and circumstances in which neither warrants nor probable cause is needed. Among the established exceptions to the Fourth Amendment are "good faith" (Ball, 1978), "child welfare" (Coleman, 2005), and "exigent circumstance" (Katz, 1990). However, these exceptions are more applicable to general citizens and not to people who are inmates in a correctional facility. Regardless of the more narrower focus and the lesser rights that inmates enjoy, there are a few basics of Fourth Amendment jurisprudence that need to be discussed.

In general, most legal scholars recognize that the Fourth Amendment has two clauses. The first clause, often referred to as the *reasonableness clause*, simply demands that searches not occur unless some reason exists for the search. The second clause, which many people refer to as the *warrant clause*, demands that all warrants be supported by probable cause. The two clauses of the Fourth Amendment may seem easy to interpret at first; however, this is not the case and many legal scholars debate the link between the two. Such views are largely dictated by some combination of the judicial philosophy of a particular legal scholar and the individual facts of a case. Thus, there is often little consistency when deciding if mere probable cause is enough to search a person's home, business, or belongings, or a warrant is actually required (Davies, 1999).

While these circumstances may appear discouraging, some basic rules can be given. Unless some exception exists, such as exigent circumstances, law enforcement will need a search warrant to conduct a search of a person's home. A search of a person while walking down the street or riding in an automobile need be based only on probable cause (Samaha, 2012). There is an exceedingly practical reason for this distinction. If law enforcement wants to search a dwelling, officers can go through the normal procedures, present evidence of probable cause to a judicial official for a warrant, and then later present the warrant during a search of the premises. However, if a law-enforcement officer wishes to search a person on the street or a person riding in a vehicle, it would be inherently difficult to get a search warrant. After all, there is little guarantee that the person would still be there after the police left to get a warrant. One court case that illustrates such a distinction is *California v. Carney*. In that case, an agent of the Drug Enforcement Administration (DEA) possessed information that Carney had given marijuana to a person in exchange for sex in Carney's mobile home. After personally observing Carney take a "youth" back to his mobile home, the DEA agent stopped and questioned the youth after the youth had left the mobile home. The youth's story corroborated what the DEA agent had previously heard, so the agent requested that the youth knock on the door of the mobile home. Carney responded to the knock at the door and stepped out of the mobile home. After Carney stepped outside the mobile home, the DEA agent searched the premises and found marijuana. The Supreme Court ultimately ruled that the DEA agent, in that case, did not need a search warrant, as the home was also being used for transportation and was not in a place that was regularly used for residential purposes. Thus, the Court seemed to draw a line between actual fixed residences and residences that could be quickly moved.

In addition to whom or what can be searched, the courts have also considered what exactly constitutes a search. Originally, courts recognized what is called the *trespass doctrine* when deciding if an actual search occurred. If law enforcement could observe either a person's actions or contraband that they carried out on the street, these items were considered in "plain view." Law enforcement was able to view these items without trespassing. However, if law enforcement came upon a person's property without permission or a warrant and discovered contraband, officers would not be able to seize those items, because they had trespassed to find them (Harper, 2008). While this doctrine seems to make good sense, new technology frustrated this doctrine. In *Olmstead v. United States,* four people were convicted of violating the National Prohibition Act. To help gather evidence against these individuals, prohibition agents had placed taps along telephone wires into the homes of the appellants, as well as of the business office that they frequented. The Court ruled that no illegal search occurred because the agents had not actually physically trespassed onto the property of any individual. Yet, the *Olmstead* ruling was a relatively short-lived precedent. Perhaps the Supreme Court failed to properly contemplate the extent of its ruling and how the new technology of the telephone challenged existing legal doctrines, because it was Justice Brandeis' dissenting opinion in *Olmstead* that would become the future standard for dictating whether an unconstitutional search had occurred (Harper, 2008).

Prior to becoming a Supreme Court justice, Justice Brandeis had discussed what he believed to be a sacred right, the right to privacy. Although a right to privacy cannot explicitly be found in the Constitution, Brandeis argued that this right essentially meant that Americans should enjoy the right to be left alone (Harper, 2008). Thirty-nine years after *Olmstead*, in its ruling in *Katz v. United States,* the Supreme Court overturned its earlier position and ruled that searches should be guided by the *privacy doctrine* instead of the trespass doctrine. Ultimately, rather than deciding whether law enforcement officers had simply gone somewhere they were not authorized to go, courts need to decide whether a person, by their actions and deeds, indicated that they desired some form of privacy. In *Katz*, the appellant had walked into a public phone booth and shut the door. This indicated to the Court that he intended to conduct his conversation in private. Thus, if law enforcement agents wanted to tap a phone, they could still do so, but in the future, they would need a warrant. Finally, in Justice Harlan's concurring opinion in *Katz,* he identified a two-prong test for determining whether a person had demonstrated a desire for privacy. First, a person must have demonstrated that they had some expectation of privacy, which courts recognize as a subjective showing of privacy. Second, society as a whole must also recognize that an activity should guarantee privacy, which courts recognize as an objective showing of privacy.

A later case, *Kyollo v. United States,* further demonstrates how the privacy doctrine works. In that case, a law-enforcement officer suspected that Kyollo was growing marijuana inside his home. While the officer had a suspicion that illegal activity was going on, he did not have enough evidence to establish the probable cause needed for a warrant. Instead of trying to obtain further evidence through typical investigative means, the officer obtained a thermal imaging device that allowed him to see heat signatures that were not detectable by the naked eye. After a thermal image inspection, the officer noticed that an unusually large heat source was present around the area of Kyollo's garage that was not present in any of the neighboring homes. Combined with tips from informants and utility bills that showed that Kyollo paid a larger-than-usual electric bill, a warrant was obtained to search Kyollo's residence. Ultimately, more than 100 marijuana plants were found in the home. However, despite the officer's suspicions being confirmed, the Court ruled that Kyollo's rights had been violated. The thermal imaging device allowed the officer to observe something in the house that was not ordinarily visible. By using this type of technology, the officer had essentially looked inside Kyollo's house, which was not permitted without a search warrant.

The Application of the Fourth Amendment in Correctional Institutions

The previously discussed cases clearly demonstrate the fierce debate over peoples' rights to be secure in their houses, persons, papers, and effects against unreasonable searches and seizure, thus placing restrictions on the power of agents of law enforcement and criminal justice. However, this debate takes a different turn when we shift our discussion to correctional settings. Incarcerated individuals, it is argued, should not have a reasonable expectation of privacy. After all, this expectation was forfeited during arrest and sentencing. As we discussed earlier in this chapter, people have a high expectation of privacy in their homes, but can expect less privacy in mobile homes and public places. Yet, the Fourth Amendment says nothing about jails, prisons, and other public spaces operating under the order of the state. Consequently, a reduced expectation of privacy by those individuals sentenced to incarceration should not come as a surprise. In fact, what is considered as a reasonable expectation of privacy for most people in free society is different from the expectations of privacy in a correctional institution (Belbot & Hemmens, 2010). The expectations of privacy in these institutions is reduced to minimal and apply not just to inmates but to all those who enter it, including visitors, workers and correctional officers. This is due to the primary goal of prisons and jails, a goal that is guided by elevated security needs and the constant need for surveillance and monitoring for the sake of public safety.

The *Katz* ruling may have changed the standard in Fourth Amendment protection from the trespass doctrine to the privacy doctrine and required the government to obtain warrants for listening on people's phone calls, but such a protection never extended within the walls of correctional facilities. In *Lanza v. New York,* Lanza had visited his brother, who was incarcerated in a New York jail. Six days after the visit, Lanza's brother was granted parole, which was described as "under rather unusual circumstances." During a subsequent investigation by a legislative committee, Lanza was given immunity from prosecution and ordered to testify. Lanza ultimately refused to testify and was later convicted in state court for willfully refusing to answer questions from a legislative investigation. Part of the evidence used against Lanza was a recording of his conversation with his brother in the aforementioned New York jail, which was made without either person's knowledge. Lanza argued that introduction of this recorded conversation violated his Fourth Amendment rights. The Court ruled that people's homes, businesses, and other similar areas should be free of government intrusions without warrants, but jails and prisons have no such protections. Indeed, the very mission of jails and prisons is to provide surveillance of the people inside. Thus, there should be no expectation of privacy in a conversation that occurred in a correctional facility and the recorded conversation was properly allowed into evidence.

While probable cause and warrants are specifically mentioned in the Constitution and the notion of privacy is perhaps an extension of the views of the founding fathers, more modern police tactics and the increasing concentration of American citizens in larger cities have resulted in an increasing number of encounters between citizens and law enforcement. Furthermore, many police departments discovered that using "nonarrest investigatory detentions" was a useful tool to combat crime (Dix, 1985). Perhaps the best-known moniker for this type of police-citizen encounter is known as a *Terry stop*, which comes from the name of the Supreme Court case, *Terry v. Ohio*, which officially sanctioned this law-enforcement tactic as constitutionally permissible. In *Terry*, a police officer (Martin McFadden) was patrolling in downtown Cleveland dressed in plainclothes. While on patrol, Officer McFadden noticed two men (Chilton and Terry) walk repeatedly in front of a store. On several occasions, one or both of the men would stop and stare into the window of the store. McFadden had been an officer and detective for nearly 40 years and would later state that, based on his experience, the two men seemed to be "casing a job, a stick-up." Thus, believing that a crime might be imminent and one or both of the men might possess a firearm, McFadden approached both men, who had been joined by a third man (Katz), who did not participate in the suspicious activity. Officer McFadden identified himself as a police officer and asked for the men's names. After Terry gave an incommunicable response, Officer McFadden spun Terry around and patted him down. During his pat-down, McFadden felt an object that he believed to be a pistol, but the object could not be removed. McFadden then ordered the three men into a store and had Terry remove his coat in which McFadden was able to remove a pistol. Afterward, McFadden found that Chilton possessed a pistol as well, but Katz was unarmed.

Terry and Chilton were ultimately arrested for carrying concealed weapons, an arrest they believed was unconstitutional, since there was no probable cause for them to be stopped, frisked, and then later searched. In justifying the actions of McFadden, the Supreme Court created an entirely new standard: *reasonable suspicion*. The Court acknowledged that when police officers stop people to investigate crimes, there is the possibility that these people may have weapons. This possibility can create a legitimate sense of apprehension within police officers. Thus, if an officer has a reasonable suspicion that criminal activity is taking place and a belief that a suspect is armed, that officer can conduct a pat-down of a suspect to determine if they have a weapon. If officers feel something which they legitimately believe to be a weapon, they may conduct a limited search of a person to determine if a weapon is actually present. In later cases, the Supreme Court ruled that police officers cannot do a pat-down for contraband, such as drugs, since that does not directly affect officer safety (Samaha, 2012). The implications of stop-and-frisk policies can be troubling to some people. Within *Terry v. Ohio*, Justice Warren, who wrote the majority opinion, noted that stop-and-frisk policies can be used to discriminate against minorities. Justice Douglas, who dissented in the case, argued that the lower standard of reasonable suspicion conflicted with the Fourth Amendment and went against why the amendment had been originally enacted. Some people have argued that the judicial affirmation of stop-and-frisk policies have further emboldened law-enforcement officers to stop people merely for being minorities (Harris, 1994). Perhaps the quintessential example of such a policy is in New York City, where the aggressive use of stop-and-frisk has been generally credited with reducing crime and at the same time, seriously aggravating race relations within America's most populous city (Gelman, Fagan, & Kiss, 2007). The first lawsuit addressing Fourth Amendment issues for prisoners that gained traction in the federal courts was *United States v. Hitchcock,* which ultimately was decided by the Ninth Circuit in 1973. In that case, Hitchcock was already serving a life sentence for murder in Arizona State Prison. His cell was searched without a warrant and documents were obtained and later used in his trial for six counts of presenting fraudulent income tax refund claims. Hitchcock argued that his prison cell should be protected from unreasonable searches and seizures, just as anybody else's home should be, and a warrant should have been required to search his cell. Citing *Lanza v. United States,* the Ninth Circuit Court ruled that no person should have an expectation of privacy while incarcerated in jail or prison. Therefore, according to that court, Hitchcock's rights were not violated.

In 1984, the Supreme Court addressed searches of inmate cells in *Hudson v. Palmer.* In that case, Palmer was a prisoner at the Bland Correctional Center in Virginia, serving time for forgery, uttering, grand larceny, and bank robbery. While he was in custody, Palmer was subject to a search he referred to as a "shakedown," which Palmer believed was used to harass him. Two correctional officers, one of whom was Hudson, had performed a search of Palmer's cell for contraband. While performing the search, the correctional officers found a torn pillowcase in the trash can within Palmer's cell. The officers cited Palmer with destruction of state property, a charge he claimed to be false. Palmer sued, claiming that the officer purposely destroyed some of Palmer's property during the search of his cell and prison locker. The claim that Palmer could sue for the loss of his personal property was not outlandish. In an earlier case, *Parratt et al. v. Taylor,* the Supreme Court had ruled that if individual states did not have procedures through which state prisoners could make claims for loss of property, then inmates wishing to make such claims could sue in federal court. However, Palmer's claim that his Fourth Amendment protection of being free from unreasonable searches and seizures, was a little bit harder to make. Initially, the Fourth Circuit Court of Appeals had ruled that prisoners had a "limited privacy right" and that a "shakedown" search meant to harass an inmate was unreasonable. Ultimately though, the Supreme Court would hold differently.

In *Palmer,* the Supreme Court ruled that while prisoners maintain many constitutional rights while they are incarcerated, the Fourth Amendment protection against unreasonable searches was not one of those rights. To the Court, the very nature of imprisonment means stripping inmates of their rights for the sole purpose of maintaining the institutional security of a correctional facility. Given the need of correctional administrators and officers to ensure that correctional facilities are free of weapons, drugs, and other contraband, inmates simply cannot enjoy the same Fourth Amendment protections that people enjoy when they are not an inmate in a state correctional facility. Furthermore, the Court ruled that the "unpredictability" of random searches of cells was necessary and the most effective method by prison administrators to ensure that dangerous and/or illegal items did not end up in the hands of inmates. Additionally, the Fourth Circuit had previously ruled that searches of inmate cells should be conducted only due to an established policy or based on reasonable suspicion, so that correctional staff would not harass inmates. The Supreme Court thought such a plan was ill advised and that prisoners would find ways to predict when searches would occur. Thus, correctional officials should be permitted the flexibility to search whenever they deemed necessary. Additionally, in the 1984 case *Block v. Rutherford,* the Court ruled that correctional officials are allowed to conduct irregular "shakedown" searches without the occupants of the cells present.

Not only can inmates have their cells and belongings searched, but their persons can be searched in many different ways as well. One of the common images people have of newly admitted inmates to a correctional facility is the various ways they are searched, including strip searches and body-cavity searches. In *Bell v. Wolfish* (1979), a case that addressed several constitutional issues associated with incarceration, a group of inmates at New York City's Metropolitan Correctional Center (MCC) challenged the practice of subjecting inmates to strip searches and visual body-cavity searches after inmates had contact visits with people who did not work at the facility. A district court had approved the practice of strip searches, but ruled that a body-cavity inspection should have prior probable cause. The Second Circuit Court of Appeals affirmed the judgment of the lower court. That court noted that there had been only one instance in which contraband was found in a body-cavity search. Thus, the Second Circuit ruled that the practice was a "gross violation of personal privacy" and the utility of the government's intrusion did not justify the violation of inmates' rights. Yet, the Supreme Court ultimately disagreed. While concurring with the lower courts that body-cavity searches are a significant intrusion to privacy of inmates, the Court ruled that such searches were reasonably related to a security interest of the correctional facility. Even though contraband had been found only once through this method, the Court reasoned that the possibility of these searches may have acted as a deterrent, so inmates did not attempt to smuggle contraband in their body cavities.

Although the Supreme Court allowed the practice of strip searches and body-cavity searches, lower courts have tackled various regulations on these practices. In *Tribble v. Gardner,* the Ninth Circuit stated that if body cavity searches were conducted every time an inmate is moved within a maximum security facility and there was no security concern, that would constitute a violation of the Fourth Amendment. In 1991, in the case of *Vaughan v. Ricketts,* the Ninth Circuit ruled that body-cavity searches must be based on some reasonable suspicion that an inmate has contraband within a body cavity. Additionally, such a search must be conducted by trained staff who will perform the search in a hygienic manner. In *Farmer v. Perrill,* the Tenth Circuit ruled that correctional officials must provide some justification for visual strip searches of inmates in public. In a 2004 California case, *People v. Pifer,* a court allowed searches of inmates using x-rays, noting that such a search is both less invasive and less traumatizing to an inmate.

In some instances, a Supreme Court decision can have problematic concerns for correctional facilities. The case of *Atwater v. City of Lago Vista* concerned a woman who was arrested and taking into custody for driving a vehicle without having properly secured her children in car seats, a crime in which a guilty verdict carries no possibility of serving any time in a correctional facility. The Supreme Court ruled that the arrest was valid and that police officers are permitted to arrest people for the commission of minor crimes. As a result of this ruling, jail administrators now must process these people, many of whom present little to no danger to correctional staff or inmates, an additional burden on their primary mission of maintaining secure correctional facilities. In 2012, in *Florence v. Board of Chosen Freeholders of the County of Burlington*, Albert Florence was arrested for a non-indictable offense and at jail processing, was given a strip search. He argued that strip searches of non-indictable offenders violated their Fourth Amendment rights and should be done only if there is some reasonable suspicion to support the search. The Supreme Court ruled that such a policy was impractical. Not all jail facilities have access to inmates' records, and strip search procedures need to strike a reasonable balance between an inmate's privacy and a jail's needs — the most important of which is maintaining the institutional security of the facilities. Ultimately, the need of jails to provide institutional security trumps the interests of inmates, even if they are most likely only going to be in jail for a very short time.

Cross-Gender Searches

In addition to whether particular searches are constitutionally permitted, the courts have had to turn their attention to the manner in which these searches are carried out. One problem arises when correctional staff of opposite genders perform these searches. In *Timm v. Gunter*, a group of inmates in the Nebraska State Penitentiary (NSP) challenged women prison guards for performing pat-down searches and seeing male inmates while in the shower or using the bathroom. As a NSP policy, pat-down searches, which take approximately 10 seconds, are performed on inmates during shakedowns, when inmates move between different areas of the penitentiary, and whenever deemed necessary for security purposes. Strip searches are performed when inmates enter or leave the visiting area and in other instances when it is deemed necessary. Beginning in 1983, prison administrators had opened all job positions at NSP to applicants on a gender-neutral basis. The only restriction placed on women correctional officers is that they were not allowed to conduct strip searches of male inmates. To comply with this policy, women correctional officers were not allowed to work in Unit 5, the only part of the prison in which strip searches were routinely performed. In an earlier proceeding, a federal magistrate ruled that male inmates should be given access to showers that were not visible by women guards. Furthermore, if a male prisoner was subject to a pat-down search, an inmate could demand that a male guard pat down that inmate's groin area. A district court affirmed the decision.

As a result of the magistrate's decision, prison administrators developed a new policy, which required that before conducting a pat-down search, a women officer ask an inmate if he preferred a male officer to perform the search. If so, the search would be delayed until a male officer arrived. Due to the new policy and the magistrate's ruling prohibiting women guards from observing male inmates in various situations where they might be nude or partially nude, this policy restricted women correctional officers from different assignments. While these accommodations were made, a group of male inmates initiated a new lawsuit against prison officials, asserting that their rights to equal protection were being violated, since women inmates at the Nebraska Center for Women were provided much greater protections from male correctional officers than male inmates were receiving from women correctional officers at NSP. Yet by enforcing these policies, it severely restricted the employment opportunities of women as correctional officers at NSP, and they were brought in as a defendant class within the lawsuit.

In a district court proceeding for the new lawsuit, that court ruled, in an effort to accommodate all parties, that genital and anal areas should not be searched during a pat-down search. As a result, women correctional officers could pat down male inmates. Further, it was decided that male inmates were allowed to request a pat-down from a male officer, as long as it did not provide a disruption or security risk. Regarding the viewing of male inmates while in various stages of undress, women correctional officers needed to make "minor accommodations of courtesy." Finally, NSP needed to make physical and scheduled modifications to accommodate prisoner privacy. Ultimately, the Eighth Circuit Court reversed this decision. That court noted that the decision was difficult because it required the balancing of seemingly conflicting interests: the constitutional rights of inmates and workplace discrimination against women. Yet, prison regulations can infringe on inmates' constitutional rights so long as they are related to a legitimate penological interest. During the proceedings before the District Court, there was testimony that in the previous year, 100 inmates were found with weapons and more than 75 inmates possessed illegal drugs. In the previous five years, more than 100 inmates were caught with escape equipment. Thus, pat-downs were obviously a necessary part of maintaining security. Women correctional officers received training to conduct pat-down searches in a professional manner, and were instructed to limit their pat-down search contacts with genital or anal areas to light and brief contacts. James Timm himself testified that he had never experienced inappropriate treatment from any women correctional officers, and most inmates at NSP did not reject pat-downs by women officers. Thus, the Eight Circuit ruled that pat-down searches by female officers were permissible. Along similar lines, because surveillance of prisoners is necessary, many precautions were already taken to give male inmates some privacy while in various stages of undressing. Thus, allowing women correctional officers to supervise men when they might be undressed was not problematic either, although the restriction of women correctional officers from Unit 5 was permissible (due to the high number of strip searches). Ultimately, the court ruled that male and female inmates are fundamentally different and present different security concerns. Therefore, it is not impermissible to maintain different sets of security regulations for male and female inmates.

While the *Timm* case was concerned with the pat-downs, the issue of strip searches of male inmates conducted by women correctional staff was the centerpiece of *Byrd v. Maricopa County Sheriff's Department,* a case before the Ninth Circuit Court of

Appeals in 2010 and 2011. In that case, Charles Byrd was detained in the Maricopa County Jail, a minimum-security facility, while awaiting trial. Jail officials ordered a search of the entire housing unit in which Byrd was incarcerated, which housed approximately 90 inmates. No emergency existed at the time the search was conducted; the search was prompted by several fights that had occurred within the facility and a suspicion of contraband. During the search, Byrd was ordered to remove all of his clothing except for a thin pair of jail-issued pink boxer shorts. He was searched by a female cadet from the officer academy, in the presence of male detention officers. During the search, the female cadet twice touched Byrd's penis and scrotum through his boxer shorts, and the cadet ran her hand up Byrd's buttocks to separate his cheeks to look for contraband inside Byrd's anus. At a trial before a district court, Byrd's initial lawsuit was limited to the issue of whether the search was reasonable; it did not address whether the search by an officer of a different sex was reasonable. The district court found in favor of the female cadet, and a three-judge panel of the Ninth Circuit affirmed the ruling of in a vote of two to one. Afterward, the Ninth Circuit reheard the case *en banc* with 11 judges. In a previous case, the Ninth Circuit had ruled that, absent exigent circumstances, a strip search of a male inmate by a women correctional officer was unreasonable. To counter this, Maricopa County officials tried to contend that Byrd had not been subject to a strip search; because he was wearing a pair of boxer shorts, the search was only a pat-down, they claimed. The full panel of the Ninth Circuit was ultimately unconvinced of such a distinction, since Byrd's genitals and anal region were clearly searched. It was finally ruled that the search of Byrd was unconstitutional.

Searches of Visitors and Employees in Correctional Facilities

Not only are inmates subject to searches, but people who visit prisoners can also be subject to searches. As Molina (2006) noted, visiting a prisoner can be akin to attempting to board an airplane. Pat-downs and walking through metal detectors are common. Additionally, as a person drives onto the property of a penal facility, they can expect to have their vehicle inspected or searched. Policies can vary by jurisdiction, however. A brochure titled "Visiting a Friend or Loved One in Prison," distributed by the California Department of Corrections, outlines the state's search policies and procedures at different points. Not all correctional facilities have correctional staff posted at facility gates before a parking lot, the brochure advises, but correctional staff may conduct a visual inspection of vehicles, including the trunk of a car, and drug-detection dogs can be used to assist a search outside of a car. Any additional search of a vehicle requires consent, a search warrant, or reasonable suspicion that a visitor is attempting to smuggle contraband or any unauthorized items into a correctional facility. Once inside a facility, rules become stricter. Visitors' outer clothing, such as jackets or sweaters, as well as any jewelry, must be removed before going through a metal detector. All belongings can be searched but any search beyond this must be justified by a suspicion that a visitor is attempting to bring contraband into the facility. If such a situation exists, that person must be informed in writing of the reason for the search and the name of the prison official who ordered the search. A visitor has the right to refuse the search, but he or she will not be allowed to visit on that day and may have future visits limited if the belief lingers that person is smuggling contraband into a facility. The only way that a visitor may be searched without giving consent is if a search or arrest warrant is procured or if a person is an immediate and significant threat to correctional facility security (California Department of Corrections, ND).

Strip searches of visitors can be done only in very limited circumstances. The issue was discussed in a case before the First Circuit Court of Appeals, *Cochrane v. Quattrocchi*. In that case, Dawn Cochrane had been a regular visitor of her father, an inmate in the Rhode Island Adult Corrections Institute, "since she was very young." While Cochrane seemed to be a model visitor, her father was hardly a model inmate. Despite several years of visiting without incident, on June 10, 1989, Cochrane was told that she would not be allowed to visit her father on that day or ever again unless she submitted to a strip search. Cochrane ultimately signed a consent form to a strip search, which was performed by two female correctional officers in a bathroom. After removing her clothing, Cochrane had her hair and ears checked. Cochrane was instructed to squat, hold her head towards her chest and cough while the two officers stood from behind. Although she had signed the consent form, Cochrane "was emotionally shaken by the experience." Afterward, she filed a civil rights lawsuit claiming battery, intentional infliction of emotional distress, false imprisonment, and assault. Cochrane argued that the search was merely retaliatory for the actions of her father, who had spent most of his life in adult correctional facilities and admitted to taking contraband drugs approximately 10 to 20 times while he was incarcerated. In the month of October 1988, Cochrane's father overdosed on cocaine while in custody. After being questioned by a police officer about the incident, Cochrane's father mentioned that he had received the drugs from a Deputy Quattrocchi or his son, who was also a correctional officer at the facility. After learning that Cochrane's father had blamed him, Quattrocchi became angry and promised Cochrane's father that some form of retribution would be coming. At trial in a district court, it was ruled that there is no constitutional right for people to visit prisoners and no violation occurred because Cochrane had ultimately consented to the search, which the district court ruled was reasonable in scope.

The First Circuit Court noted that every circuit court that had considered the issue of prison visitation had ruled that prison visitors retain their Fourth Amendment protection from unreasonable searches and seizures. However, citing the 1985 Supreme Court case *New Jersey v. T.L.O.*, the First Circuit Court stated reasonableness "depends upon the context within which a search takes place." As with so many other searches within correctional facilities, the First Circuit Court ruled that a balance needed to be struck between the institutional security of the facility and the Fourth Amendment rights of a prison visitor. Yet prison visitors have a diminished expectation of privacy and cannot expect to reasonably claim they should have the same rights that they would have either in their home or simply walking on the street. At the same time, the First Circuit noted that strip searches are an "extreme intrusion" and some reason should exist for the search. As mentioned previously, there had been no prior evidence that Cochrane was anything but a model visitor. During the district court proceedings, Quattrocchi stated that an informant had provided information that Cochrane was smuggling drugs into the facility. During direct examination during the trial, Quattrocchi stated that he could not remember until the day of trial the name of the informant who provided the information. Based on the First Circuit's interpretation of the testimony, there was little specificity or reliability to indicate that the informant actually provided credible evidence supporting a claim that Cochrane should be strip-searched. Thus, the issue should have been decided by a jury. Furthermore, the Ninth Circuit had previously ruled, in *Blackburn v. Snow,* that consenting to a strip search that was unreasonable under the circumstances takes away the ability of a visitor to reasonably consent. Since there was presumably no evidence to support the suspicion that Cochrane was carrying contraband, the First Circuit ruled that a jury could reasonably conclude that Cochrane did not consent to the search.

Not only are visitors to correctional facilities forced to surrender their right of privacy when they enter a correctional setting; employees also have a reduced expectation of such a privacy privilege. Correctional institutions have clear policies that make employment conditional on consenting to searches of their persons, bodies, and vehicles (Belbot & Hemmens, 2010). Employees agree to forfeit their right to privacy in their lockers, desks, and even lunch boxes, as they are required to bring lunches in transparent plastic bags or containers. They are also subjected to random searches upon entering and exiting a facility.

Although many places may not pay correctional officers well, these officers have a tremendous responsibility, to maintain a safe correctional facility environment, and to prevent contraband from reaching the hands of inmates. For this reason, many correctional officers may face scrutiny that people with so-called "ordinary" jobs do not face. Correctional officers, like most other state and federal workers, do have common civil-service protections (Clear, Reisig, & Cole, 2016), but otherwise have diminished rights compared with other professions. In *Anderson v. City of Philadelphia* (1988), the Third Circuit Court of Appeals ruled that it is permissible to require correctional officers to take and pass a polygraph test as a precondition of employment. In addition to polygraphs, correctional officers can be expected to take drug tests before being hired and randomly during their employment, or if a reasonable suspicion exists that they have used drugs. Such rules were approved by the Ninth Circuit Court of Appeals in *American Federation of Government Employees v. Roberts,* a case regarding the drug testing of correctional workers employed by the Federal Bureau of Prisons. As that court noted, the Supreme Court in *National Treasury Employees Union v. Von Raab* had in 1989 already allowed a similar plan for drug testing of workers in the Customs Department. According to the Ninth Circuit, there seemed a far greater need to test corrections workers. Thus, such programs were permissible.

In addition to these standard testing procedures, correctional officers have many other limitations on their Fourth Amendment rights. As noted in a decision before the Court of Appeals of Georgia, *Bradley v. State*, once a corrections officer drives inside the guard line, into the parking lot of a correctional facility, their car can be searched. Additionally, in a case before the Appellate Division of the Supreme Court of New York, *Matter of Seelig v. Koehler*, while upholding a random drug-testing program, that court noted several regulations of correctional officers who worked in the New York City Department of Corrections. Among these rules was one that stated that an officer could be searched at any time while on duty and force could be used if necessary. Any package that an officer carries in or out of a correctional facility can be searched. Additionally, the lockers of correctional officers can be searched at any time. Such regulations were revisited in many states after two convicted murderers escaped from a prison in Dannemoro, New York. After the escape, it was revealed that the two fugitives received various degrees of help from prison staff. Citing the incident, the Corrections Commissioner of Vermont announced new regulations that would involve searches of bags and personal effects, but would not allow pat-downs or strip searches. In New Hampshire, correctional staff must be searched and pass through metal detectors before entering a correctional facility. Additionally, correctional staff must bring in belongings, such as meals, in clear containers (Stoffers, 2015).

Conclusion

As noted in Chapter 2, prior to the 1960s, courts generally practiced a "hands-off" approach when dealing with incarcerated individuals. The Supreme Court's approach relied heavily on the notion that correctional practitioners and penal administrators are well qualified to perform their protective duties, and thus should not be burdened by Supreme Court decisions that threaten their autonomy. This was reinforced by the notion that prisoners were not entitled to any protections or redress under the law, as they were merely *slaves of the state* (*Ruffin v. Commonwealth*). Once convicted of a crime, an offender forfeited his or her liberty, and for the time of his sentence he becomes a slave of the state, and as such also forfeits the right for privacy. Branham and Hamden (2005) also note that once convicted and sentenced, offenders were thought to become *civiliter mortuus*, and all their possessions may be treated as if they were dead. Consequently, when the Supreme Court shifted to the "hands-on" approach, judges were expected to consider the limitations of the bill of rights when dealing with individuals under the care of correctional institutions. In particular, judges are constantly debating cases in light of the goals of punishment, the methods of achieving such goals, and the goals and limitations of correctional and penal administrators. Incapacitation is the most primal goal of punishment, which means that the state limits offenders movements so that they cannot cause further harm to society. This is achieved via 24/7 surveillance, while keeping an incarcerated individuals safe from harm to themselves, other inmates, correctional staff, and the public. Since incarcerated individuals are held in governmentally funded institutions, they are considered to be held in public domain, and as such, are subject to reasonable search and seizure. The question that this chapter has tried to answer is: how do we define what is "reasonable"? The cases discussed in this chapter illustrate how the goals of surveillance and safety determine what is reasonable and what is not. As a result of the previously discussed cases, as well as many more brought before the Supreme Court and several federal appeals courts, incarcerated offenders have learned to reduce their expectations of privacy. Serving the best interest of all parties involved—inmates, correctional officers, prison workers, and the community—inmates can be subject to random searches of their bodies, belongings, and living quarters without a warrant or even probable cause, or suspicion, as the goal of safety is held higher than all the other constitutional rights. Yet searches should not exceed their declared aim of providing safety, and will be called into question if they are considered harassment or humiliating. Interestingly enough, the same standards also apply to visitors and workers in these institutions, even though they are by definition free citizens. The desire to prevent contraband while maintaining safety overrides their privacy.

Discussion Questions

1. Discuss the similarities between American colonists and imprisoned individuals today in regard to the safeguards of the Fourth Amendment. Why is this amendment relevant to the protection of incarcerated individuals?

2. What are the two main clauses under the Fourth Amendment that legal scholars regard as the most crucial ones? Why are these two clauses difficult to interpret?

3. What are some of the penological issues that may conflict with the Fourth Amendment under correctional conditions of confinement? Discuss the correctional context of security and the punitive principle associated with the limitation of rights under this amendment.

4. What is the correctional justification for limiting prisoners' protection from search and seizure, and why do many correctional institutions limit the related due-process rights of incarcerated individuals? Discuss these issues in reference to at least one penological goal. Support your argument with relevant judicial rulings.

5. How do the privacy and trespass doctrines apply to correctional management? What is the view of the courts regarding these doctrines within the penal system, and how have they been addressed by correctional administrators?

6. Should convicted offenders held in correctional institutions maintain their right to privacy, and to be secure in regard to their cells, papers, and belongings? Discuss the issue of reasonable search in correctional institutions and how it serves the aims of corrections.

7. How does the decision in the case of *Palmer v. Taylor* demonstrate the court's support of institutional requirements of security, and what penological implications does it emphasize?

8. What are the legal requirements for body-cavity searches? What is the logic for such requirements?

9. Why do body-cavity searches of prisoners require probable cause, while strip searches do not? Discuss the rationale of this exception while referring to relevant cases.

10. What are the legal issues that courts have had to deal with in cross-gender searches? Discuss the troubles such searches may breed while referring to relevant cases.

11. Discuss the case of *Byrd v. Maricopa County Sheriff's Department*. What were the main elements that provoked the litigation, and how did the court ultimately respond to such litigation? Explain the logic behind the judges' decision.

12. What is the logic in searching visitors and employees in correctional facilities? Discuss the constitutional dilemma presented by the fact that these are not convicted offenders. How does the court tend to view such searches?

13. Discuss the notion of *slaves of the state* and its relevance to judicial decisions regarding issues of the Fourth Amendment. How does this notion resonate with the penological ideologies of retribution, deterrence, and incapacitation?

List of Cases Cited

American Federation of Government Employees v. Roberts, 1994. 9 F. 3d 1464.

Anderson v. City of Philadelphia, 1988. 845 F. 2d 1216.

Atwater v. City of Lago Vista, 2001. 532 U.S. 318.

Bell v. Wolfish, 1979. 441 U.S. 520.

Blackburn v. Snow, 1985. 771 F. 2d 556.

Block v. Rutherford, 1984. 468 U.S. 576.

Bradley v. State, 2008. No. A08A1118.

Byrd v. Maricopa County Sheriff's Dept., 2011. 629 F.3d 1135.

California v. Carney, 1985. 471 U.S. 386.

Cochrane v. Quattrocchi, 1991. 949 F. 2d 11.

Farmer v. Perrill, 2002. 288 F. 3d 1254.

Florence v. Board of Chosen Freeholders of the County of Burlington, 2012. 132 S. Ct. 1510.

Hudson v. Palmer, 1984. 468 U.S. 517.

Katz v. United States, 1967. 389 U.S. 347.

Kyollo v. United States, 2001. 533 U.S. 27.

Lanza v. New York, 1962. 370 U.S. 139.

Matter of Phillip Seelig v. Koehler, 1990. 76 N.Y.2d 87.

National Treasury Employees Union v. Von Raab, 1989. 489 U.S. 656.

New Jersey v. T.L.O., 1985. 771 F. 2d 556.

Olmstead v. United States, 1928. 277 U.S. 438.

Parratt et al. v. Taylor, 1981. 451 U.S. 527.

People v. Pifer, 2004. 8 Cal. Rptr. 3d 731.

Ruffin v. Commonwealth, 1871. 62 Va. 790.

Terry v. Ohio, 1968. 392 U.S. 1.

Timm v. Gunter, 1990. 917 F. 2d 1093.

Tribble v. Gardner, 1988. 860 F. 2d 321.

United States v. Hitchcock, 1973. 467 F.2d 1107.

Vaughan v. Ricketts, 1991. 950 F. 2d 1464.

Chapter 8

Due Process and Other Associated Rights

Due process is a collection of procedural steps guaranteed by the United States Constitution, set down to ensure fairness to defendants in the criminal justice system. Essentially, due process demands that the government provide defendants the opportunity to demonstrate their innocence or challenge violations of the various constitutional safeguards put in place to ensure that innocent defendants are not convicted of crimes that they did not commit. So essential is due process that the courts have deemed issues relating to it as *fundamental fairness*, and ruled that the more a person has to lose, the more fair process needs to follow.

The Fifth Amendment to the Constitution covers the concept of due process. It states:

> *No person shall be held to answer for a capital, or otherwise infamous crime, unless on a presentment or indictment of a Grand Jury, except in cases arising in the land or naval forces, or in the Militia, when in actual service in time of War or public danger; nor shall any person be subject for the same offence to be twice put in jeopardy of life or limb; nor shall be compelled in any criminal case to be a witness against himself, nor be deprived of life, liberty, or property, without due process of law; nor shall private property be taken for public use, without just compensation.*

This language seems to have very little application to correctional institutions and the management of incarcerated individuals. After all, due process applies to the judiciary process, a process prisoners have already finished by the time they are incarcerated. However, the Fifth Amendment does in fact apply to the discipline of incarcerated individuals and the process by which they are disciplined. The prison environment is highly rigid and uncompromising in prioritizing the safety and order of the institution. Nonetheless, many inmates do enjoy some liberties, such as work, visitations, vocational and educational programs, and these are considered benefits to those who comply with prison regulations and maintain good behavior. When such compliance is absent, though, discipline must follow—and in this case, the due process clause of the Fifth Amendment comes into play in various ways that will be the focus of this chapter.

Acceptance of the Fifth Amendment's application to prisoners was slow to spread across various states. A common complaint against the American legal system has been its failure to provide criminal defendants, especially minorities, with adequate defense. It was only after the United States Supreme Court embraced the incorporation doctrine, with the "due process clause" of the Fourteenth Amendment that applied this clause of the Bill of Rights to the individual states. For example, in the case *Wolf v. Colorado*, in 1949, which applied the Fourth Amendment protection against unreasonable searches and seizures to the individual states (Samaha, 2012). While most of the Bill of Rights has been applied to the states via the Fourteenth Amendment, the courts were slow to apply such protections to prisoners. As Call (1995) notes, federal courts were often reluctant to provide prisoners with due process rights. This reluctance came from the courts' reasoning that prisoners lacked expertise in institutional security, but also from a concern that recognizing prisoners' due process rights would lead to a dramatic increase in prisoner lawsuits — a concern that was in fact prophetic. Ultimately, the Supreme Court and other courts recognized that inmates have some degree of due process rights.

Inmates who allege due process violations can cite a number of amendments. Although the Fifth Amendment has been cited, prisoners overall have been more likely to challenge under a similar clause in the Fourteenth Amendment, which states:

> *No State shall make or enforce any law which shall abridge the privileges or immunities of citizens of the United States; nor shall any State deprive any person of life, liberty, or property, without due process of law; nor deny to any person within its jurisdiction the equal protection of the laws.*

Inmates alleging due process violations typically cite the Fourteenth Amendment, rather than the Fifth, because the *Civil Rights Act* exists to enforce the Fourteenth Amendment. Of particular importance in the Civil Rights Act is 42 U.S.C. § 1983, commonly known as Section 1983, which states, "Every person who under color of any statute, ordinance, regulation, custom, or usage, of any State or Territory or the District of Columbia, subjects, or causes to be subjected, any citizen of the United States or other person within the jurisdiction thereof to the deprivation of any rights, privileges, or immunities secured by the Constitution and laws, shall be liable to the party in an action at law, Suit in equity, or other proper proceeding for redress...." There is no comparable legislation that enforces violations of the Fifth Amendment, hence very little legal action by prisoners cites this amendment.

Whenever a person files a lawsuit, to maximize the scope of their claim, the plaintiff will usually allege that a series of violations has occurred. Such is often the case with prisoner lawsuits. Additionally, the notion of what protections "due process" encompasses can be vague and is not necessarily limited to the Fifth and Fourteenth Amendments. For instance, while the Fifth and Fourteenth Amendments may guarantee a defendant or prisoner a right to certain hearings, another amendment, the Sixth Amendment, secures other equally important rights that can affect the fairness of the procedural safeguards that are guaranteed by due process. The Sixth Amendment states:

> *In all criminal prosecutions, the accused shall enjoy the right to a speedy and public trial, by an impartial jury of the State and district wherein the crime shall have been committed, which district shall have been previously ascertained*

by law, and to be informed of the nature and cause of the accusation; to be confronted with the witnesses against him; to have compulsory process for obtaining witnesses in his favor, and to have the Assistance of Counsel for his defense.

As one can see, although rooted in different amendments, issues found in the Fifth, Sixth, and Fourteenth Amendments can often overlap in prisoner lawsuits. Another important aspect that emerges from the Sixth Amendment is the right of the accused to legal counsel for their defense. This is an important aspect that has far-reaching implications on how correctional institutions address such element of the Bill of Rights, in their daily dealings with incarcerated offenders.

Access to Legal Counsel and Law Libraries

Whenever an offender appeals their conviction, they are asserting that some error took place in the process, and that this error violated their constitutional rights. However, to file an appeal, an offender needs more than just a list of allegations. To file a complete appeal, an offender (or any person bringing an appeal) needs to include a copy of the transcript of the court proceedings in which the alleged error took place. While this may seem easy, court transcripts cost money. One of the ways in which court reporters make money, in addition to being paid an hourly rate for their services during legal proceedings, is by selling transcripts; often, this is not cheap. Along with many other accommodations for indigent defendants, the criminal justice system must provide these defendants with court transcripts. Such a right was established by the Supreme Court in *Griffin v. Illinois*, in which Justices Black, Warren, Douglas, and Clark held that the due process and equal protection clauses of the Fourteenth Amendment were violated by the state's denial of appellate review solely on account of a defendant's inability to pay for a transcript. The ruling created a more level playing field for all defendants, regardless of their financial ability to pay for transcripts that can assist in their appeal.

Many inmates simply lack legal knowledge, of course, and even those who do have some idea how the law works often face an uphill battle in the courts. Because many correctional facilities do not provide inmates with legal representation, select inmates with some legal knowledge essentially become self-appointed "jailhouse lawyers" who provide assistance to other inmates, for varying fees or other compensation. Correctional facilities attempt to regulate such practices, but in *Johnson v. Avery*, the Supreme Court ruled that correctional facilities were not allowed to enact an absolute prohibition against inmates providing this service unless the state provides "a reasonable alternative" for legal assistance.

One example of a legitimate regulation of inmates providing legal representation to other inmates is when it interferes with other prison rules. For instance, in *Shaw v. Murphy*, Kevin Murphy had sent a letter to another inmate to assist that inmate with his defense for the assault of a correctional officer. Due to a fear of inmates engaging in illegal activities, most correctional facilities prohibit inmates from communicating via letters or at least read this type of correspondence before delivering it. In Murphy's case, the administration read the letter and charged Murphy with a disciplinary infraction for insolence and interfering with due process. Murphy claimed that this was a violation of his right, under the free speech provision in the First Amendment, to provide legal assistance to other inmates. A unanimous Supreme Court, led by Justice Clarence Thomas, who wrote the majority opinion, ruled that no such right existed and allowing such activity would undermine prison administration.

While incarcerated individuals can seek the assistance of other inmates in their legal defense and other matters, the Supreme Court ruled in both *Bounds v. Smith* and *Younger v. Gilmore* that prison authorities must provide prisoners with adequate law libraries or assistance from people trained in the law. Justice Marshall, who wrote the majority opinion in *Bounds,* emphasized that its decision was not involving the Supreme Court too deeply in the administration of corrections. So long as correctional officials provided prisoners with a law library, the Court's ruling stated, correctional officials did not need to provide inmates with any other legal counsel. These rulings set a precedent used in later cases on due process for prisoners. In 1989, in *Murray v. Giarratano*, the Supreme Court ruled, citing *Bounds* and *Younger*, that death-row inmates were not entitled to free legal counsel for appellate matters.

A more pressing question emerged from the *Bounds* and *Younger* decisions: what constitutes an "adequate" law library in a prison? This was considered in *Lewis v. Casey* in 1996. In that case, a group of 22 inmates of the Arizona Department of Corrections argued that their legal library materials were inadequate, as was the training of library staff. Legal materials were out of date, photocopying services were limited, and inmates who were on lockdown or in administrative segregation were often blocked from library access. In considering *Lewis*, the Supreme Court ruled that the previous decision in *Bounds* did not create an "abstract" right to a law library. Instead, the decision had merely stated that creating a legal library was only one way in which correctional facilities could provide legal assistance to inmates. Thus, there should be no strict guidelines on what a prison legal law library must include; rather, inmates must prove that their due process rights were actually harmed in some manner. Merely pointing out the alleged inadequacy of materials in a particular library did not satisfy such a standard.

Another case called for the examination of inadequate legal materials seized by correctional staff, who considered certain legal documents as contraband. In *Monroe v. Beard*, heard by the Third Circuit Court of Appeals, 15 current and former inmates had been involved in a scheme to file fraudulent Uniform Commercial Code (UCC) claims against various prosecutors and prison officials. Once filed, such liens are very difficult to remove. As a result of several such liens having been filed (one for $14.5 million and $3.5 million), which required a federal court order to remove, the Pennsylvania Department of Corrections ordered that any UCC forms found in inmates' belongings be confiscated. The Third Circuit Court ruled that such a dismissal was proper because the inmates were unable to show how such a confiscation infringed on the inmates' due process rights.

While jailhouse lawyers and legal libraries are essential to upholding the right to legal defense guaranteed under the Sixth Amendment, the court in their decisions has kept sight of the penological and administrative goals of corrections and by doing so, has enabled correctional administrators to place limitations on this right when it is seen to pose a threat to the management of the institution.

Procedural Due Process in Disciplinary Hearings and Actions

Because their rights are already curtailed by being in jail or prison, incarcerated individuals have a heightened interest in maintaining what freedoms and privileges they do have while incarcerated. Such desires have led to frequent and contested litigation revolving around how incarcerated individuals are disciplined. On the face of things, incarceration seems punitive enough. Why do we need to discipline incarcerated individuals on top of the punishment they have received—deprivation of their freedom?

Nowadays, correctional institutions are very different from the first penitentiaries, such as the Walnut Street Jail in Pennsylvania, and Auburn Prison in New York. Modern prisons (aside from super-maximum-security facilities) allow inmates more freedom of movement. When visitors tour correctional facilities, they are often surprised to see inmates roaming the yards and engaged in various activities such as work, study, treatment sessions, and the like. For the most part, inmates are not handcuffed or chained, and many inmates are free to walk through different parts of a correctional facility unescorted by correctional officers. This allows individuals to develop a sense of responsibility and accountability, while also learning to function and interact with both other inmates and staff in a constructive manner. Yet, such freedom comes with a risk of violence and violation of prison or jail regulations and these violations call for discipline—which in turn can be challenged by inmates.

It is worth noting that Cripe, Pearlman, and Kosiak (2013) argue that some incarcerated individuals are sociopaths, to one degree or another. As such, they tend to get in trouble, not only on the outside but also while incarcerated. But rather than accept and acknowledge responsibility for their wrongdoing, they blame others and avoid any accountability for their actions. As a result, when charged with infractions and violations of prison rules, "they dispute the charges or the authority of prison officials to place any sanctions upon them." (ibid: 203) This in turn leads to disciplinary appeals, and frivolous litigation. Nonetheless, when the court is asked to discuss issues of institutional disciplinary action, they must treat all cases as valid. Typically, the courts' analysis focus on the question of whether there has been a deprivation of life, liberty, or property that warrants the protections guaranteed under due process.

In *Block v. Rutherford*, for example, a group of pretrial detainees who were detained in the Los Angeles County Central Jail challenged several conditions of their confinement. One was a policy of the jail that forbade contact visits with spouses, relatives, children, and friends, which constitutes deprivation of basic liberties without due process, in addition to random and irregular "shakedown" searches by jail officials. The inmates argued that this policy denied their due process rights guaranteed by the Fifth Amendment. Citing its previous decision in *Bell v. Wolfish,* the Supreme Court noted that any penal policy that was "reasonably related" to the security of a facility should face minimal court intervention and be largely delegated to correctional facilities to determine its reasonability. According to the Court, it is entirely reasonable for a correctional facility to institute a "blanket prohibition" on contact visits. Contact visits can lead to a variety of problems for correctional staff and are a common way for contraband to be introduced into a facility. Furthermore, the Court noted that nothing within the Constitution specifically granted inmates the right to receive visitors, especially if correctional officials determine that visitors to a facility represent an undue security risk.

A decade earlier, in *Wolff v. McDonnell,* McDonnell, an inmate in the Nebraska Penal and Correctional Complex filed a Section 1983 motion, claiming violation of civil rights guaranteed by the Fourteenth Amendment. The prison maintained a system in which discipline for "serious" violations of correctional policies was either loss of good-time credits or time in solitary confinement. For minor misconduct, correctional officials would take away other inmate privileges. According to the Nebraska Treatment and Corrections Act, inmates were to be "consulted"—rather than given a full hearing—whenever they were charged with misconduct, and it was this lack of hearing before instituting discipline that McDonnell claimed violated his right to due process. Ultimately, the Court, citing a case from the previous year (*Preiser v. Rodriguez*), ruled that any restoration of good-time credits must come through a writ of habeas corpus and not through a Section 1983 motion. However, if granted, inmates may sue for damages under Section 1983.

Regarding the denial of due process in disciplinary hearings, the Court ruled that correctional facilities could not completely deny prisoners due process. Indeed, as the Court noted, prisoners may have limited rights, but they cannot be stripped of those rights completely. The Court stated that prison disciplinary proceedings are not part of a criminal prosecution, and therefore "the full panoply of rights" guaranteed under the Constitution that an inmate would expect when they are accused of a crime does not apply. That said, some accommodation must be made for the institutional needs of correctional facilities and the general protections of the United States Constitution. While the Constitution does not specifically protect good time credits for inmates, such a procedure was described in Nebraska statutory law. Since the state of Nebraska outlined procedures for the punishment of inmates in disciplinary procedures, there still must be some minimal level of protections for inmates in these procedures. Thus, the Court ruled, rather than a mere "consultation" on a disciplinary infraction, an inmate must have some form of hearing on the matter.

McDonnell had also argued that inmates in disciplinary hearings should receive the same range of protections that parolees enjoy whenever they faced the possibility of parole revocation, as outlined in a 1972 case, *Morrissey v. Brewer.* Just as parolees had a right to counsel in revocation hearings, McDonnell argued, so should inmates facing disciplinary action. On this point, however, the Court ruled that the revocation of parole and the loss of good-time credits were not equivalent. When parole is revoked, the person must report to a jail or a prison. An inmate who receives a reduction in good-time credits may only have their release delayed and in some instances, an inmate can recoup good-time credits through future good behavior. Additionally, the Court noted that, by their nature, disciplinary proceedings in correctional facilities need to be handled in a swifter manner than the usual adversarial process. If an inmate charged with a disciplinary procedure is allowed to drag out the process, this could reduce the security within a correctional facility. Additionally, allowing inmates to confront their accusers may cause further violence in a facility or may limit correctional facilities from properly disciplining inmates. In conclusion, the Court decided, inmates should expect to receive prior notice of any disciplinary charges against them as well as a written report detailing the evidence against them and the ultimate findings of a disciplinary board. So long as it does not endanger the security of the facility, an inmate should be allowed to call witnesses who may testify on their behalf as well as be provided the chance to introduce any documentary evidence in their defense. If correctional officials believe that certain witnesses will not provide relevant information or may be pressured to provide false testimony, then correctional officials may reasonably restrict such evidence from being presented.

Not long after *Wolff v. McDonnell*, the Supreme Court again considered the due process rights of inmates in correctional facilities in the case of *Baxter v. Palmigiano*. The case originated from a lawsuit filed by inmates at California's San Quentin State Prison. As in *Wolff*, the inmates filed suit under Section 1983 of the Civil Rights Act, likewise criticizing the prison's disciplinary process. Initially, the Ninth Circuit Court of Appeals had ruled that inmates had a right to a notice of charges against them, to be able to testify in their own defense and call witnesses, to confront and cross-examine witnesses, to face a neutral and detached hearing body, and to receive a decision based solely on the evidence presented at the hearing. The Ninth Circuit also ruled that inmates should be allowed access to counsel or a "counsel substitute" whenever inmates faced "serious" disciplinary action, such as placement in solitary confinement. Yet, just after the Ninth Circuit ruled, the Supreme Court delivered its decision in *Wolff v. McDonnell*. Thus, the Ninth Circuit had to grant a rehearing to reconsider the case with the newly decided precedent. After the rehearing, the Ninth Circuit modified its decision to align more with *Wolff*, but it stood by its decision regarding the right to counsel and ruled that anytime an inmate was facing prison discipline for a violation that could also be considered punishable in state criminal proceedings, that inmate retained a right to counsel. Ultimately though, the case reached the Supreme Court, which disagreed and ruled that inmates do not have a right to retained or appointed counsel in disciplinary hearings.

A similar issue arose before the Supreme Court in *Hewitt v. Helms*. In that case, in the aftermath of a riot at the Pennsylvania State Prison, the plaintiff, an inmate in the facility named Helms, was removed from his prison cell in the general population and held in administrative segregation pending investigation of Helms' role in the riot. The following day, Helms received a notice of disciplinary charges against him. Four days later, Helms attended a hearing committee, in which he acknowledged in writing that he had been given an opportunity to present a defense. After the hearing, no finding of guilt was made, but Helms remained in administrative segregation because separate criminal charges had been filed against him. While those charges were ultimately dropped, a review committee determined that Helms should remain in administrative segregation because he posed a threat to institutional security as well as to other inmates. Subsequently, a second misconduct report was filed against Helms. After a correctional officer and Helms provided testimony, Helms was found guilty and sentenced to six months in administrative segregation. Helms' suit argued that his due process rights had been violated. While a district court provided summary judgment for the state, the Third Circuit Court of Appeals ruled that Helms had a "protected liberty interest in continuing to reside in the general population." Helms' victory was short-lived, however, as the Supreme Court ultimately ruled that an "informal, non-adversary evidentiary review" was sufficient to rule that an inmate represents a security threat and should be placed in administrative segregation. Since Helms had received both notice of the disciplinary charges and an opportunity to present his side of the story, the Court ruled that Helms' due process rights had not been violated.

One common assumption in the United States is that legal codes are right and necessary. To comply with the principles of legality and due process, however, Americans are entitled to know what actions are prohibited. To some degree, this has become part of prison regulations as well. Inmates must be informed which actions will be tolerated and which will not. Arbitrary application of rules by prison administrators has led to countless prisoner lawsuits. At the same time, correctional administrators resist codifying too many regulations, as these might grant too many rights to inmates. This issue was considered before the Supreme Court in 1995 in *Sandin v. Conner*. An inmate in a Hawaii prison, Conner, was found guilty of misconduct and sentenced to a period of time in solitary confinement. The offense that landed Conner in solitary confinement stemmed from an encounter with a correctional officer who had performed not only a strip search of Conner, but a cavity search as well. Conner was not happy with the manner in which he had been treated and "retorted with angry and foul language directed at the officer." Eleven days later, Conner received notice that he had been charged with disciplinary infractions as a result of the encounter. Conner later appeared at a disciplinary hearing and requested that he be allowed to call witnesses on his behalf. His request was denied, and Conner was ultimately found guilty of the violations and sentenced to 30 days in solitary confinement. In a later review by a prison administrator, Conner had one of the charges against him (the only charge that was "serious") dropped, and his disciplinary record was expunged. Furthermore, the violation did not add any time to Conner's sentence and ultimately, he was paroled before his lawsuit even reached the Supreme Court. In considering whether Conner's due process rights had been violated, the Court determined that serving time in solitary confinement was not an "atypical" punishment for inmates and was not a significant deprivation of an inmate's liberty. Thus, unless prison regulations specifically provide such a right or an inmate might serve more time in a correctional facility as a result of the sentence, inmates are not entitled to full due process rights while they are incarcerated.

Disciplining inmates is critical to maintain order and security inside a correctional facility, but also highly relevant for community corrections and supervision, such as probation and parole. Convicted individuals, sentenced to probation or other forms of community supervision, enjoy reduced freedoms. The reduction in freedoms may be perceived by the offenders as an additional punitive measure taken to restrict their movement, but also has further penological justification to it. In particular, many times the courts will side with the correctional policies and practices when these demonstrate genuine concern about the welfare of the individual and the safety of the officer, and other members of the community, while further pursue rehabilitative goals. These issues of disciplinary actions resulting in reduction of freedoms and privileges was discussed earlier in Chapter 3.

Confidential Informants

Confidential informants are often used in internal security investigations to prevent escapes, import of contraband, gang affiliation and activity, and to prevent further institutional crime and maintain the safety of inmates, guards, and correctional staff. The Supreme Court has not ruled on the standards for using evidence from confidential informants; however, lower courts have held that hearing officials must, at minimum, satisfy the reliability of information provided by another inmate in confidence.

In 1982, *McCollum v. Miller* (usually referred to as *McCollum I*), the Seventh Circuit had remanded the case because there was no evidence from the record if three of the four petitioners had their charges set aside or if the length of their sentence would be reduced. Furthermore, in *McCollum I*, the Seventh Circuit considered the issue of whether the four inmates should have been informed of the identities of the confidential informants and whether they should at least have been apprised of the dates and times when they allegedly committed their actions of extortion. Ultimately, the Seventh Circuit ruled that the costs outweighed the benefits: there would be a realistic possibility of death or injury to other inmates if this information was disclosed to the four inmates. Furthermore, the Seventh Circuit believed that if confidential informants did not receive anonymity, violent crime and acts of extortion would increase in the penal facility. Yet, the Seventh Circuit was reluctant to let such a process stand completely unchallenged. There was still a concern that disciplinary hearings of this nature were not the traditional adversarial proceedings indicative of American jurisprudence and instead were merely inquisitorial and ultimately not consistent with due process. Thus, *McCollum I* also wanted to investigate (on remand) what procedural safeguards were feasible for prison administrators at Marion to protect both the inmates' safety and their right to at least some due process.

About four years later, in another case filled by McCollum, *McCollum v. Williford*, the Seventh Circuit Court of Appeals considered the issue of the use of confidential informants within prison facilities. In this case, four inmates had filed habeas corpus petitions, which were denied, that argued the inmates were denied due process of law in prison disciplinary hearings at the federal penitentiary at Marion, Illinois. Three of the four inmates (one of whom was McCollum, for whom the case is named) had been charged with the exact same disciplinary infractions. During the months of June, July, and August of 1980, these three inmates had allegedly coerced other inmates, by threatening them and their friends with harm, into paying for commissary items and participating in homosexual acts. The fourth inmate who had been charged, Ramirez-Rodriguez, was believed to be "the ringleader of the gang of extortionists." His charges differed in that he allegedly had "pressured" other inmates rather than merely threatened to harm them. These charges were based on information that had been received from "various confidential sources." Few details about the specific nature of the charges were provided because prison administrators believed that providing any details to the four inmates who had been charged could compromise the case and endanger the sources, as the inmates had already shown a proclivity for victimizing other inmates and so might retaliate against the informants. The prison disciplinary committee found all four inmates guilty of the charges. Ramirez-Rodriguez had to forfeit 224 days of credits for good behavior and was placed in "disciplinary confinement" for an indefinite period of time, albeit with periodic reviews of his status. The other three inmates served 30 days in disciplinary confinement and were later released from the restrictive unit.

In the three and a half years between *McCollum I* and *McCollum v. Williford*, the Seventh Circuit had the opportunity to hear several other cases concerning confidential informants. In *Jackson v. Carlson,* a consolidated appeal of cases filed by five federal prisoners, disciplinary hearing decisions were upheld after a refusal to disclose the identity of confidential informants. In three of the cases, prison employees were able to provide eyewitness testimony regarding the incidents that led to the hearings, so the testimony of the confidential informants was not needed. In one case where the testimony of correctional employees was not included, the inmate charged was given notice of the date of the hearing, hour, place, and it was clear the inmate knew the identity of their alleged victim. In a similar case, an inmate could have reasonably inferred the identity of the confidential informant, based on details disclosed in the hearing, and the fact that a member of the disciplinary committee stated for the record that the confidential informant had been reliable in previous instances. In a subsequent case, *Davison v. Smith*, also in 1983, the Seventh Circuit stated specifically that in any prison disciplinary decision that relies completely on the testimony of confidential informants, some showing needs to be made of their reliability. In that case, an in camera review was conducted in which a prison investigator supplied information that led the district court, which heard the case before it proceeded to the Seventh Circuit, to conclude that "there were sufficient additional indicia of reliability." Based on these decisions on several cases, the Seventh Circuit developed four ways to indicate the reliability of confidential informants: (1) an oath of an investigating officer that a report he or she compiled (based on confidential informer testimony) is true; (2) corroborating testimony; (3) a statement on the record by the chair of a disciplinary committee that he or she had "firsthand knowledge" that sources of confidential information had a "past record of reliability"; or (4) in camera review of materials was conducted.

Standard of Proof

Another component of due process, along with fair procedures, is that there should actually be a showing of guilt before a person can be convicted of a crime. Furthermore, in a criminal court, a defendant's guilt must be proven *beyond a reasonable doubt*. Yet, as we have repeatedly seen, prison hearings do not operate in the same way as American criminal courts. The issue of what establishes guilt in a prison hearing was litigated before the Supreme Court in *Superintendent v. Hill*. In that case, Hill and Crawford were inmates at Massachusetts Correctional Institution-Cedar Junction, a state prison in Walpole, Massachusetts. Hill and Crawford were involved in a fight with a third inmate, for which Hill and Crawford were charged with assault. Both Hill and Crawford denied assaulting the inmate and the victim of the altercation denied that Hill and Crawford were the source of his injuries. However, a prison guard had observed that both Hill and Crawford were fleeing the scene and thus concluded that they were responsible. Hill and Crawford were found guilty, lost 100 days of good-time credit, and were sentenced to 15 days in solitary confinement. After several appeals, the case reached the Massachusetts Supreme Judicial Court. That court ruled that the evidence before the prison disciplinary board was not constitutionally adequate. Yet, the United States Supreme Court overturned the decision, noting that the evidence presented at the hearing was indeed "meager," but prison disciplinary hearings are essentially decided on a standard of "some evidence." Ultimately, the Court ruled that "the record is not so devoid of evidence that the board's findings were without support or otherwise arbitrary." Thus, it seems clear that prison disciplinary hearings require decidedly less proof than the traditional "beyond a reasonable doubt" required in criminal trial proceedings.

Double Jeopardy

Within the Fifth Amendment is the protection "nor shall any person be subject for the same offense to be twice put in jeopardy of life or limb." Commonly known as the *double jeopardy clause*, this protection prevents a person from being tried in a criminal court a second time for the same offense (Westen, 1980). Much like the rest of the Bill of Rights, for many years, many states refused to enforce the clause, arguing that the Bill of Rights did not apply to the states. However, that ended in 1969, when the Supreme Court ruled in *Benton v. Maryland* that the double jeopardy clause of the Fifth Amendment did apply to the states. While the Court applied the clause to the states, several exceptions exist, many of which are not terribly relevant to our discussion here. Yet one distinction is important. As Dawson (1992) notes, the "dual sovereignty doctrine" exists, which allows separate prosecutions to be carried out by state and federal courts against a person, even if both prosecutions relate to the same alleged criminal transaction. Thus, the double jeopardy clause gives people protection from prosecutions only in the same type of court or forum. This issue was litigated before the Ninth Circuit Court of Appeals in *United States v. Brown*. In that case, Reggie Brown was in prison serving a 15-year sentence for robbery. While incarcerated, Brown participated in a prison riot and at a disciplinary hearing was charged with assault on a correctional officer, riot, attempted murder, and destruction of government property. Brown was convicted only of assault; he was docked 41 days of good-time credit and transferred to another correctional facility with a higher security designation. Subsequent to Brown's punishment and transfer, he was indicted in federal court for assaulting a federal officer and destruction of government property, charges based on the same incident for which he had been charged in the prison disciplinary hearing. Brown argued that this violated his protection against double jeopardy. Ultimately, the district court denied his motion, and the Ninth Circuit affirmed the decision. The Ninth Circuit reasoned that the disciplinary hearings were part of Brown's original sentence for armed robbery and his obligation to conform to prison rules for the duration of his original sentence. If Brown's motion had been granted, a correctional facility would often have to choose whether it was more important to pursue the immediate institutional security of a prison facility or to hold out for the possibility of a later criminal prosecution. The Ninth Circuit believed that this would compromise correctional institution security.

Due Process and the Classification of Inmates

Many people would consider incarceration a miserable experience. It is, aside from the death penalty, the most punitive measure the United States imposes against criminal offenders. Yet the experience can vary greatly depending on how and where a person serves time: weekends only in a jail or detention center, for instance, or a minimum-security prison where inmates are allowed to walk off of penal facility grounds, or, on the other end of the spectrum, "supermax" (super-maximum security) custody where inmates are kept in isolation for 23 hours a day (Clear, Reisig, & Cole, 2016). While some "lifers" or "career criminals" view prison as home, many inmates do not feel the same way. Many prisoners would prefer to serve a longer stretch of a time in an easier facility rather than a shorter period in a tougher facility. When a prisoner is transferred to a different facility, especially one with more-stringent security and a greater likelihood of more violent prisoners, is a contentious issue. It is extremely important to determine how such decisions are made and whether these decisions comply with notions of due process; the Supreme Court has considered this topic, of prisoners' classification according to risk levels, on three separate occasions.

In *Meachum v. Fano*, six inmates were incarcerated at the Massachusetts Correctional Institution at Norfolk, designated a medium-security facility. In less than three months during 1974, nine serious fires occurred at the facility. Primarily based on the reports of informants, six inmates were identified as the probable culprits. All six were removed from general population and placed in administrative detention, an area normally used to process new inmates. Afterward, all six inmates received notice and were represented by counsel at a hearing before the classification board to determine if the inmates should be transferred to a maximum-security facility. The defendants were allowed the opportunity to present evidence in their defense, but did not learn the identity of the informants or what testimony they had provided. After the hearing concluded, one inmate was placed in administrative segregation for 30 days, three were transferred to a maximum-security facility, and the last two were transferred to a mixed facility containing both medium- and maximum-security designations. The decision of the board was later reviewed by the commissioner for classification and treatment and the commissioner of corrections. Upon review, five of the six prisoners were ultimately placed in a maximum-security facility, and one was remanded to a mixed-security facility. All six prisoners filed a Section 1983 motion arguing that they were being transferred to a "less favorable institution without an adequate fact-finding hearing." Eventually, the Supreme Court ruled that, given that all six inmates had previously been convicted of a crime and were being deprived of their liberty in accordance with the Constitution, then so long as they were not held in conditions that violated the Eighth Amendment's protection against cruel and un-usual punishment, the inmates remained wards of the state or federal correctional agency that held them. Absent any specific state or federal law specifying what pro-tections inmates have from being transferred to another correctional facility, the Court decided, the inmates had no due process protections from transfer.

While the decision in *Meachum* certainly added clarity to this issue, the Supreme Court still had two more issues to sort out when considering the transfer of inmates to different correctional facilities. In *Montanye v. Haymes*, Haymes had enjoyed a prestigious position as an inmate clerk in the law library at the maximum-security Attica Correctional Facility. After Haymes engaged in behavior that prison authorities considered rabble-rousing, Haymes was transferred to Clinton Correctional Facility, a different maximum-security prison. Haymes acknowledged that prisoners could be transferred freely for administrative purposes, but if inmates were transferred for disciplinary reasons, they should be entitled to a hearing. Ultimately, the Court dis-agreed with Haymes' argument and stated that prison officials are free to transfer in-mates for any reason, since there is no constitutional protection preventing correctional facility transfers. In a related case, *Olim v. Wakinekona*, the Court further ruled that states were allowed to transfer their own prisoners to prisons in other states. According to the Court, just as a prisoner cannot expect to serve time in a particular prison, that prisoner cannot expect to serve time in any particular state.

In *Vitek v. Jones*, the Supreme Court had a slightly different issue to consider. Jones was convicted of robbery and sentenced to three to nine years in a Nebraska state prison. Six months after Jones was incarcerated, he was transferred to the penitentiary hospital. Two days later, he was placed in solitary confinement. While in solitary, Jones set his mattress on fire and severely burned himself. Jones was treated in a burn unit of a private hospital. Upon his release from the hospital, Jones was transferred to a mental hospital. This was based on a Nebraska statute that stated that if a physician or psychologist deems a prisoner to suffer from a "mental disease or defect" and "cannot be given proper treatment" while incarcerated in a regular correctional facility, the state director of correctional services can transfer the inmate to a state mental hospital.

While at first glance, this case may seem similar to the two previous ones, the Supreme Court considered the case different. According to the Court, unlike a mere transfer from one correctional facility to another, a transfer to a state mental hospital may mark a person with a special stigma that could last the rest of his or her life. Thus, prisoners who face a transfer to a state mental hospital have certain liberty interests that are guaranteed by the Fourteenth Amendment. Among these rights are: (1) written notice that a transfer is being considered; (2) a hearing with notice in which the evidence supporting the transfer is given and a prisoner can provide evidence on his or her own behalf; (3) the opportunity to call witnesses and to confront witnesses called by the state; (4) an independent decision maker; and (5) effective and timely notice of all rights that a prisoner has in such proceedings.

Conclusion

Given that the management of correctional facilities is a delicate situation, balancing security and inmates' rights, it's possible to view due process appeals as an attempt to pressure prison administration for more humane conditions and the legal protection granted by the constitution—but also as a means to gain power and status among fellow inmates, as someone who challenged the system.

Disobeying prison rules means to challenge the institution, and an attempt to adjust to the institution demands, rules and regulations. It is also essential that we acknowledge the importance of the procedural reaction in which appealing inmates operate—they learn that one must follow certain process and procedure to be heard, and regardless of the outcome, the process is part of normative socialization. Using the rationale of Foucault (1983), inmates' taking a legal action against their jailers is a form of opposition that is essential to generate an evolving dialogue. Such dialogue is essential for change and the betterment of prison management, as well as for improving the conditions of confinement. Yet, as we reviewed in this chapter, the courts have generally not been willing to accommodate such appeals, and more often than not, the courts have maintained the approach of letting those prison administrators who understand their institutions deal with their own security demands.

The majority of cases discussed in this chapter reveal that the courts are not interested in interfering with correctional practices geared toward the maintenance of safe and secure environment for both prisoners and correctional personnel. Similarly, correctional administrators argue that sentenced prisoners lose some of their constitutional rights when they are remanded to the responsibility of state or federal correctional authority. Although due process rights are essential check-and-balances to the powers of the government and may generate a dialogue between prisoners and correctional administrators such dialogue should be limited. Indeed, the limitation of the due process is discussed under the 13th amendment—slaves of the state—discussed previously in Chapters 2 and 7, and will be discussed again in Chapter 13.

Discussion Questions

1. The due process clause of the Fifth and Fourteenth Amendments normally applies to defendants. Discuss the relevance of due process to sentenced prisoners. In your opinion, should convicted and sentenced offenders enjoy due process rights?

2. Discuss the effects of the introduction of due process rights in correctional settings on the scope and magnitude of judicial intervention in correctional management. Specifically, what effect did the due process clause have on prisoners' litigation?

3. Discuss the importance of providing prisoners with the right to access court transcripts free of charge. Do you think that such right be available to convicted offenders? Explain the due process importance of this practice.

4. Why is it important that prison administration monitor and examine written correspondence between prisoners? In your response, explain Justice Clarence Thomas's stand.

5. Discuss the importance of having access to law libraries in prisons. How does this practice help serve due process?

6. Discuss the procedural due process issues that revolve around disciplinary hearing committees. What is the guiding rule that provided the logic to judicial rulings associate with correctional disciplinary hearings?

7. Discuss the issues that revolve around confidential informants in disciplinary hearings. What is the main problem that threatens due process rights in using prison informants? In your discussion make references to relevant cases.

8. Discuss the four ways established by the Seventh Circuit court to indicate an informant level of reliability. How do these criteria help protect due process rights of prisoners charged before a disciplinary committee?

9. Discuss the double jeopardy issue that was challenged in the case of United States v. Brown. In your opinion, was the federal court right to add additional punishment to the ones already imposed on Brown?

10. What is the importance of adequate classification system that follows due process regulations? In your response, discuss the relevant cases that examine the issues revolving around classification and transfer of prisoners between correctional facilities. Do you think convicted offenders should have the right to veto the security level in which they serve their sentence/transferred into?

List of Cases Cited

Baxter v. Palmigiano, 1976. 425 U.S. 308.

Bell v. Wolfish, 1979. 441 U.S. 520.

Benton v. Maryland, 1969. 395 U.S. 784.

Block v. Rutherford, 1984. 468 U.S. 576.

Bounds v. Smith, 1977. 430 U.S. 817

Davison v. Smith, 1983. 719 F.2d 896.

Griffin v. Illinois, 1956. 351 U.S. 12.

Hewitt v. Helms, 1983. 459 U.S. 460.

Jackson v. Carlson, 1983. 707 F.2d 943.

Johnson v. Avery, 1969. 393 U.S. 483.

Lewis v. Casey, 1996. 518 U.S. 343

McCollum v. Miller, 1982. 695 F.2d 1044.

McCollum v. Williford, 1986. 793 F.2d 903.

Meachum v. Fano, 1976. 427 U.S. 215.

Monroe v. Beard, 2008. 536 F.3d 198

Montanye v. Haymes, 1976. 427 U.S. 236.

Morrissey v. Brewer, 1972. 408 U.S. 471.

Murry v. Giarratano, 1989. 492 U.S. 1

Olim v. Wakinekona, 1983. 461 U.S. 238.

Preiser v. Rodriguez, 1973. 411 U.S. 475.

Sandin v. Conner, 1995. 515 U.S. 472.

Shaw v. Murphy, 2001. 532 U.S. 223

Superintendent v. Hill, 1985. 472 U.S. 445.

US v. Brown, 1995. 59 F.3d 102.

Vitek v. Jones, 1980. 445 U.S. 480.

Wolf v. Colorado, 1949. 338 U.S. 25.

Wolff v. McDonnell, 1974. 418 U.S. 539.

Younger v. Gilmore, 1971 404 U.S. 15.

Chapter 9

Eighth Amendment: Physical Aspect of Punishments

Punishing offenders was never intended to be pleasant. The reactions of those harmed by criminal acts is something that cannot be predicted. After all, revenge is a violent natural reaction to being attacked. Humans can react to an attack on their person or belongings in an uncontrolled manner and according to their ability and means at their disposal. Constitutional protections for those accused of criminal conduct are a kind of safeguard against such instinctive emotions and reactions. Yet, the Constitution does not provide unity in punishment; if anything, it can be applied discriminatorily against different offenders who commit the same crime.

This chapter and the next one, both covering the Eighth Amendment, examine how the Constitution protects the accused from being punished in a cruel and unusual manner. It is vital to our discussion that we understand that at heart, the Eighth Amendment focuses on securing the dignity of offenders who are convicted of crimes and subjected to the treatment of our penal institutions. It is an important amendment, as it limits how far the state can go in punishing offenders and helps define what basic conditions should be available to those forced to reside in correctional institutions. This amendment is also a reflection of American society's level of humanity and its willingness to support rehabilitation and reintegration. These ideas are not immediately understood in the text of the Eighth Amendment; however, subsequent court decisions have teased out its ramifications for the entire rehabilitation, reentry, and reintegration process, because this process plays a large part in whether incarcerated individuals perceive their punishment as just.

The Eighth Amendment reads:

> *Excessive bail shall not be required, nor excessive fines imposed, nor cruel and unusual punishment inflicted.*

Correctional practices do not deal with bail, which is the domain of the courts, nevertheless the Eighth Amendment is relevant to penology by addressing fines and cruel and unusual punishment. Bail is also relevant to jail populations, as those who are denied bail or who cannot post it may be subjected to punitive practices and harsh confinement conditions that may not be appropriate for people who have yet to be convicted of a crime. However, most cases that incarcerated individuals bring before the courts tend not to deal with monetary compensation, but rather focus on the conditions of confinement. These cases can range from not having enough food, hot water for showers, or health services, to issues of personal and institutional safety, abuse, and capital punishment.

Why should we care about the conditions of confinement and the safety of those offenders who have harmed us? Answering this question may reveal that there is much more than just locking offenders away, and that we should be interested in the way inmates are treated once behind bars. The importance of it lies in our own social values and the way we want to be perceived as a moral society. Further, maintaining the human dignity of offenders has an important public health aspect to it, as will be discussed later in this chapter and in the following chapter.

The cases presented and examined in this chapter are concerned with whether punishment was excessive or disproportionate to the offense committed. In the next chapter, we will consider the Eighth Amendment specifically as it pertains to conditions of confinement, and whether they constitute a cruel and unusual punishment. The Eighth Amendment has also been cited in cases alleging discrimination due to disability and sickness, and some alleging cruelty in the prevention of necessary medical treatment. In each of these cases, the courts must determine whether an inmate has been treated in a manner that does not reflect the standards of American society. At the same time, prison administrators may be required to demonstrate that they acted in good faith and that they did not deliberately create conditions that would bring more suffering to the inmate. The issue of deliberate action will be discussed again in the following chapter.

We begin the discussion in this chapter with the most controversial form of punishment, the death penalty, and examine the legal debate around it in an attempt to determine if it aligns with the cruel and unusual clause. We then turn to corporal punishment against incarcerated offenders, and the views of justices on the legality of such practices, and discuss issues of proportionality in sentencing, such as length of sentence and sentencing of habitual offenders. We conclude the discussion of the Eighth Amendment in this chapter with a short discussion on bail.

Death Penalty

The death penalty has had a controversial history in the United States. Only one year after English settlers arrived at Jamestown, the first execution was carried out by colonial authorities. Since that time, more than 20,000 people have been executed in the United States (Bohm, 2003). Although capital punishment came to the lands that would become the United States nearly as soon as European colonialists, protests against this form of punishment arrived almost simultaneously. Indeed, many colonists fled to America to avoid religious persecution, as well as the high number of executions conducted in European countries. Furthermore, many religious groups, perhaps most prominent among them the Quakers, advocated for a complete abolition of the death penalty. While these groups failed in that goal, it is noteworthy to mention that in 1682, the colony of Pennsylvania, a state with a high population of Quakers, limited the application of capital punishment to only the crimes of murder and treason (Friedman, 1993). Yet, as time went on and 13 colonies became 50 states, different parts of the country had widely diverging death penalty statutes. Ultimately, this lack of uniformity would be part of the impetus for the Supreme Court to step in and affect drastic changes in the imposition of capital punishment in the United States. Although capital punishment is highly controversial and is considered the ultimate punishment, it is less common than many people may think. For example, according to the Death Penalty Information Center, in the four decades from 1976 to March 2016, 1,431 individuals were executed, with the a spike in executions occurring between 1997 and 2002, with 1999 having the highest number of executed prisoners in that decade, 98 people, which is less than 0.00004% of the total incarcerated population that year. Nonetheless, this does not diminish the importance of the related cases that come before the Supreme Court.

The first case that substantially affected the modern imposition of the death penalty was *Furman v. Georgia*. This case paved the way for other capital punishment cases and initiated the pendulum of debate over its constitutionality. By a 5–4 decision, the Supreme Court ruled that the imposition of the death penalty in one case of murder and in two other cases for the crime of rape, constituted cruel and unusual punishment. However, beyond that the imposition of the death penalty was unconstitutional; the five justices who ruled that the death penalty was unconstitutional could come to no agreement as to why. Two justices, Justice Brennan and Justice Marshall, stated that the death penalty itself constituted cruel and unusual punishment. Justice Douglas, while not quite so unequivocal, ruled that the death penalty as imposed was discriminatory against certain minority populations, because they were more likely to receive this form of punishment. Given that there is no practical solution to this problem, Douglas' argument would essentially rule that the death penalty is always unconstitutional. Justice Stewart noted that many states, at that point in time, actually mandated the death penalty for certain crimes, which he found problematic. Additionally, he noted, "I simply conclude that the Eighth and Fourteenth Amendments cannot tolerate the infliction of a sentence of death under legal systems that permit this unique penalty to be so wantonly and so freakishly imposed." Justice White argued that juries seemed to arbitrarily give the death penalty in some cases while refusing to consider it in others. White also noted the infrequency with which the death penalty was imposed. As for the four dissenting justices in the case, they made three primary arguments in support of the constitutionality of death penalty. The first was that the death penalty is mentioned in the Constitution, which in their view implied its constitutionality. The second argument was that the death penalty has been a punishment throughout the history of the United States. The third argument was that the majority of the Supreme Court was impermissibly overruling the will of the states that utilized capital punishment as a penalty. As Clear, Cole, and Reisig (2013) note, the impact of the *Furman* decision was substantial. The Court invalidated capital punishment statutes in 39 states and the District of Columbia, as well as a federal statute that authorized the death penalty for certain crimes (11 states did not have the death penalty at that time).

While *Furman v. Georgia* essentially placed a moratorium on capital punishment, it was certainly not the end of the issue. Three years later, in 1975, Justice Douglas, a long-time liberal on the Supreme Court bench, retired. Additionally, Justices Stewart and White, who had ruled in *Furman* that the death penalty as applied at that time was unconstitutional, had also stated that they could imagine that states could write death penalty statutes that would be considered constitutional. Specifically, Justices Stewart and White had argued that different safeguards needed to be put in place to protect the rights of defendants who might be subjected to the death penalty. Furthermore, both justices were adamant that state statutes that mandated the death penalty for certain crimes needed to be abolished. Stewart and White had noted in *Furman* that the issue of whether the death penalty was constitutional per se had not been presented in *Furman*, only the circumstances surrounding the implementation of the death penalty at that time. In the years following *Furman*, 35 states and the federal government enacted new statutes, authorizing the death penalty for certain crimes and different circumstances. Many of these statutes took into account the many procedural problems that had led the Court in *Furman* to rule the death penalty unconstitutional (Ducat, 2013).

In 1976, in *Gregg v. Georgia*, the Supreme Court ruled in a 7–2 decision that the death penalty itself, as a punishment, was constitutional. Beyond that ruling, the Court had other decisions to make regarding the constitutionality of the application of the death penalty. The Court ruled that state statutes that use a bifurcated trial process, where the first phase of trial determined guilt and the second phase of a trial (often referred to as the penalty phase) were constitutional. To decide whether a convicted person is eligible for the death penalty, these states may have slightly different policies, but in general, the state must assess aggravating factors (such as whether a murder was heinous, atrocious, or cruel) and mitigating factors (such as abuse suffered as a child, or abuse by the victim). If the aggravating factors outweigh the mitigating factors, a jury would probably vote in support of the death penalty and if the mitigating factors outweigh the aggravating ones, the jury would probably vote for some alternative punishment to death, such as life in prison without a possibility of parole. Furthermore, a state (or the federal government) should make some provision of oversight of a decision to give someone the death penalty—such as an automatic appeal to an appellate court.

While some states seemed to learn the lessons imparted in *Furman* when developing new capital punishment statutes, other states did not. The parameters to determine what crimes warrant the death penalty were defined in two landmark cases decided in 1976, *Woodson v. North Carolina* and *Roberts v. Louisiana*. In both, it was decided that if a person was found guilty of a crime and in particular, a capital crime that warrants the death penalty, then the automatic penalty would be death. Much like the decision in *Furman*, the Supreme Court ruled in *Woodson* and *Roberts* that a separate choice must be made beyond a guilty verdict to determine the appropriateness of the death penalty. Not all capital crime convictions carry a mandatory punishment of death and the decision on the death penalty should be decided separately from that of the guilty verdict (i.e., two decisions are made for guilt and for the application of the death penalty). In a similar decision, the Supreme Court ruled in *Sumner v. Shuman* that inmates who are serving a sentence of life without parole cannot receive an automatic death sentence for any murders that are committed while they are incarcerated. As an extension of these decisions, in *Ring v. Arizona*, the Supreme Court ruled that a person could not be sentenced to death without a jury deciding that execution was the proper penalty, given the circumstances of a particular case. No longer could judges alone hand down death sentences.

While *Gregg v. Georgia* maintained that the death penalty as a punishment was constitutional, the case hardly settled the issue, and challenges to capital punishment continue unto the present day. One question that does seem to have been settled is, What types of crimes are eligible for the death penalty? In early United States *common law*— part of the British law that is derived from custom and judicial precedent rather than statutes—many crimes were punishable by death. Among those crimes, which many people would not even consider crimes, much less punishable by death, were blasphemy, idolatry, and witchcraft (Bohm, 2003). Historically, one crime that many governments have punished with death is treason and in some countries, merely speaking against the government can be considered treasonous. While the United States is not that extreme, Hurst (1945) noted that as far back as the foundation of the United States Constitution, Americans wanted to maintain a high level of harm for someone found guilty of treason. Today, although the United States can legally punish traitors with death, very few people have been charged with treason and even fewer have been convicted.

Beyond treason, the most commonly litigated death-penalty crimes in America today are various forms of criminal homicide and sexual assault. In the case of *Coker v. Georgia*, Coker had escaped from prison, where he was serving sentences for murder, rape, kidnapping, and aggravated assault. While on the run from authorities, Coker broke into a family home, where he threatened the couple, the Carvers, with violence, then tied up Mr. Carver and raped Mrs. Carver. After the sexual assault, Coker kidnapped Mrs. Carver, fleeing in the Carvers' car with some of the couple's money. Coker was eventually caught, convicted of rape and kidnapping, and sentenced to death. In a 6–3 decision, the Supreme Court ruled that punishing rape with the death penalty was disproportionate to the offense and therefore constituted cruel and unusual punishment.

While the decision in *Coker* seemingly closed the door on the possibility of people being put to death for sexual assault against adults, the Supreme Court later considered whether the sexual assault of a child could warrant the death penalty. In the 2008 case of *Kennedy v. Louisiana*, the appellant had been convicted of the rape and sodomy of his eight-year-old stepdaughter. The attack tore the victim's perineum and caused numerous injuries that required invasive emergency surgery to repair. On the basis of a 1995 Louisiana law that made the rape of a child under the age of 12 a capital crime and considering the brutality of the attack, the jury that convicted Kennedy gave him a death sentence. In a 5–4 decision, the Supreme Court ruled that despite the brutality of the crime, the death penalty was not a proportional punishment to child rape. The Court viewed a distinction between "intentional first-degree murder" and crimes that were not homicide. Additionally, relying on a previous court decision in *Roper v. Simmons* (which will be discussed later), the Court ruled that for the death penalty to be constitutional, there had to be a national consensus that a crime should be punishable by death. In the *Kennedy* decision, the Court noted that only six states had a law that punished child rape with the death penalty. Ultimately, the Court ruled that the imposition of Kennedy's death sentence was unconstitutional.

As it stands now, the only crimes for which a person can be given the death sentence (outside of the military justice system) are treason, some limited forms of espionage (rarely implemented), and intentional murders in the first degree that either have aggravating factors or are perpetrated against a member of a protected class of people, such as an on-duty police officer. Yet, based on the narrow 5–4 decision in *Kennedy* and the resulting societal reaction to the decision, there is always the possibility that this issue could be revisited. As Barnes (2008) notes, during the 2008 presidential elections, senators Barack Obama and John McCain both criticized the Court's *Kennedy* decision. Both men noted that such a brutal rape seemed "heinous" and believed that laws could be written that should be considered constitutional. Yet, the seeming rarity of such a punishment might very well violate the standard set in *Furman*. Only six states (Georgia, Louisiana, Montana, Oklahoma, South Carolina, and Texas) permitted the death penalty in cases of child rape. No one in the United States has been executed solely for rape since 1964, and only Kennedy and one other man (also convicted in Louisiana) has received a death sentence under this type of statute.

While people can make many moral objections to the death penalty, one of the most common is that the imposition of the death penalty can be biased, and this has inspired much litigation. Many people have lobbied against the death penalty for convicted rapists because the penalty has most often been reserved for African-American men who raped White women (Kleck, 1981). Furthermore, African Americans who kill Whites are significantly more likely to receive the death penalty than African Americans who kill African Americans (Chemerinsky, 1995).

In 1987, the Supreme Court considered evidence of this kind in *McCleskey v. Kemp*. In that case, Warren McCleskey was an African-American man who was convicted of armed robbery and murder. After a jury found McCleskey guilty, in the penalty phase of the trial, the jury found two aggravating factors that the jury believed warranted the imposition of the death penalty. Among the many claims McCleskey made in a habeas corpus motion challenging his conviction was that the imposition of the death penalty was discriminatory. To support this claim, McCleskey's attorneys cited a study by David Baldus and two other law professors (Baldus, Pulaski, & Woodworth, 1983) who analyzed 2,000 murder cases litigated in Georgia during the 1970s. The defendants who killed a White victim received the death penalty in 11% of cases, while those who killed African-American victims received the death penalty in only 1% of cases. Many other similar results were found that demonstrated that African-American defendants who killed White victims were more likely to receive the death penalty. Justice Powell, who wrote the majority opinion for the 5–4 Court decision, noted that the cited statistics were troubling and seemed to make a very good case that the death penalty was imposed in a racially biased manner. Yet, statistics, except perhaps in DNA cases, are rarely used in court cases. While compelling, the Court had to consider whether there was actual bias in the imposition of McCleskey's sentence alone, not how the death penalty is imposed overall. Since there was both ample evidence of McCleskey's guilt and aggravating factors supporting a death sentence, the Supreme Court let McCleskey's death sentence stand.

In addition to establishing for what crimes a person can be executed and what procedures must be put in place, the Supreme Court has also established what types of people can be executed. One issue that has been litigated is whether a person who is mentally ill or insane can be executed. Legally, if a person is mentally ill, she or he may lack competency to stand trial or may be acquitted by reason of insanity, mental illness may also be used to mitigate the circumstances, and may as a result have an impact on the sentence imposed; for example, a person found guilty but insane may be sentenced to serve their sentence in a mental hospital rather than a correctional facility. These principles apply to people before they are sentenced; however, it is no secret that serving time in prison itself can have a debilitating effect on a person's mental well-being. Such a situation was considered in *Ford v. Wainwright*. In 1974, Alvin Ford was convicted in Florida of murder and ultimately sentenced to death. While Ford showed no signs of mental illness either before or during his trial, he had "manifest changes in behavior" while awaiting his execution. Among those behaviors was Ford's growing belief that the Ku Klux Klan meant Ford harm and wanted him to kill himself. Additionally, Ford believed that the correctional officers in his facility were part of the conspiracy and wished Ford harm as well. Ford believed that these correctional officers were killing prisoners and torturing members of Ford's family. After several evaluations with different mental health professionals, no consensus was reached as to whether Ford legitimately suffered from mental illness. Ultimately, a divided Supreme Court ruled that executing Ford would be cruel and unusual punishment. According to Justice Marshall, who wrote the majority opinion, a person must be able to comprehend not only that they are being executed, but also the reason for their execution. Otherwise, any supposed deterrent effect of capital punishment is nonexistent.

As for the issue of executing people with mental disabilities, the Supreme Court considered this in *Penry v. Lynaugh*. Johnny Paul Penry had brutally raped, beaten and stabbed Pamela Carpenter. During a competency hearing, a clinical psychologist stated that Penry was "mentally retarded." According to medical records, Penry was diagnosed with organic brain damage as a child, most likely a result of the birthing process. Throughout his life, his IQ was measured between 50 and 63. As part of the preparation for the competency hearing, the same psychologist noted that despite Penry being 22 years old, he had the mental age of six and a half years and a social maturity equivalent to a nine- or 10-year-old child. After being found competent to stand trial, Penry presented an insanity defense, based on the aforementioned reasons. A psychiatrist noted that the combination of organic brain damage and mental retardation from which Penry suffered left him with poor impulse control and an inability to learn from experience. Two psychiatrists who testified for the prosecution stated that although Penry was clearly mentally disabled, the main problem from which Penry suffered was antisocial personality. Both psychiatrists believed Penry could understand right from wrong and was thus competent to stand trial. Specifically, application of the *M'Naghten rule* that determines defendant's ability to understand the illegality of his or her actions and distinguish right from wrong, was applied. Ultimately, the jury rejected Penry's insanity defense and found aggravating factors that led to their determination that Penry should receive the death penalty. Writing for the majority of the Court, Justice O'Connor had noted that within the common law, "idiots" (the unfortunate term at the time) were not to be punished, because they lacked reason and understanding and could not discern good from evil; people who were "mentally retarded" fit into that category. Justice O'Connor further pointed out that some evidence existed at that time that many people opposed executing people with developmental disabilities, but acknowledged that there was not yet a national consensus on such an issue and thus, such a situation, of lack of national consensus, did not offend the notion of "*evolving standards of decency.*"

Penry was decided in 1989. Thirteen years later, the Court would come to a different conclusion. In *Atkins v. Virginia*, Daryl Atkins and an accomplice, William Jones, kidnapped, robbed, and murdered Eric Nesbitt, a member of the Air Force. Jones had reached a plea deal and testified that Atkins was the shooter; Atkins was convicted of capital murder and sentenced to execution. Although Atkins's IQ was disputed in the course of the trial, initial evidence was presented that he had an IQ of 59. While the jury in Atkins's trial made a similar decision to the Penry case, the Supreme Court case had a different outcome: it overturned Atkins's death sentence. The difference is largely due to the passage of time. In writing the majority opinion, Justice Stevens noted that 19 states did not allow the death penalty. Of the 31 states that had the death penalty, 21 states had laws that prohibited the execution of convicts with developmental disabilities. As Justice O'Connor had predicted, due to "evolving standards of decency," a national consensus had in time arisen that executing people with mental disabilities violates the Eighth Amendment prohibition against cruel and unusual punishment. Yet, despite the *Atkins* ruling, no clear standard has been set for determining mental disability. In *Hall v. Florida*, the Supreme Court struck down a Florida law that stated a person must prove an IQ of 70 or below as evidence of an "intellectual disability" that would preclude execution. In a 5–4 decision, the Court rejected such a "rigid rule" because it would create an unacceptable risk that people with intellectual disabilities could still be executed.

Another ongoing struggle in the courts is over the age at which people can be held criminally liable for their actions. The issue spawned the entire juvenile court system and, more recently, has focused largely on the controversial decision to waive juvenile offenders into adult courts. While the courts have not completely settled these issues, the Supreme Court has at least determined that people who commit crimes while under the age of 18 may not receive the death penalty. This push began with two Supreme Court decisions during the late 1980s. In *Thompson v. Oklahoma*, the Court ruled that executing Thompson for a murder he committed when he was 15 years old went against "evolving standards of decency." The Court then ruled a year later in *Stanford v. Kentucky* that it was permissible to execute two people who committed their crimes at the ages of 16 and 17. Then, in 2005, by a 5–4 decision, in *Roper v. Simmons*, the Court ruled that executing a person who committed his crime before he turned 18 was unconstitutional. The Court again cited "evolving standards of decency." While 20 states at that time allowed the execution of juveniles, the majority opinion noted that only six of those states had executed juveniles since 1989. Furthermore, the opinion stated that only the countries of Iran, Pakistan, Saudi Arabia, Yemen, Nigeria, the Democratic Republic of the Congo, and China had executed any juveniles since 1990.

Corporal Punishment

Like capital punishment, corporal punishment has been practiced since the founding of the United States. As a formal sanctioned punishment, however, corporal punishment was more often used against slaves and people who could not afford to pay fines (Preyer, 1982). As Friedman (1993) argues, because corporal punishment has long been associated with minorities and the poor, Americans have often been hostile to the idea of its use against all citizens. In 1809, Massachusetts was the first state to abolish corporal punishment. The federal government followed suit in 1839 and most other states abolished corporal punishment in that time period as well. One outlier was Delaware, which last used corporal punishment in 1952 and finally abolished the practice in 1986 (Hall, 1995).

As for corporal punishment's place inside correctional facilities, prior to 1968 it was still used against inmates for entirely disciplinary reasons. That practice essentially stopped in 1968 after a decision by the Eighth Circuit Court of Appeals in *Jackson v. Bishop*. In that case, several inmates challenged the constitutionality of corporal punishment in the Arkansas Prison System. The practice had been allowed for years within the system, but only in 1962 were any policies put in place dictating when inmates would be subjected to this form of punishment. Officially, corporal punishment was authorized only for "major offenses," such as "homosexuality, agitation, insubordination, making or concealing weapons, refusal to work when medically certified able to work, and participating in or inciting a riot." To punish inmates for these infractions, inmates were struck with a leather strap that was between 3.5 and 5.5 feet in length, 4 inches wide and a quarter of an inch thick. These leather straps were attached to wooden handles approximately 8 to 12 inches in length. By the guidelines, the Board of Inquiry for the Arkansas Prison System would decide how many lashes should be given, but the number was not to exceed 10 lashes. After a previous court case, in 1965, *Talley v. Stephens*, it was decided that whippings would only be administered by the warden of a correctional facility.

At the time of the decision in *Jackson*, future Supreme Court Justice Harry Blackmun was the chief justice of the Eighth Circuit Court of Appeals. Writing for the majority of the Eighth Circuit, Blackmun noted that whipping inmates was a humiliating practice that only two states, Arkansas and Mississippi, officially used. He also noted there were multiple instances of irregularities in the administration of corporal punishment, and, a number of wardens had either resigned or been terminated upon discovery of these incidents. Citing a Supreme Court decision from 1879, (*Wilkerson v. Utah*, which at that time held that execution by firing squad was not unconstitutional), Blackmun noted that what exactly constitutes cruel and unusual punishment is not always clear, but punishments that are torturous should be considered cruel and unusual punishment. Despite whatever safeguards the Arkansas Prison System put in place to regulate corporal punishment, Blackmun stated that the practice of whipping inmates could be easily abused and seemed an unnecessary and counterproductive practice. Therefore, the Eighth Circuit held that whipping inmates constituted cruel and unusual punishment.

Although corporal punishment is no longer given as a sentence at the state or federal level and it is no longer used for discipline in prisons, it is still permitted in some school districts and correctional facilities. In these facilities, it has not been banned completely because correctional officers are generally prohibited from carrying most forms of weapons. Physical force remains one of the only ways of handling noncompliant or aggressive inmates, and this is primarily how corporal punishment is used today.

Issues of Proportionality in Sentencing: Cruel and Unusual Sentences

Sentencing practices have diverged widely throughout American history. The dominant philosophy in sentencing has shifted depending on the era, and the country has seen phases of determinate, indeterminate, and mandatory sentencing (Clear et al., 2013). While the Supreme Court has engaged in a seemingly endless exercise of examining the various permutations of the death penalty, it has shown great deference to the varied other sentencing practices across the United States. According to Samaha (2012), some Supreme Court justices have held that there should be consideration of proportionality when providing judicial oversight of state and federal sentences, but more often, the Court has allowed sentences to stand without criticism.

Before habitual-offender statutes collectively became known as "three-strikes laws," many states had some version of laws that sentenced offenders for a longer period of time after each repeated violation. These came to the attention of the Supreme Court in the case of *Rummell v. Estelle*. William Rummell had been previously convicted of two felonies involving theft: the fraudulent use of a credit card for $80 worth of goods and services and uttering a forged check for $28.36. In the case that went to the Supreme Court, Rummell had been convicted of obtaining $120.75 through false pretenses, as well as violating a Texas recidivist statute. He was sentenced to life in prison (with the possibility of parole). The Supreme Court upheld the sentence—even though the thefts involved a total of $229.11. The Court noted that it was not necessarily important that the three crimes seemed minor, but Rummell had engaged in criminal behavior on three different occasions and had seemingly failed to learn his lesson to not engage in crime. In a similar case, *Lockyer v. Andrade*, the Supreme Court upheld two sentences of 25 years to life for shoplifting $150 worth of videotapes from Kmart. Again, the Court reasoned that the sentence was not for the theft alone, but more the criminal record of Andrade, who had been previously convicted of theft, residential burglary, transportation of marijuana, petty theft, and parole violation.

In its statement on *Rummell*, the Supreme Court noted that sentencing someone to a life sentence in prison for failing to pay a parking ticket would be cruel and unusual punishment. Yet, beyond such a hyperbolic hypothetical, it remains unclear at what point the Supreme Court would deem a sentence disproportionate to the offense. One real example came before the Court in *Harmelin v. Michigan*. In that case, Ronald Harmelin was convicted of the possession of more than 650 grams of cocaine. Based on a Michigan statute, Harmelin was given a life sentence without the possibility of parole, despite the crime being his first offense. By a 5–4 decision, the Court upheld Harmelin's sentence.

Though it has left the sentences of adults unchallenged, recently, however, the Supreme Court has made some determinations regarding the sentencing of juveniles. In *Graham v. Florida*, the Supreme Court ruled that the only juvenile offenders who could receive a sentence of life without parole were those convicted of murder. A mere two years later, in *Miller v. Alabama*, the Court ruled that states could no longer deny the possibility of parole for juvenile offenders who had been convicted of murder. In both decisions, the Court reasoned that juvenile offenders are fundamentally different and more likely to be rehabilitated.

One of the byproducts of the evolution of sentencing has been sentencing guidelines. They can take many forms, but essentially they attempt to impart fairness to the system. However, in recent years, many critics have argued that sentencing guidelines have inhibited judicial discretion and resulted in some defendants receiving more stringent sentences than were deserved. As a result of sentencing guidelines, the Supreme Court has had to consider two issues.

The first issue is how aggravating factors relate to sentencing. This came up in 2000 with *Apprendi v. New Jersey*. In that case, Apprendi had fired a gun at an African-American family. The judge concluded that Apprendi's actions were a hate crime that warranted a sentence enhancement, which Apprendi challenged. When the case came before the Supreme Court, it ruled in Apprendi's favor because the aggravating factor of bias had been improperly handled. For any judge to enhance a sentence based on aggravating factors (such as bias, in this case), the Court decided, those aggravating factors must be admitted to by the defendant (Apprendi did not) or a jury must decide beyond a reasonable doubt that the aggravating factors were present (Apprendi had arranged a plea deal, so the case never went before a jury). Furthermore, if a person being sentenced has a criminal record or a previous conviction, that can be taken as a matter of record and does not need to go before a jury. The Supreme Court made similar decisions in *Blakely v. Washington* and *United States v. Booker*, two other cases that challenged sentences lengthened by aggravating factors. Although a judge alone, without a jury, cannot use aggravating factors to lengthen a sentence, in *Gall v. United States*, the Supreme Court ruled that a judge alone can consider mitigating factors that would shorten a sentence. In this case, Gall was a former drug dealer who had quit of his own volition; his crime had been discovered only after he had quit dealing, and he willingly cooperated with the government. He was given a sentence of probation rather than incarceration, a decision that was appealed by the government.

Stripping Citizenship as Cruel and Unusual Punishments

Returning to the notion of "evolving standards of decency," the phrase was famously coined by Chief Justice Earl Warren in the decision in *Trop v. Dulles*. It has since been used in a multitude of court cases considering government actions such as the imposition of the death penalty. Albert Trop's case was another instance in which the Supreme Court defined cruel and unusual punishment. Trop, a natural-born citizen of the United States, served in the Army during World War II. In 1944, he deserted his post while stationed in Casablanca, Morocco. After deserting, Trop surrendered to military police. He was court-martialed and found guilty. His punishment was three years' hard labor, forfeiture of pay, and a dishonorable discharge. While that may have seen as the end of his punishment, in 1952, when Trop applied for a United States passport, he was denied. Four years prior to Trop's desertion, the *Nationality Act of 1940* was passed; it included provisions that any member of the United States Armed Forces who deserted could lose their citizenship. Trop filed suit in federal court seeking a ruling that he was still a United States citizen. Trop lost in district court and the Second Circuit affirmed the decision. Ultimately, in a 5–4 decision, the Supreme Court ruled that stripping an American citizen of citizenship was cruel and unusual punishment. Nine years later, in *Afroyim v. Rusk*, the Supreme Court ruled that the citizenship clause of the Fourteenth Amendment prevented the government from involuntarily stripping citizenship under any circumstances. This decision overruled a previous decision in *Perez v. Brownell*, which had permitted the federal government to strip the citizenship of a man who had lived in Mexico and voted in that country from 1944 to 1947 to avoid serving in the military.

In addition to citizenship issues, the Supreme Court has also held that it is cruel and unusual punishment to punish people for certain status offenses. In *Robinson v. California*, Robinson was on a street in Los Angeles one night when he encountered two police officers. While examining Robinson, the officers noticed multiple scars and scabs on Robinson's arms, suggesting he was probably using intravenous drugs. According to the police officers, Robinson admitted to engaging in such behavior. Robinson was not charged with drug possession, but was instead charged with "being addicted to the use of narcotics," which at that time was a misdemeanor in California. Ultimately, the Supreme Court ruled that punishing such offenses was unconstitutional, reasoning that if the state were permitted to criminalize addiction, it could possibly make it a criminal offense to be "mentally ill, or a leper, or to be afflicted with a venereal disease." The Court noted that civil commitment statutes—detention with the intention of preventing future dangerous or harmful behavior usually used with mentally ill offenders who pose danger to themselves or others—might be appropriate to regulate such behavior, but making such behavior or statuses a punishable crime was a violation of the Eighth Amendment.

Bail

While the Eighth Amendment is most associated with the prohibition against cruel and unusual punishment, also important is the first clause, which states, "Excessive bail shall not be required." Yet, bail affects most defendants, as more than 90 percent are granted bail. For people charged with minor crimes, bail is very important because with the problems of modern prison overcrowding and a clogged court system, these defendants might end up spending far more time in jail awaiting trial than they would be given for punishment of their actual charged crime—never mind that some of these people will be found not guilty. While most people receive bail, there is no specific right to bail—only a prohibition against excessive bail.

In *Stack v. Boyle*, 12 members of the Communist Party were charged with violating the *Smith Act* of 1940 against subversive activities. After initially being granted bail ranging from $2,500 to $100,000, the District Court settled on $50,000 for each defendant. All 12 defendants argued that this amount was excessive. The only evidence the federal government provided in justifying the amounts, which were high compared with the amounts set for similar crimes, was that four people who had previously been convicted of the Smith Act had forfeited their bail. The Supreme Court defined excessive bail as any amount more than necessary to guarantee the defendant's appearance at trial. The factors used for evaluating the appropriate amount of bail— and whether it should be set at all—should be the seriousness of the offense, the evidence against the defendant, the defendant's ties to the community and the length of time in residence there, the defendant's criminal history, and whether a defendant has previously failed to appear in court.

Considering all these factors, the court may come to a bail amount that is simply too high for the defendant to pay. There is also the worry that a defendant may not only skip bail, but present some danger to the judicial process itself. For instance, there have been multiple instances of organized crime figures intimidating, harming, or killing witnesses. When this is deemed a risk, some defendants may not be granted bail, but are placed in preventive detention. In such a case, *United States v. Salerno* (1987), Anthony Salerno, a former boss of the Genovese crime family, challenged his denial of bail, arguing that this constituted cruel and unusual punishment and violated his due process rights because he was essentially being punished before being found guilty. The Court ruled against Salerno, citing the *Bail Reform Act of 1984*, which had established clear criteria for bail and a provision for the denial of bail if the government provided clear and convincing evidence that a defendant posed some danger. In Salerno's pretrial hearing, the government had shown evidence that Salerno was likely to flee or threaten members of the community.

Jail

Jail inmates may live in limbo, many of the inmates in these facilities have not yet convicted but are nonetheless incapacitated. Because of this, the Eighth Amendment rights of jail inmates have led to some very specific legal challenges. The case of *City of Revere v. Massachusetts General Hospital* deals with the responsibility of jails to provide adequate treatment and safety for resident non-convicts. In that case, a Massachusetts police officer shot and wounded Patrick Kivlin after he was ordered to stop fleeing from the scene of a burglary. The officer took Kivlin to the hospital, where he received treatment for his wounds and was later released. Kivlin then returned to the hospital for further treatment and was hospitalized for a few more days. Afterward, the hospital billed the Revere police department for the cost of both visits, but the chief of police argued that Kivlin should pay for the medical treatment received. After the case was dismissed in the Suffolk County superior court, the hospital took it to the state supreme court, arguing that the Eighth Amendment prohibition against cruel and unusual punishment requires a police department to pay for the medical costs of a person that an employee of that department injures. The court found in the hospital's favor. Later, though, the Supreme Court reversed the decision, ruling that a municipality is not constitutionally required to reimburse a hospital for treatment of a suspect wounded by its city police. It further stated that city police do not have any financial responsibility over medical treatment to pretrial detainees or other people in their care. To avoid cruel and unusual punishment in similar cases, governmental agencies only have to ensure that medical care is provided but do not require to pay for such care (see Anderson et al., 2010). This case demonstrates the limited interpretation of the Eighth Amendment as it pertains to pretrial detainees. In another case, *Heflin v. Stewart County*, the family of Heflin, a 20-year-old pretrial detainee who committed suicide, brought suit against officials in Tennessee for failing to resuscitate Heflin and save his life. Citing the previous cases of *Bell v. Wolfish* and *Estelle v. Gamble* (discussed in the next chapter), the Sixth Circuit Court of Appeals held that pretrial detainees have a constitutional right to the same protection afforded convicted prisoners with serious medical needs. To ignore the medical needs of prisoners would invoke an Eighth Amendment claim of cruel and unusual treatment that is a result of deliberate indifference, which means that governmental officials, such as correctional or police officers, acted in a manner that disregards the potential consequences of their actions, either consciously or recklessly. We discuss this term in more length in the next chapter.

Conclusion

Through the discussion of cruel and unusual punishment, as core concepts of the Eighth Amendment, physical punishments were examined and discussed in an attempt to gain a better understanding of such practices as they pertain to the deterrent effect of punishments. Yet, it seems that judges are not always unified in their rulings and at times even prefer to refrain from imposing such severe punishments. Their debate is that of a higher moral call, in which they need to acknowledge not just the primal desire of revenge and retribution, but that of a moral and humane society that values life. It is within this context that the chapter discussed the mitigating circumstances of those who have committed capital crimes, and their perceived accountability. Specifically, the Supreme Court has made its ruling to address issues of mental capacity, either as a result of mental illness, mental retardation, and young age. The discussion further examined the cruelty of sentences in lieu of the actual crime committed, and how justices interpret those.

As discussed the first death penalty to receive the attention of the Supreme Court was *Furman v. Georgia*. This case paved the way for other capital punishment cases and initiated the pendulum of debate over its constitutionality. In this case, the Supreme Court ruled that the imposition of the death penalty in one case of murder and in two other cases for the crime of rape, constituted cruel and unusual punishment. As discussed, this was not an easy case as the presiding Justices were not unanimous in their decision. Two of the justices stated that the death penalty itself constituted cruel and unusual punishment. While Justice Stewart noted that many states, at that point in time, actually mandated the death penalty for certain crimes, which he found problematic. The case also highlighted the disparity of the death sentences with Justice White arguing that juries seemed to arbitrarily give the death penalty in some cases while refusing to consider it in others. White also noted the infrequency with which the death penalty was imposed. This case resulted in the invalidation of capital punishment statutes in 39 states and the District of Columbia, as well as a federal statute that authorized the death penalty for certain crimes (11 states did not have the death penalty at that time). Yet, as we have seen through the page of this book, the judicial pendulum never stops its swing, and in 1976, the Supreme Court ruled that capital punishment was constitutional in the case of *Gregg v. Georgia*. However, it was also established that those sentences to death will have the right to an automatic appeal and access to an appellate court; thus establishing a check-and-balance mechanism that will minimize disparities in the application of the capital punishment. Another provision that was established was the result of a decision made in the case of *Ring v. Arizona*, where the Supreme Court ruled that a person could not be sentenced to death without a jury deciding that execution was the proper penalty, given the circumstances of a particular case. No longer could judges alone hand down death sentences.

Similar to capital punishment, corporal punishment was a common method of punishment that received much attention and was mostly abolished as the main form of punishment during the 1840s. However, corporal punishment remained a practice in many correctional facilities across the nation. Accordingly, several inmates challenged the constitutionality of corporal punishment, calling it cruel and unusual. Supreme Court Justice Harry Blackmun, who was the chief justice of the Eighth Circuit Court of Appeals, noted that what exactly constitutes cruel and unusual punishment is not always clear, but punishments that are torturous should be considered cruel and unusual punishment. As discussed, in some instances, correctional officials cannot refrain from the use of force in trying to gain control over disobedient prisoners, and such infraction tend to result in corporal punishments. However, these are not a result of deliberate indifference. When prisoners can prove that such actions were executed with a malicious intent to cause harm and add punitiveness, than the courts will have to reevaluate these cases.

While the Supreme Court has engaged in a seemingly endless exercise of examining the various permutations of the death penalty, it has shown great deference to the varied other sentencing practices across the United States. Some Supreme Court justices have held that there should be consideration of proportionality when providing judicial oversight of state and federal sentences, but more often, the Court has allowed sentences to stand without criticism. Some of these sentences are highly disproportional to the criminal conduct, as discussed in the chapter. This may raise the question on the Supreme Courts tendency to follow a more punitive approach that neglect the aims of rehabilitation and deterrence and focus more on the need to incapacitate and reattribute. Illustration of this approach taken by the courts is highly visible in cases of habitual-offenders. However, the courts placed limits on punishments that aim to strip citizens from their citizenship as a result of a criminal conduct.

Finally, while correctional practices do not deal with bail, which is the domain of the courts, the Eighth Amendment is relevant to penology by addressing fines and cruel and unusual punishment. In that regard the Supreme Court defined excessive bail as any amount more than necessary to guarantee the defendant's appearance at trial.

In the following chapter we continue our discussion on the Eighth Amendment while turning the attention to the conditions of confinement and judicial intervention in correctional institutions management and practices.

Discussion Questions

1. Discuss the importance of the *Furman v. Georgia* case. What effects did it have on the implementation of capital punishment?

2. Discuss the difficulties surrounding the application of the death penalty to individuals with low IQ. In your discussion explain the concept of "evolving standards of decency." While doing so, refer to relevant cases and explain the chronological development that is associated with these cases and their effect on the above concept.

3. Discuss the constitutional issues revolving around corporal punishment. Specifically, explain how does the application of corporal punishment infringe on constitutional rights of the accused? In your opinion, should correctional facilities completely abolish corporal punishment?

4. Discuss the issue of variation in sentencing as a potential violation of the 8th Amendment clause of cruel and unusual. In your discussion, explain the paradox in proportionality between the actual crime and the punishment received while referring to relevant cases. In your opinion, is there a justification for disproportionate sentences in cases of habitual-offenders?

5. Discuss the cases of *Trop v. Dulles*, *Afroyim v. Rusk*, and *Perez v. Brownell*. In your opinion, was the court right to decide that the government cannot strip citizenship under any circumstance? Do you think such ruling may also apply to cases of treason?

List of Cases Cited

Afroyim v. Rusk, 1967. 387 U.S. 253.

Apprendi v. New Jersey, 2000. 530 U.S. 466.

Atkins v. Virginia, 2002. 536 U.S. 304.

Blakely v. Washington, 2004. 542 U.S. 296.

City of Revere v. Massachusetts General Hospital, 1981. 463 U.S. 239.

Coker v. Georgia, 1977. 433 U.S. 584.

Hall v. Florida, 2014. 134 S.Ct. 1986.

Heflin v. Stewart County, 1992. 958 F. 2d 1214.

Ford v. Wainwright, 1986. 477 U.S. 399.

Furman v. Georgia, 1972. 408 U.S. 238.

Gall v. United States, 2007. 552 U.S. 38.

Graham v. Florida, 2010. 560 U.S. 48.

Gregg v. Georgia, 1976. 428 U.S. 153.

Jackson v. Bishop, 1968. 404 F. 2d 571.

Kennedy v. Louisiana, 2008. 554 U.S. 407.

McCleskey v. Kemp, 1987. 481 U.S. 279.

Miller v. Alabama, 2012. 132 S. Ct. 1733.

Penry v. Lynaugh, 1989. 492 U.S. 302.

Perez v. Brownell, 1958. 356 U.S. 44.

Ring v. Arizona, 2000. 536 U.S. 584.

Roberts v. North Carolina, 1976. 428 U.S. 325.

Robinson v. California, 1962. 370 U.S. 660.

Roper v. Simmons, 2005. 543 U.S. 551.

Rummel v. Estelle, 1980. 445 U.S. 263.

Stanford v. Kentucky, 1989. 492 U.S. 361.

Stack v. Boyle, 1951. 342 U.S. 1.

Sumner v. Shuman, 1987. 483 U.S. 66.

Talley v. Stephens, 1965. 247 F. Supp. 683.

Thompson v. Oklahoma, 1988. 487 U.S. 815.

Trop v. Dulles, 1958. 356 U.S. 86.

United States v. Booker, 2005. 543 U.S. 220.

United States v. Salerno, 1987. 481 U.S. 739.

Wilkerson v. Utah, 1879. 99 U.S. 130.

Woodson v. North Carolina, 1976. 428 U.S. 280.

Chapter 10

Eighth Amendment: Conditions of Confinement

In the previous chapter, we discussed how the Eighth Amendment applies to the imposition of punishment on people who have been convicted of a crime. In this chapter, we will discuss a slightly different aspect of the Eighth Amendment, specifically how it applies to the conditions in which people are incarcerated. Since the early 1800s, when America began its experiment with incarceration as the primary punishment for serious criminal offenders, controversy has surrounded the conditions of confinement in correctional facilities, with critics saying that such conditions add more suffering to the punishment of being confined. Prison and jail conditions have been a constant source of litigation, based on the claim that the conditions themselves constitute cruel and unusual punishment.

Throughout this book, we have documented the rights of prisoners under a variety of circumstances, such as of the restriction of free speech rights or subjection to search and seizure. However, on a more basic level, many inmates have challenged the various physical conditions in which they live. Similar to how children depend on their parents, prisoners are completely dependent on correctional officials. By law, prisoners are not allowed to leave, and in many instances, cannot do anything to improve the conditions in which they live. As a punishment, incarceration serves the goal of incapacitation, restricting the ability of offenders to further violate laws. American society has for the most part agreed that incarceration is not intended to be used as a means to vengeance and retribution. Thus, the limiting of freedom via incarceration is the punishment; any substandard living conditions while incapacitated can, many have argued, violate the Eighth Amendment prohibition against cruel and unusual punishment. While some people do believe that prisoners have it easy, the reality is quite different and this has forced the court system to take what some would consider extreme action. In some instances, entire prison systems have been placed under court control. When this happens, correctional administrators lose their authority to make decisions and must submit plans to a court for approval. If a court believes a plan is inadequate, that court will provide correctional administrators with a list of changes that need to be made (Levitt, 1996). In other circumstances, courts have continually monitored various prison managements, asking them to meet certain goals, such as a reduction in the prison population (Sturm 1993). As Robbins and Buser (1977) pointed out, this is a clear departure from the "hands off" policy that federal courts used to practice regarding penal policy. One of the key turning points in policy was the 1963 Supreme

Court decision *Jones v. Cunningham*, in which the Supreme Court ruled that prisoners in state facilities could file writs of habeas corpus challenging the constitutionality of their conditions of confinement. After this precedent was set, a massive increase in litigation involving correctional facility conditions followed.

The federal courts' broad intervention, ruling that the total conditions of a prison system could violate prisoners' Eighth Amendment rights, can be seen in three important cases: *Holt v. Sarver, Ruiz v. Estelle*, and *Pugh v. Locke*. These three cases evaluated the prison systems of Arkansas, Texas, and Alabama, respectively. In broad rulings, the judges found in all three states a variety of deplorable conditions, including prison overcrowding, too few guards to prevent inmate violence, lack of health care and rehabilitation programs, unsafe working environments, and generally unsanitary conditions. As a result, the prison systems were placed under court supervision for many years. As stated in *Pugh*, the conditions were so horrible that "it is impossible for inmates to rehabilitate themselves or to preserve skills and constructive attitudes already possessed even for those who are inclined to do so." As a remedy, various federal courts have developed concrete orders for correctional officials, often requiring increased funding to correctional facilities. Federal courts have acted as overseers for many state prison systems for years.

Ruling on an Arkansas case, *Hutto v. Finney*, the Supreme Court approved of a federal court order that limited inmate stays in administrative segregation to 30 days. In a more recent case in California, *Brown v. Plata*, the federal courts noted that California's prisons were designed to house 80,000 inmates, yet these facilities held almost twice that number, a total of 156,000 inmates. This overcrowding prevented inmates from receiving adequate treatment and secure conditions, a situation the court considered cruel and unusual. A federal district court ordered the California Department of Corrections to reduce the system's prison population to 137.5% of capacity (releasing about 40,000 prisoners) and develop a compliance plan subject to court approval. Ultimately, the Supreme Court approved of the order, which capped the number of prisoners in state prisons.

While conditions have seemingly improved within many prison systems, few people could reasonably argue that additional improvements cannot be made. Furthermore, many prison systems are still overcrowded and under court order to monitor and reduce populations. While these court cases (and others) examined overall prison conditions, it is important to discuss a few different specific issues that courts have considered.

Health Care Issues

One of the most important cases regarding the provision of health care to inmates is *Estelle v. Gamble*. It is also notable for establishing the standard by which many different inmate needs should be evaluated. An inmate in Texas, J.W. Gamble, was performing his job assignment in prison when a bale of cotton fell on him as he was unloading a truck. Gamble continued to work, but after four hours, he became stiff and was allowed to go to the prison hospital for treatment of his back pain. In the days following his injury, he received various medications and saw physicians a total of 17 times. Eventually, prison administrators, based on advice from prison medical staff, ordered Gamble back to work after he was deemed fit for duty. Gamble refused, arguing that his medical condition prevented him from working. Gamble was placed in administrative segregation and had to appear before a prison disciplinary committee.

Gamble sued the medical director of the state corrections department and two correctional officials, claiming that he had received inadequate treatment for his back injury, and that this violated his Eighth Amendment protection from cruel and unusual punishment. The Supreme Court ultimately denied Gamble's claim, countering that it seemed that prison officials had provided him with a great deal of medical care. According to the Court, a failure to perform x-rays or additional diagnostic techniques was at most medical malpractice, which if pursued legally, should be filed in a state court. Justice Thurgood Marshall, writing the majority opinion, noted that "an inmate must rely on prison authorities to treat his medical needs; if the authorities fail to do so, those needs will not be met." That said, Marshall continued, for an inmate to successfully argue that a lack of medical care constituted cruel and unusual punishment, that inmate needed to establish that prison administrators acted with *deliberate indifference*. Furthermore, an inmate had to include some proof of a state of mind that authorities were deliberately indifferent to serious medical needs; an inadvertent failure was not evidence of such a state of mind. This concept was developed further in *Wilson v. Seiter*, when the Court rejected a suggested rule that "short-term" or "one-time" prison conditions required a proof of state of mind, but when considering "continuing" or "systemic" conditions, such a state of mind should be implicit and need no proof. Deliberate indifference is not an easy concept to define and interpret and as such, the courts have been faced with this challenge time and again due to frequent inmate lawsuits. However, as noted in *Gittlemacker v. Prosse*, complaints of improper or inadequate medical treatment need to go beyond tortious medical malpractice. Indeed, according to *Jordan v. Fitzharris*, for a claim of improper or denied inmate medical care to violate the Eighth Amendment, it must "shock the general conscience or ... be intolerable to fundamental fairness."

One interesting issue is if an inmate seeks to avoid medical treatment. In *Washington v. Harper*, Harper was incarcerated in the state of Washington for a robbery conviction. During his time as an inmate and while briefly under parole, Harper was given antipsychotic drugs. When not taking the drugs, he engaged in violent conduct and his mental health deteriorated. Harper argued that the due process clause of the Fourteenth Amendment required a hearing before any inmate could be involuntarily administered medication. Ultimately, the Court ruled that such decisions should be made by a medical professional when the behavior of an inmate can threaten the institutional security of a correctional facility. While the Court allowed inmates who pose a threat to institutional security to be involuntarily medicated, the Court ruled in *Riggins v. Nevada* and *Sell v. United States* that the state or a correctional facility could not involuntary medicate an inmate simply so that the inmate could be ruled competent to stand trial. The Court ruled that this should be done only in narrow and appropriate circumstances, which had not been presented to the Court.

Two state court opinions further highlight the ability of inmates to refuse medical care. In *Singletary v. Costello*, the Fourth District Court of Appeal of Florida ruled that an inmate engaging in a *hunger strike* could refuse any medical care that correctional officials sought to apply to offset the effects of malnutrition. In that case, Costello had dropped from 189 pounds to just over 159 pounds over a three-month period. A physician had described Costello as in need of emergency treatment and "in danger of imminent death." A similar decision was reached in California in the 1993 case of *Thor v. Superior Court (Andrews)*, when the Supreme Court of California ruled that a quadriplegic inmate could make the decision to refuse to be fed. Both courts noted that a medical patient who was not incarcerated would be allowed to make the decision to refuse medical care. Unless allowing a prisoner to make a decision that ended his or her life somehow threatened institutional security, there was no reason to intercede.

As American society (and others, for that matter) have become increasingly aware of the dangers of smoking and secondhand smoke, bans on smoking in workplaces and public places have become increasingly common. This issue has also reached correctional facilities. In *Helling v. McKinney*, McKinney was an inmate in a Nevada state prison. For a time, he had a cellmate who smoked five packs of cigarettes a day. McKinney filed a Section 1983 motion, arguing that by placing him in a cell with someone who smoked, the state was endangering McKinney's health and this constituted cruel and unusual punishment. Ultimately, the Supreme Court ruled that McKinney could be allowed to pursue a claim that a prison condition could damage not only his current health, but his future health as well. To pursue a successful claim, a prisoner must show both an objective factor that something is harming him and a subjective factor that prison authorities are engaging in deliberate indifference towards that harm. However, during the legal process, McKinney was transferred to a new facility and prison authorities made new smoking policies, which greatly restricted where inmates could smoke and thus allowed nonsmoking inmates to be free from the dangers posed by secondhand smoke. While the Court did not explicitly state that McKinney should lose his lawsuit, the Court noted that under the new circumstances of McKinney's smoke-free confinement environment, making a case would be difficult, as the state removed him from his previous environment and thus reduced the ability of McKinney to demonstrate that the Nevada prison system acted with deliberate indifference.

Another rising health care concern prison administrators have routinely had to deal with is prisoners with the human immunodeficiency virus (HIV) and the accompanying medical condition (when HIV worsens) acquired immune deficiency syndrome (AIDS). The necessary medical care, stigma, and possibility of people with these diseases infecting others have been considerable societal concerns. Such problems are exacerbated in correctional settings, where they are considered a serious health threat. Without adequate treatment, infection is almost synonymous to a delayed death sentence. In 2008, nearly 22,000 prisoners who were incarcerated in American correctional facilities were diagnosed as HIV-positive and almost 6,000 prisoners had AIDS. Although states and correctional facilities have different policies regarding the testing of inmates for these diseases, these numbers are actually a significant decrease from the 1990s. Managing these inmates presents a challenge. Inmates need care and clearly have rights, yet there are legitimate concerns about the potential for other inmates to be infected. The general trend seems to be only to segregate inmates with AIDS and HIV-positive inmates who display symptoms of the condition; however, this is not a universal standard (Clear et al., 2013).

While not a corrections case, in *Bragdon v. Abbott*, the Supreme Court ruled that people who have HIV are substantially limited in their major life activities. Thus they are afforded protection under the *Americans with Disability Act (ADA)*, which states: "No individual shall be discriminated against on the basis of disability in the full and equal enjoyment of goods, services, facilities, privileges, advantages, or accommodations of any place of public accommodation by any person who operates a place of public accommodation." Although the Court ruled that people who have HIV are covered under ADA, the Court noted that only medical caregivers can determine if a particular individual would constitute a "direct threat" to themselves or others. While complying with the ADA may require only additional accommodations or costs in general society, such accommodations and costs can be problematic in a correctional facility.

Some of these issues were considered in the case *Gates v. Rowland*, which was heard by the Ninth Circuit Court of Appeals. The case was a class action Section 1983 lawsuit by inmates at the California Medical Facility (CMF). Two major issues existed: (1) inmates complained that HIV-positive inmates were being held in segregation; and (2) HIV-positive inmates were denied the opportunity to work in prison food services. In the latter issue, these inmates claimed that they had a handicap, and Section 504 of the federal Rehabilitation Act of 1973 prohibited any institution that received federal funding from discriminating based on a handicap. As for the former issue, according to the Ninth Circuit, the placement of HIV-positive inmates in segregation was dictated by state law, which required placement by the Unit or Institution Classification Committee. For such placement, one or more of the following criteria must be found: a documented history of high-risk behavior in the last 12 months; participation in anal or oral intercourse; assault during which an HIV-positive inmate bled; or a displayed propensity for or likelihood of engaging in any of these behaviors. Additionally, the Ninth Circuit Court ruled that for an inmate to be denied participation in food services, there must be a determination that the inmate was unable to perform the required duties for such a position and/or no reasonable accommodations could be made so that such an inmate could perform food services duties.

Another case, *Harris v. Thigpen*, was heard by the Eleventh Circuit Court of Appeals. This case originated in Alabama and was a class action lawsuit by a group of inmates who claimed that the mandatory policies of testing and segregation of inmates who had HIV violated their First, Fourth, Eighth, and Fourteenth Amendment rights. Alabama is one of many states that tests all inmates for a variety of diseases upon admission to a correctional facility. Male and female inmates who test positive for HIV are sent to special segregated wings at the Limestone Correctional Facility for men and the Julia Tutwiler Prison for Women. In their suit, the inmates claimed that the mandatory testing policy was an unreasonable search and seizure; that segregation constituted cruel and unusual punishment and a de facto announcement of their positive status, and thus a violation of privacy; and that their limited access to the prison library and legal materials, due to segregation, represented a violation of their First Amendment right to access those materials.

After a trial in a district court, the inmates' claims were dismissed. Upon review by the Eleventh Circuit, the court noted that although inmates maintained a right to privacy, this need had to be balanced against the needs of the correctional facility. In this case, the correctional facility sought to prevent the spread of HIV and AIDS by segregating those prisoners. While the court acknowledged that many correctional facilities allowed HIV-positive inmates to remain in the general population, this was not yet a consensus position. Furthermore, testing inmates for this purpose was not an unreasonable search. Regarding the Rehabilitation Act, the district court had found that inmates with AIDS were not qualified for many programs because they represented an unacceptable risk to other inmates. However, such practice was a clear violation of the Rehabilitation Act which prohibits discrimination on the basis of disability in programs conducted by federal agencies, as well as in programs receiving federal financial assistance. Such a determination rests on an earlier decision by the Supreme Court in the case of *School Board of Nassau County v. Arline*. In that case, the Court held that if a person had an infectious disease, for the purposes of Section 504 of the Rehabilitation Act, an individualized inquiry must be made to determine, based on "reasonable medical judgments given the state of medical knowledge at the time." In doing so, the Court ruled that whether the "probabilities the disease will be transmitted and will cause varying degrees of harm." According to the Eleventh Circuit in *Harris*, the district court could come to the same conclusion, but such a determination needed to be made on each individual, not a class of inmates. Thus, the Eleventh Circuit remanded the case and ruled that a blanket policy of segregation could not simply block HIV-positive inmates from participating in prison programs. Regarding the issue of access to legal materials, the Eleventh Circuit determined that inmates who are segregated for medical reasons should still have access to these materials.

In *Muhammad v. Carlson*, Muhammad, who had been tested and diagnosed with AIDS, challenged his segregation to the AIDS unit. He argued that by essentially being placed into administrative segregation, he was punished without a hearing. However, the Eighth Circuit Court of Appeals ruled that Muhammad's admission to segregation was medically directed and not the result of any disciplinary infraction. For this reason, Muhammad was not entitled to a hearing.

While the placement of an inmate in a segregated HIV or AIDS unit may be constitutional and not a de facto violation of privacy, in *Woods v. White*, a case heard before a federal district court in Wisconsin, ruled that medical personnel of a correctional facility were not allowed to discuss an inmate's HIV or AIDS diagnosis with nonmedical personnel or other inmates. While segregation may be necessary or medical staff can converse with other medical staff, inmates still have a privacy interest that must be protected.

Prisoners with disabilities pose additional challenges in other contexts as well. In *Pennsylvania Department of Corrections v. Yeskey*, Yeskey had been sentenced to serve 18 to 36 months in a Pennsylvania correctional facility. The sentencing judge recommended that Yeskey could be admitted to a boot camp reserved for first-time offenders. If Yeskey successfully completed the program, he would be paroled after only 6 months. However, because Yeskey had a documented medical history of hypertension, he was refused admission to the program. Yeskey filed suit, arguing that his exclusion from the boot camp violated the ADA. Ultimately, the Supreme Court agreed with Yeskey and ruled that any voluntary programs in correctional facilities (or alternatives to incarceration) are protected under the ADA because an inmate could receive a benefit from these programs. In this case, the benefit was clear. Successful completion of the program could result in a significant reduction in sentence length.

Unlike AIDS or HIV, which are not communicable airborne diseases, tuberculosis is a highly infectious airborne disease. Its presence in correctional facilities poses many challenges to correctional administrators and staff, and has resulted in numerous appeals to the courts. For this reason, prevention measures can be more onerous than mere segregation. One example of such a case is *Jolly v. Coughlin*. Paul Jolly was an inmate in Attica Correctional Facility. When Jolly was admitted, he refused to be tested for tuberculosis, citing his beliefs as a Rastafarian. To test for tuberculosis, the department of corrections used a purified protein derivative (PPD) test, which involved injecting a small amount of purified protein into a person's skin. Jolly argued that such a test was a sin in the Rastafarian religion because it involved accepting artificial substances into one's body. After Jolly refused the test, he was placed in what correctional officials called "medical keeplock." Jolly was confined to his cell except for a ten-minute shower once a week. Medical keeplock is not a professional term, but rather a common term used by prisoners and correctional officials to describe a form of administrative segregation for inmates without medical significance, who refuse testing or medical treatment for potentially infectious disease. Inmates who tested positive for "active" tuberculosis were placed in "respiratory isolation." On the other hand, inmates who tested positive for "latent tuberculosis" were not placed in medical keeplock or respiratory isolation. Thus Jolly's placement was not truly preventative, as if he had presented a true risk, he should have been in respiratory isolation; medical keeplock was mere punishment. Jolly claimed that his segregation violated his free exercise of religion under the *Religious Freedom Restoration Act* of 1993 and his Eighth Amendment protection from cruel and unusual punishment. Along with his suit, Jolly filed a preliminary injunction against his placement in medical keeplock. The court found that when a prisoner expresses a legitimate religious objection to a general prison policy, the department of corrections is obligated to engage in the least restrictive method to further the policies of the department of corrections. Since there were alternatives to the PPD test, such as chest x-rays, the Second Circuit granted the injunction and noted that Jolly had a high likelihood of success in his lawsuit— the standard for obtaining an injunction.

Maintaining a Safe Environment

Whenever a person owns property, it is his or her duty to keep it safe from hazards. If a guest or even a trespasser is injured through such a failure in care, they can sue and, if successful, collect damages from the property owner. In *Daniels v. Williams*, a prisoner slipped on a pillow that had been negligently left by a sheriff's deputy. The prisoner filed a Section 1983 motion, arguing that the state's failure had deprived him of his liberty interest from bodily injury without due process of law, which the prisoner claimed violated the Fourteenth Amendment. The Court disagreed with the prisoner's argument and stated that this was a simple negligence claim that should be filed in a state court. According to the Court, the due process clause was designed to protect individuals from abuses of power by government officials, not simply a lack of due care or negligence.

Aside from medical care, inmates are also beholden to correctional officials to be protected from violence. Many people in correctional facilities have been incarcerated for violent crimes, so it should come as little surprise that inmates will engage in violence against one another. Much as with health care, though, the question is when protection from violence becomes a federal issue.

In *Davidson v. Cannon*, Davidson was a prisoner in a New Jersey state prison. While he was incarcerated, he sent a note to Sergeant Cannon that stated another inmate (McMillian) had threatened violence against Davidson. Cannon did not read the note but was informed of its substance; he failed to notify other officers of the threat and forgot about the note before he went off-duty. Two days later, McMillian attacked Davidson and caused serious bodily injuries. New Jersey state law forbids a prisoner from suing the state or an employee of the state if they are attacked by another prisoner. Since Davidson could not make a claim in state court, he filed a Section 1983 motion in the U.S. district court for the District of New Jersey against Cannon and prison officials, arguing that his Eighth Amendment and Fourteenth Amendments rights had been violated. He had sustained injuries due to the negligent failure of both Cannon and prison officials to protect him. While Davidson was awarded damages during a bench trial by the district court, which held that Davidson had been deprived of his liberty interests in personal security without any due process, thus upholding his Fourteenth Amendment claim, Davidson's Eighth Amendment claim was dismissed. Ultimately, the Third Circuit Court of Appeals would reverse the decision, in part because Davidson had taken no other action, such as requesting protective custody. Furthermore, Davidson testified that he had not foreseen actually being attacked by McMillian and had only sought to protect himself from potential blame if McMillian started another fight. The Supreme Court affirmed. The Court decided in *Davidson v. Cannon* on the same day it heard the arguments in *Daniels v. Williams*, regarding the negligent placement of the pillow by the deputy sheriff on a staircase that caused the petitioner to slip over and sustain injuries. In both instances, the Third Circuit held that the Fourteenth Amendment due process clause was not intended to address the lack of due care by an official who causes unintended injury or injuries through negligence. Rather, the Fourteenth Amendment was designed to prevent abusive and intentional governmental conduct. According to the Supreme Court these two cases, *Davidson v. Cannon* and *Daniels v. Williams*, did not rise to the level of due process violations. Specifically, the Supreme Court stated that: "... respondent's lack of due care, while leading to serious injuries, simply does not approach the sort of abusive government conduct that the Due Process Clause was designed to prevent." Accordingly, the Court made it clear that the due process clause protects against deliberate deprivations of life, liberty, and property. Detainees and prison inmates were advised to seek remedy in state and/or civil tort action, rather than trying to invoke the Fourteenth Amendment.

While violence and victimization may be part of the prison experience, certain inmates might be especially vulnerable in these conditions. In *Farmer v. Brennan*, Dee Farmer was a transsexual inmate with feminine characteristics who was incarcerated among male inmates in a federal prison. Farmer was placed in the general population for certain periods of time and placed for longer periods of time in segregation. After being transferred to a higher-security facility, Farmer was beaten and raped by another inmate. Farmer filed suit and sought damages from the federal government, arguing that prison officials' failure to protect him was deliberate indifference and amounted to cruel and unusual punishment that he suffered. A district court ruled, and the Seventh Circuit Court of Appeals affirmed, that for prison officials to be held liable under these circumstances, they must be "reckless in a criminal sense" and have "actual knowledge" of a potential for danger. However, the Supreme Court reversed this decision and ruled that whether an obvious danger existed should have been a subjective question of fact that should have been decided during a trial.

A theme that emerges repeatedly throughout this book is that correctional officials and officers have great latitude in abridging the rights of inmates when it comes to maintaining a secure environment. This extends to the amount of force correctional officers are allowed to use against inmates, to promote institutional security and to end disturbances. The Supreme Court considered the issue in *Whitley v. Albers*. In that case, during a riot at the Oregon State Penitentiary, a correctional officer was taken hostage. In the process of freeing the hostage, a correctional officer fired a shotgun and hit Albers in the knee. Albers filed a Section 1983 motion arguing that, in receiving this injury, his Eighth and Fourteenth Amendment rights had been violated. The Supreme Court denied Albers' claim and ruled that although the level of force seemed slightly excessive or unnecessary, the shooting was the result of a good faith effort to maintain or restore discipline. To the Court, the shooting was not malicious, sadistic, or intended to harm. The Court revisited this issue in 1992 in *Hudson v. McMillian*. Hudson was an inmate in a Louisiana state prison. While incarcerated, two guards (McMillian and Woods) handcuffed and shackled Hudson after he argued with the guards. Mezo, a supervisor on duty, told McMillian and Woods "not to have too much fun" while McMillian and Woods beat Hudson. Hudson filed a Section 1983 motion, arguing that the beating was not legitimate to maintain institutional security and should be considered cruel and unusual punishment. Hudson prevailed at trial, but the Fifth Circuit Court of Appeals reversed because Hudson's injuries were minor. Finally, the Supreme Court reversed the Fifth Circuit's ruling and held that excessive force may constitute cruel and unusual punishment, even if the injuries suffered are minor.

While the discipline that inmates face at the hands of correctional officers is a constant area of contention, another issue that inmates have challenged is the practice of "double bunking" or "double celling." Within the original Pennsylvania and Auburn models of incarceration, inmates were held in isolation. Yet, as America's incarcerated population has continually increased, holding inmates alone in their cells is typically reserved for disciplinary reasons, such as administrative segregation or supermax prisons. Various inmates have argued that they should be allowed single cells without being disciplined. One case that considered this issue is *Rhodes v. Chapman*. In that case, several inmates in a maximum security prison in Ohio brought a class action Section 1983 suit arguing that the practice of double celling was a violation of their rights. Ultimately, the Supreme Court ruled that the practice of double celling was not cruel and unusual punishment. As the Court noted, to be unconstitutional, conditions of confinement must not be wanton or an unnecessary infliction of pain or grossly disproportionate to the severity of a crime that warrants incarceration. According to the Court, double celling was merely a standard condition of confinement, and no evidence was presented that indicated the inmates had been harmed by the practice.

One issue that has come to the attention of the courts has been whether inmates must attend mandatory educational classes in prison. In *Rutherford v. Hutto*, James Rutherford was an inmate in an Arkansas prison. Due to a lack of formal education, Rutherford was 43 years old and illiterate, with only a "slight ability to read and write and some elementary understanding of simple arithmetic." Rutherford argued that his enforced attendance of classes being held at the Cummins Unit, Arkansas Department of Correction, violates his rights protected by the First Amendment to the Constitution of the United States and also constitutes cruel and unusual punishment prohibited by the Eighth and Fourteenth Amendments. The presiding judge in the case ruled that Rutherford must attend classes and he had no constitutional right to remain illiterate or ignorant. In another case, heard before the Eighth Circuit Court of Appeals, *Jackson v. McLemore*, the court upheld a decision that an inmate who received disciplinary action for a refusal to comply with educational exercises had no constitutional right to challenge such a punishment. As the Eighth Circuit noted, states and correctional administrators have "a sufficient interest in eliminating illiteracy among its convicts to justify it in requiring illiterate convicts, including adults, to attend classes."

Suicide

One of the biggest problems in managing prisons and jails is the shock many inmates will feel when they are incarcerated. Many first-time prisoners or prisoners who suffer from mental illness find the shock of incarceration too much to bear, and may have thoughts of or attempt suicide (Clear, Cole, & Reisig, 2013). According to a report published by the Bureau of Justice Statistics, since 2000, suicide in prisons and jails is one of the top two causes of death in confinement (the other is heart disease). In jails, suicide was the number-one cause of death among inmates since 2000 (Noonan, Rohloff, & Ginder, 2015). In 2013, a third (34%) of jail inmate deaths was due to suicide (ibid.). In 2010, more than 38,000 inmates died from suicide in both jails and prisons (Han, Compton, Gfroerer, & McKeon, 2014). Because prison and jail administrators are responsible for the safekeeping of their inmates and suicide is a known risk, administrators are expected to prevent inmates from harming themselves. However, the complex question of what steps and procedures, and how much protection must be given, is a question often left to the courts.

While the Supreme Court has neglected to hear a case concerning this issue, perhaps the best statement of how courts evaluate the liability of state authorities is stated in *Rellergert v. Cape Girardeau County*, a case decided by the Eighth Circuit Court of Appeals. Generally, the courts have recognized that state liability is decided under the *Estelle v. Gamble* standard of deliberate indifference. Typically, the courts will deal with one of two scenarios. The first is when jailers fail to discover an inmate's suicidal tendencies, whether by monitoring an inmate's behavior or noting a history of suicidal tendencies when previously incarcerated. The second scenario is when jailers fail to take the proper preventative measures in suicide prevention. In the case of *Rellergert*, a parolee named Mark England had his parole revoked after failing to remain employed. While England had no reported problems during his year of incarceration, he indicated in his self-reported medical history that he had attempted suicide in the past. England was interviewed the next day by a social worker. After the interview, the social worker concluded that England seemed to be suffering from mild depression but did not seem to have suicidal symptoms and did not need mental health treatment. Despite the diagnosis, the sheriff's office decided to house England in the common area of the jail along with other inmates who were considered a suicide risk. Placement in the common area allowed a duty officer to watch England at all times, except when inmates were allowed to go to an adjacent shower and bathroom area, which could not be observed by the guard booth. When Deputy Bedell began his shift at midnight on June 20, 1987, England was incarcerated in the common area with another inmate. An hour after Bedell's shift began, a new arrival, who had been arrested for driving while intoxicated, was placed in the common area as well. At some point after 3:00 a.m., Bedell was in the booth completing the processing forms for the man who had recently been arrested. Bedell had observed England heading to the shower area. After England "did not return quickly," Bedell woke one of the inmates to check on England. The inmate, along with a jail trustee, went to check on England and found that he had hanged himself with a bedsheet. The dispatcher was alerted, and within 10 or 15 minutes "road personnel" came and checked on England. They confirmed that England was dead. Throughout, Bedell stayed in the observation booth, per jail procedures. England had been assigned only one bed sheet, but somehow obtained another one. Bedell observed England heading to the shower area, but did not recall seeing a bedsheet.

Rellergert, the son of England, filed a Section 1983 suit arguing that his father's Fifth, Eighth, and Fourteenth Amendment rights had been violated. The county sheriff and Deputy Bedell were found liable at trial. The Eighth Circuit noted, "It is deceivingly inviting to take the suicide, ipso facto, as conclusive proof of deliberate indifference." As the court noted though, such a belief does not comply with the deliberate indifference standard. A motivated person can commit suicide despite safeguards against such actions. The court noted that the deliberate indifference standard required that actions be taken to prevent suicides, but there were no strict criteria as to what standards should be put in place. The county had a policy in place, by placing inmates in a common area, to help monitor their behavior. Additionally, while Bedell could have been more prudent, he was not allowed to leave his post and had other duties than solely observing England. The court concluded that Bedell's actions did not constitute deliberate indifference and overturned the trial court's verdict.

In *Heflin v. Stewart County*, Hugh Allen Heflin hanged himself in his jail cell only a few hours after he was arrested. Heflin had been placed in a single-occupant cell; he left his shower running and gagged himself with a rag to muffle any sound he made during his suicide. After suspecting something was wrong in Heflin's cell, a jail officer found Heflin's body. The county sheriff and two emergency medical technicians (EMTs) arrived shortly after jail officers discovered Heflin's hanging body. The EMTs checked for vital signs and after finding none, left Heflin's body hanging. After the county medical examiner was summoned and performed a preliminary check, the medical examiner "directed" that Heflin's body could be cut down. Subsequently, Heflin was officially declared dead.

After these events, Heflin's parents and sister sued Stewart County and jail personnel. The plaintiffs claimed jail administrators were doubly negligent: for failing to classify Heflin as a suicide risk, a violation of his Eighth and Fourteenth Amendment rights, and for not immediately cutting him down upon discovery and delivering emergency first aid. This latter failure, leaving Heflin's body hanging, illustrated "deliberate indifference" to Heflin's medical need, Heflin's family claimed. At trial, the District Court dismissed the first claim, but ultimately found the defendants liable for the second count. Such a finding was buttressed by evidence that the county had a policy to leave suicide victims hanging until an official order was given to cut down the person. The Sixth Circuit Court would later reverse a part of the decision concerning the awarding of attorney's fees, but it ultimately affirmed the rest of the decision, which assigned blame to Stewart County.

In *Logue v. United States*, Reagan Logue was held in the Nueces County jail in Corpus Christi, Texas, while awaiting trial in federal court. The day after he arrived in the facility, Logue attempted suicide by slashing veins in his left arm. As it turned out, the injury was minor, but Logue was admitted to the psychiatric floor of the hospital in which he was treated. According to a physician at the facility, Logue was "actively hallucinating and out of touch with reality." After a psychiatrist completed an evaluation, the doctor recommended that Logue be committed to a medical facility. The next day, a judge in the federal district court in which Logue's case was set to be heard approved the transfer. However, before the necessary paperwork could be completed, federal officials decided to transfer Logue back to the Nueces County jail. The deputy marshal who had originally arrested Logue and returned him to the Nueces County jail advised the chief jailer at the facility that a special cell, with all dangerous objects removed, should be prepared for Logue, in light of his previous suicide attempt. However, the deputy marshal did not advise the chief jailer that constant surveillance should be provided. The day after being returned to jail, Logue used the bandage on his self-inflicted arm wound to hang himself.

After Logue's death, his mother and stepfather sued under the Federal Tort Claims Act. In a trial before a federal district court, the court found that the United States was liable for the negligence of the employees of the Nueces County jail for "inadequate" surveillance of Logue. Additionally, the court found that the deputy marshal was negligent for a failure to make the necessary arrangements for the constant surveillance of a federal prisoner who had a high likelihood of self-harm. Later, though, the Fifth Circuit Court of Appeals would reverse and remand the decision. In its judgement, the Fifth Circuit had no real issue with a finding of negligence, but instead ruled that Nueces County should be considered a contractor of the United States and since the Federal Torts Claims Act specifically omitted plaintiffs from collecting damages from contractors, Logue's family could not collect damages from the federal government. The Supreme Court then affirmed the judgment of the Fifth Circuit, but it remanded the case to consider the negligence of the deputy marshal specifically, rather than the county government, and determine if that would allow the Logue family to collect any damages, as that would involve a federal employee.

In *Myers v. County of Lake*, Steven Myers (16 years of age at the time) was housed in what is described as an "open" juvenile facility in Indiana, after he had been found delinquent. While in custody, Myers stole a staff member's car. As a result of this offense, Myers was transferred to a more secure facility, the Lake County Juvenile Center (LCJC). This was not Myers's first stay at LCJC, and his caseworker recommended that Myers be transferred to a facility in Maine "specializing in intelligent children who treated ordinary detention facilities as challenges to overcome." Eight days after a state court authorized the transfer but before Myers was moved to Maine, Myers hanged himself with a bed sheet. Myers did not die, but suffered "severe and permanent brain damage."

Even though all parties involved were citizens of Indiana, Myers's family sued in federal court, arguing that the "deliberate indifference" of employees at LCJC in preventing suicide risks violated the due process clause of the Fourth Amendment and thus constituted a violation of Myers's civil rights, which would support a Section 1983 claim. During pretrial motions, a federal magistrate ruled that the Myers family had not produced enough evidence to support a federal Section 1983 claim. Such a ruling left only a negligence claim under state law, but the federal magistrate ruled that because the federal claim was dismissed shortly before the trial would start, the trial for a state negligence claim would still commence in a federal court.

At trial, the Myers family produced evidence that LCJC was understaffed and underfunded. Additionally, Lake County had signed a consent decree 12 years prior, specifying that one full-time psychologist be employed for every 44 inmates. If the number of inmates fell below 44, the county still had to provide one full-time psychologist. When Myers was incarcerated, LCJC provided only a part-time employee who saw inmates only on Tuesdays and Thursdays. This resulted in many newly arrived inmates not receiving proper psychological services or new inmate screening in a timely manner. Myers was incarcerated in LCJC for nearly a month and never saw a psychologist. Additionally, employees of LCJC did not check files for newly admitted inmates who had previously been to the facility. If staff had checked Myers's file, they would have found that on his previous stay, Myers had shown "pronounced suicide ideation" and had previously been placed on suicide watch. Furthermore, Myers had been on suicide watch while at the facility in which he had stolen a staff member's car. At trial, the clinical director at a third facility Myers had been incarcerated in testified it was "painfully obvious" that Myers suffered from depression. Ultimately, a jury concluded that LCJC was negligent and awarded the Myers family $600,000 in damages. While the Seventh Circuit Court of Appeals noted that the case probably should have been held in a state court, there was no evidence to suggest that the outcome would have been any different. Thus, the Seventh Circuit affirmed the judgment.

Conclusion

Cases that challenged the Eighth Amendment and other related constitutional rights examine excessively and disproportionately punishing conditions of confinement, as well as the treatment found in jails and prisons. Such cases are of great importance to the penological discussion in which the goals of punishment, their justification, and attempted consequences should be evaluated. Following a utilitarian approach that strives to prevent future crimes, the Eighth Amendment and its cruel and unusual clause forces us to focus attention on the proportionality of the punishment, thus suggesting that cruel and unusual conditions may be driven by a desire for vengeance and retribution, rather than simply incapacitation. It is in this context that the courts have been called to determine if prisoners are being treated in a manner that does not reflect the standards of an evolving society (Anderson, Mangels, & Dyson, 2010), and hence may be viewed as retributive and unjustly cruel and unusual. After all, society and its values determine the goals of any penal institution, and those in turn influence the multifaceted challenges such institutions must confront and respond to (Goldberg, 2015). However, such challenges also mandate the examination of correctional practices and how prison officials perform their daily duties. Of particular interest is the requirement that prison officials, as discussed in this chapter and previous chapters, demonstrate that their actions were taken without malice, and to demonstrate that they have not acted in a manner that is "deliberately indifferent," and create conditions that may intentionally harm prisoners under their custody. The courts have also examined the responsibility of states and the government to provide adequate care for individuals directly under its care. This is one way punishment is justified under the social treaty/contract, in which individuals surrender their powers to the government with an expectation and trust that they will be protected by it. Punishment that is perceived as unjust thus violates the social balance created by the treaty, and thus will not help in deterring and preventing future wrongdoing.

Discussion Questions

1. Discuss the relevance of the 8th Amendment to the examination of physical conditions of confinement. Should there be any minimum requirements by which state prisons confine convicted offenders? Why should the courts care about the conditions in which convicted offenders are being confined?

2. Discuss the importance of the *Brown v. Plata* case. Search the internet for information about this case, and explain its potential relevance to rehabilitation, public health, and other potential consequences of incarceration.

3. Explain the importance of the legal term *deliberate indifference*. Discuss its relevance to correctional practices while referring to relevant cases.

4. Discuss the issues that revolve around medical treatment to inmates who are going on a hunger strike. How did the court decide in these cases, and what was its logic?

5. What are some of the issues revolve around prisoners who are HIV-positive and prisoners with AIDS? In your discussion refer to relevant cases, and explain how such medical conditions may affect the conditions of confinement and risk violating these prisoners' 8th Amendment rights.

6. How does the American with Disability Act (ADA) protect the rights of prisoner diagnosed with HIV/AIDS? Explain the importance of this act to the day-to-day dealing of prison authorities with these prisoners.

7. In your opinion, should prisons conducted mandatory blanket blood tests for all incoming prisoners in the name of public health and concern to prison staff and other inmates? In your response, please discuss the relevant case/s that dealt with such issue, and explain the importance of the court ruling.

8. Discuss the relevance of the Rehabilitation Act to the treatment of prisoners diagnosed with chronic medical conditions and disabilities. What protections does this act provide to these prisoners, and why is it important to maintain constitutional rights guaranteed under the 8th Amendment?

9. Correctional facilities are required to provide safe confinement environment to both prisoners and staff. Present some of the issues that were brought before the Courts and explain how they were dealt with. What is the leading logic used by the Courts in assessing the safety of the correctional facility?

10. Discuss the issues revolving around the use of force by correctional officials. While referring to relevant cases, explain what is the guiding rule by which the Courts examine and determine the legitimacy of use of force?

11. Should jails and prisons be held liable when a prisoner commit suicide? In your response, refer to relevant cases, and explain the unique position taken by the courts in such cases.

List of Cases Cited

Bragdon v. Abbott, 1998. 524 U.S. 624.

Brown v. Plata, 2011. 131 S. Ct. 1910.

Daniels v. Williams, 1986. 474 U.S. 327.

Davidson v. Cannon, 1986 474 U.S. 344.

Estelle v. Gamble, 1976. 429 U.S. 97.

Farmer v. Brennan, 1994. 511 U.S. 825.

Gates v. Rowland, 1994. 39 F.3d 1439.

Gittlemacker v. Prasse, 1970. 428 F. 2d 1.

Harris v. Thigpen, 1991. 941 F.2d 1495.

Heflin v. Stewart County, 1992. 968 F2d 1214.

Helling v. McKinney, 1993. 509 U.S. 25.

Holt v. Sarver, 1969. 300 F. Supp. 825.

Hudson v. McMillian, 1992. 503 U.S. 1.

Hutto v. Finney, 1979. 437 U.S. 678.

Jackson v. McLemore, 1975. 523 F.2d 838.

Jolly v. Coughlin, 1996. 76 F. 3d 468.

Jones v. Cunningham, 1963. 371 U.S. 236.

Jordan v. Fitzharris, 1966. 257 F. Supp. 674.

Logue v. United States, 1973. 412 U.S. 521.

Muhammad v. Carlson, 1988. 845 F.2d 175.

Myers v. County of Lake, 1994. 30 F. 3d 847.

Pennsylvania Department of Corrections v. Yeskey, 1998. 524 U.S. 206.

Pugh v. Locke, 1976. 406 F. Supp. 318.

Rellergert v. Cape Girardeau County, Missouri, 1991. 924 F.2d 794.

Rhodes v. Chapman, 1981. 452 U.S. 337.

Riggins v. Nevada, 1992. 504 U.S. 127.

Ruiz v. Estelle, 1975. 679 F 2d. 1115.

Rutherford v. Hutto, 1974. 377 F. Supp. 268.

Sell v. United States, 2003. 539 U.S. 166.

School Board of Nassau County v. Airline, 1987. 480 U.S. 273.

Singletary v. Costello, 1996. 665 So. 2d 1099.

Thor v. Superior Court (Andrews), 1993. 855 P. 2d 375.

Washington v. Harper, 1990. 494 U.S. 210.

Whitley v. Albers, 1986. 475 U.S. 312.

Wilson v. Seiter, 1991. 501 U.S. 294.

Woods v. White, 1988. 689 F. Supp. 874.

Chapter 11

Access to Federal Courts

As we have previously documented, for years, the federal courts allowed the states to maintain their own correctional systems with very little to no interference (the so-called "hands-off" period). However, as federal courts continued to hear cases filed by state inmates and the federal correctional system grew as well, federal courts became increasingly active in hearing disputes between inmates and various correctional authorities. As a result, the federal government (Congress and the President) began to insert itself into this process as well. This chapter will discuss some of the various laws that have regulated various parts of corrections, as well as various general laws that have affected corrections in some manner.

Limits on Litigation

Even though federal courts will now consider state claims, a person cannot immediately file suit in federal court after being convicted. Instead, a person must exhaust all appeals in state court before seeking the intervention of the higher authority of the federal courts. By their nature, appeals are supposed to examine what legal errors may have occurred in a case. However, many inmates have made use of writs of habeas corpus in federal courts. A power guaranteed by the Constitution, *habeas corpus* comes from Latin and literally means "you have the body." This means that whenever an inmate files a habeas corpus petition, they are demanding to know why they are being incarcerated or conversely, asking correctional officials (or the state) to justify why they are being held in custody or treated in one way or another. Originally, the writ of habeas corpus was designed so that people would not be incarcerated for long periods without having charges filed against them. As time went on, prisoners began to use these writs to challenge state procedures and the laws that led to their incarceration. Furthermore, unlike other appeals, which only seek to determine if legal errors were made during a defendant's trial, habeas corpus petitions allow federal courts to reconsider almost any part of a trial. As Williamson (1973) notes, the whole purpose of habeas corpus petitions is to ensure that American citizens are receiving due process and fair trials.

In the "hands-off" era, many federal courts simply ignored the bulk of inmate lawsuits. However, after federal courts began to hear these types of lawsuits, many people clamored for reforms. One of the first efforts to do this took place in 1966, when Congress applied the *abuse of the writ doctrine* to federal habeas corpus petitions. Abuse of writ doctrine is a principle that limits future petitions of writ of habeas corpus that were not raised earlier in the judicial process. Specifically, abuse of the writ doctrine prohibits subsequent consideration of claims not raised, and thus defaulted, in a prior federal habeas proceeding. The doctrine essentially allows inmates to file only a single habeas corpus motion. The exception to this policy is if an inmate alleges a new complaint and can convince a judge that it was not deliberately withheld from the original habeas corpus motion. The Supreme Court considered this issue in *McCleskey v. Zant*. McCleskey had been convicted of murder and sentenced to death. After his conviction, McCleskey filed a state habeas corpus petition that included a claim that he had been induced to make incriminating statements without the assistance of counsel. According to McCleskey, this violated his rights guaranteed under the Sixth Amendment to the Constitution and as decided in the case of *Massiah v. United States*, where relying on the *Spano rule*—confession that is a result of illegal interrogation in the absence of legal counsel (see *Spano v. New York*)—the justices held that "the defendant's own incriminating statements, obtained by federal agents under [these] circumstances…, could not constitutionally be used by the prosecution as evidence against him at his trial." McCleskey's state claim was unsuccessful. Afterward, McCleskey filed a habeas corpus motion in federal court that was unsuccessful. However, unlike the state motion, McCleskey did not include a *Massiah* claim, and the federal claim was unsuccessful. McCleskey filed yet again, a second federal habeas corpus petition that this time did include a *Massiah* claim. McCleskey tried to argue that this was not an abuse of the writ because he had new documentation supporting his *Massiah* claim that had not been included in the state petition. Yet, the Supreme Court ultimately turned down the second federal petition. The Court noted that the documentation was new, but McCleskey should have made the claim in his first federal petition. The Supreme Court reasoned that since McCleskey seemed to know his rights regarding *Massiah* in the state petition, he should have made this claim in the first federal petition.

With the federal courts increasingly intervening as guardians of the Constitution and Bill of Rights, ruling the Fourteenth Amendment application of the Bill of Rights to states became more frequent, so did the number of prisoners' rights petitions. While some people just saw this as a long-overdue process through which inmates did not lose all their constitutional rights once they entered a correctional facility, other people framed prisoners' lawsuits as an abuse of the legal system and believed that this needlessly clogged federal courts. Based on the growing perception among many people that bored inmates were abusing the court system in hopeless attempts to overturn their properly decided criminal convictions, in 1995, Congress passed the *Prisoners Litigation Reform Act (PLRA)*, which was signed by President Bill Clinton. This legislation, which took effect a year later, in 1996, has made it much harder for prisoners to gain relief in the federal courts. The act addresses two main concerns: (1) the increasing number of prisoners' lawsuits, and (2) federal judges who intervene in the operation of state prison systems and order extensive and costly reforms. The act requires prisoners to exhaust any remedies available to them through their inmate grievance system and state courts before they file any lawsuit in federal court. In that regard, the PLRA shifts the pendulum once more toward the "hands-off" doctrine. Further, the act imposes limitations on the legal fees awarded to successful prisoner-plaintiffs. While the PLRA did not completely obliterate the right of prisoners to file habeas corpus motions, guaranteed by cases such as *Ex parte Hull* (a state prison rule abridging or impairing a prisoner's right to apply to the federal courts for a writ of habeas corpus is invalid), federal courts have been essentially stopped from hearing valid constitutional claims of inmates until these inmates have complied with the abuse of writ rule and fully exhausted any state claims or grievance procedures within state correctional systems.

While some people have viewed the PLRA as a way to curtail frivolous lawsuits, others have seen it differently. The most common critique is that the PLRA simply prevents inmates from exercising their access to the courts and does not actually identify when a lawsuit is frivolous. As Schlanger (2003) notes, in 1995, inmates were only successful in 15% of the lawsuits that they filed. Thus, inmates seemed to already be at a disadvantage. However, after the PLRA, not only were inmates unlikely to succeed on the merits of their cases, they were also less likely to be able to file lawsuits. Twelve years later, Schlanger (2015) notes, from 1996 to 2008, prisoner lawsuits decreased from 23.3 per 1,000 prisoners to 10.2 per 1,000 prisoners. Overall, this represented a 60% decrease in lawsuit filings. To some people, this might indicate that the PLRA served its purpose, but Schlanger noted that the number of frivolous lawsuits has not decreased and inmates still have a low rate of success. Inmates, few of whom have legal training, already have a difficult time filing proper lawsuits, but the demands of the PLRA have made prisoner lawsuits even tougher to file, and many lawsuits are simply dismissed for procedural defects rather than substantive ones. Among the most important effects of the PLRA is that it forced inmates to exhaust all grievance procedures in the facilities in which they are incarcerated, it increased filing fees for inmates, decreased the amount of attorney's fees that could be awarded, and limited the damages awards. Furthermore, the PLRA made it more difficult to maintain court control of correctional facilities that did not comply with court orders. One particular topic of contention has been requiring inmates to pay filing fees with courts. In cases such as *Burns v. Ohio* and *Smith v. Bennett*, the Supreme Court stated that forcing indigent inmates to pay filing fees was a violation of due process because this had the practical effect of denying them access to the courts.

One of the first decisions that the Supreme Court decided after the passage of the PLRA was *Martin v. Hadix*. In that case, Hadix was among a group of inmates who filed a class action lawsuit against officials in the Michigan prison system alleging a variety of claims regarding the constitutionality of the inmates' confinement. The ruling resulted in a consent decree being entered, requiring subsequent monitoring to ensure that correctional officials continued to comply with the consent decree. At the time the consent decree was entered, the market rate for attorney fees was $150 per hour. However, the PLRA capped the rate of attorney fees at $112.50 per hour. Ultimately, the Court decided that all legal work completed before the PLRA took effect would be paid at whatever rate was negotiated. Any work completed after the PLRA took effect, even if a lawsuit was filed before, would have been subject to the cap restrictions of the PLRA.

One of the ways in which the PLRA was designed to speed up the federal court dockets was to restrict the amount of time a federal court may consider certain aspects of prisoner lawsuits. The PLRA allows prison officials working under federal court supervision to file motions to terminate injunctions or any other legal orders imposed on them by the federal courts. According to the language of the PLRA, if a federal court cannot find any "continuing conditions" that warrant further court oversight, the applicable federal court must terminate its oversight of that correctional system. Furthermore, not only must the courts make this determination, they must do so in a timely manner. The PLRA demands that a federal court hear the motion within 30 days of filing. A court may extend the deadline 60 days "for good cause," but the PLRA definitively states that if a court has a heavy caseload, that is not a legitimate reason to extend the deadline. If a court fails to rule within these parameters, any injunction or legal order is automatically terminated.

One of the most basic questions that the Supreme Court has considered is the full meaning of "exhaustion" within the grievance process. In *Woodford v. Ngo*, an inmate (Ngo) filed a grievance with the California prison system based on the conditions of his confinement, but the grievance was dismissed because Ngo had waited too long to file. Later, Ngo filed suit in a federal court. The state of California objected to the lawsuit and argued that because Ngo had missed the deadline to file a grievance, he should be prevented from filing a suit in federal court based on those same claims. While the district court agreed with the state of California and dismissed the lawsuit, the Ninth Circuit Court of Appeals reversed. The Ninth Circuit ruled that Ngo met the definition of exhaustion because he was unable to file a grievance and that Ngo should be allowed the opportunity to file suit in federal court. However, Ngo's victory was short-lived, as the Supreme Court ruled that to comply with the PLRA, an inmate must "properly" exhaust the grievance procedures, not simply wait until the deadlines have expired. According to the majority opinion of a 6–3 decision, if this lawsuit had been allowed to proceed, inmates would begin to skip the grievance process in hopes of filing suit in federal court.

An additional question concerning the concept of "exhaustion" was considered by the Seventh Circuit Court of Appeals in *Strong v. David*. In that case, Dion Strong was an inmate at Shawnee Correctional Center. On one occasion, after Strong had visited a physician, Strong accused the physician of sexually assaulting him. Strong was ordered by a lieutenant in the prison's internal affairs division to take a polygraph. The polygraph examiner concluded that Strong lied about the encounter. As a result, Strong was convicted in a prison disciplinary hearing of making a false accusation against a staff member and was later disciplined. Strong filed two grievances, including his original allegations of the sexual assault, both of which were denied. Later, Strong filed a Section 1983 lawsuit. The district court hearing Strong's case determined that Strong was alleging violations of his Eighth Amendment and due process rights. In dismissing Strong's lawsuit, the district court noted that while Strong had filed grievances, his first grievance did not cover all legal theories and did not request the same relief that he was seeking in his lawsuit. Additionally, the district court ruled that his second grievance was lacking because the claim had not been followed to exhaustion.

Precisely because the PLRA requires exhaustion before suing in federal court, the issue of what constitutes proof of exhaustion was then considered in *Jones v. Bock*. While prison inmates must exhaust their claims, inmates do not need to actually provide documentation illustrating exhaustion. Instead, the burden is on the state to provide such documentation, so that a premature lawsuit can be dismissed. Yet, the Supreme Court further ruled that a court did not necessarily have to dismiss a lawsuit if an inmate had not completed the exhaustion process. If a federal court wanted, that court could merely delay hearing the lawsuit until all required state or prison grievance hearings had concluded. Last, in *Jones*, the Court ruled that a prisoner did not have to name every defendant in a federal lawsuit in a previous administrative grievance for that claim to go forward in federal court.

In *Strong*, the Seventh Court noted that in a previous decision, *Curry v. Scott*, by the Sixth Circuit Court of Appeals, that court had required only that an administrative grievance identify each person who would ultimately become a defendant in a subsequent lawsuit. Alternatively, the Eleventh Circuit Court ruled in *Brown v. Sikes* that an inmate only had to include what information a prisoner was reasonably expected to know and a grievance did not need to include all the people who would eventually be named in a lawsuit. Thus, the Seventh Circuit noted, different circuits had different requirements concerning how much information needed to be included in a grievance before that inmate had met the PLRA criteria of exhaustion and be able to file a subsequent lawsuit in federal court. In deciding *Strong*, the Seventh Circuit took a slightly different approach. It ruled that the requirements of the state grievance system should be consulted. If a grievance system requires a certain set of facts be included in a pleading, then that will be the controlling standard. However, in *Strong*, the court noted, "Illinois has not established any rule or regulation prescribing the contents of a grievance or the necessary degree of factual particularity." Thus, the court later stated, "As in a notice-pleading system, the grievant need not lay out the facts, articulate legal theories, or demand particular relief. All the grievance need do is object intelligibly to some asserted shortcoming." Afterward, having found that Strong had met that standard in the two grievances that he filed, the Seventh Circuit ruled that Strong's federal lawsuit should have been allowed to proceed.

In a later decision, the Seventh Circuit noted one exception to the timely filing of a grievance for purposes of exhaustion. In *Riccardo v. Rausch*, Anthony Riccardo, an inmate at the Centralia Correctional Center in Illinois, filed a Section 1983 motion against Lieutenant Larry Rausch. According to Riccardo, Rausch had been negligent in assigning a bunkmate to Riccardo. The bunkmate in question, Juan Garcia, sexually assaulted Riccardo. While Riccardo's lawsuit would ultimately be unsuccessful, one of the issues presented in the case was that Riccardo had filed a grievance after the required deadline. Despite Riccardo's late filing, Illinois allowed a six-month extension if an inmate had "good cause." Although the reason was not specified, Riccardo's grievance was heard on the merits. Thus, while Riccardo was late in filing, because state law allowed him an extension to the filing date and had heard the grievance on the merits, Riccardo had met the requirements of exhaustion and was allowed to file a federal lawsuit. If the grievance had been denied for late filing, the Seventh Circuit would have ruled that Riccardo had not properly exhausted the grievance system.

In *Miller v. French*, different provisions of the PLRA were challenged. In that case, inmates at Pendleton Correctional Facility in Indiana filed a lawsuit in 1975 that challenged various aspects of their incarceration. As in so many other cases, the correctional facility then came under supervision of the courts. In 1997, a year after PLRA was passed, administrators at Pendleton filed a motion to terminate the order overseeing the correctional facility. Prisoners at Pendleton argued that the automatic stays in the PLRA were unconstitutional because Congress took away the ability of the courts to decide how long courts had to determine the fate of cases. According to the prisoners, this was a violation of the separation of powers established in the Constitution. A divided Supreme Court upheld the deadlines established in the PLRA and noted that the new guidelines did not compromise the ability of the courts to perform oversight; rather, Congress was merely imposing deadlines on the courts in which to make those decisions.

As previously mentioned, the federal courts have always demanded that people filing cases based on state matters exhaust all remedies in state courts before turning to the federal courts. In this regard, the PLRA really just codified what was already legal custom in prisoner litigation. Nonetheless, this issue came up again in *Booth v. Churner*. In that case, Booth was an inmate at the State Correctional Institution in Smithfield, Pennsylvania. Booth filed an administrative grievance with the prison system arguing that his Eighth Amendment protection against cruel and unusual punishment had been violated in several different ways. Ultimately, his grievance was denied. Booth had the opportunity to appeal the decision, but decided not to because the grievance system lacked provisions for monetary damages. Thus, Booth filed suit in a federal district court alleging the same facts that he had complained of in his administrative grievance. Because he could not be awarded monetary damages in the administrative grievance system, Booth reasoned, his suit was proper and it did not matter that he had not exhausted his remedies in the grievance system since the remedy he sought was unavailable there. The district court dismissed Booth's case and the Court of Appeals later affirmed the decision, as did a unanimous Supreme Court. According to the Court, regardless of the availability of monetary damages, an inmate must exhaust state claims before filing suit in federal court.

In a slightly different case, *Porter v. Nussle*, Ronald Nussle was an inmate at the Cheshire Correctional Institution in Connecticut. He filed a Section 1983 motion alleging that certain correctional officers at the facility had subjected him to a sustained pattern of harassment and intimidation. Furthermore, Nussle alleged that on one occasion, correctional officers had severely beaten him. Nussle did not file a grievance with the correctional facility. Instead, Nussle first filed a Section 1983 lawsuit in federal court, based on the logic that because the PLRA applied only to "prison conditions," excessive-force claims fell outside this and thus, he was not required to exhaust his remedies with the grievance system. The district court hearing Nussle's suit dismissed the case, but the Second Circuit Court of Appeals reversed, believing the legislative history of the PLRA supported Nussle's assertion. However, a unanimous Supreme Court decision disagreed and ruled that as in any other prisoner lawsuit, Nussle needed to exhaust all administrative remedies before filing suit in federal court.

Another procedure established by the PLRA is how to determine if correctional facilities are overcrowded and need to reduce population. The act specifies that if a defendant claims overcrowding and calls for a reduction in population, only a panel of three judges can make such a determination. Such a situation occurred in California. In 1990, a suit was filed by a group of prisoners with serious mental illness who did not receive adequate medical care. Five years later, in *Coleman v. Wilson*, a special master was appointed to oversee these inmates' proper care. In a later case, *Brown v. Plata*, decided in 2011 but originally filed in 2001, a group of inmates sued the California Department of Corrections, alleging that deficiencies in prison medical care violated their Eighth Amendment rights. The state of California conceded that these allegations were true but failed to take corrective action. Eventually, the inmates sued and requested a three-judge panel (the necessary condition set by the PLRA) to be convened to determine if correctional facilities were overcrowded and if population reductions were needed. A three-judge panel was established, and both of the aforementioned cases — *Coleman v. Wilson* and *Brown v. Plata* — were consolidated into one appeal. That panel of judges ruled that the state of California needed to reduce its prison population to 137.5% of design capacity within two years. If the state could not build additional facilities to reduce population, the state needed to develop a plan to reduce population by other means. When the case later came before the Supreme Court, it was ruled that the formation of the three-judge panel and its subsequent ruling was proper. This ruling resulted in an order that demanded the release of more than 40,000 low-risk prisoners from California correctional facilities within a one-year time span of 2011 to 2012.

Prison Rape Elimination Act of 2003

Sexual assault within correctional facilities has been a topic of conversation for some time. This talk is often so pervasive that many people believe sexual assault to be a common part of the prison experience. Yet how widespread this phenomenon is has often been debated (Hensley & Tewksbury, 2002). As Moster and Jeglic (2009) found, correctional research has reported that sexual assault in prison varies from 0.3% to 14% of inmates experiencing an assault. Thus, it appears that there is some divergence in the reported rate of incidents. Regardless of the precise numbers, many people have concluded that sexual assault in correctional facilities represents a problem. As an effort to combat this problem, in 2003, Congress passed the *Prisoner Rape Elimination Act (PREA)*, which was signed by President George W. Bush. The legislation mandates zero-tolerance policies for sexual assault within correctional systems, allocates funds to conduct research and various forms of program development, and requires the collection of national data on the occurrence of sexual assaults and rapes.

While PREA made some strides in reducing levels of sexual assaults and rapes in correctional facilities, it was limited by the PLRA, which presented some limitations to the full adoption of the PREA. Specifically, and as discussed earlier, the PLRA was enacted by Congress in response to the sharp increase in prisoner litigation in the federal courts and as such, was designed to decrease the incidence of litigation within the court system. Thus, the enactment of the PREA, which encourages reporting of sexual-assault incidents and therefore presumably use of the courts, can be seen as being impeded by the PLRA. For instance, in *Hancock v. Payne*, a group of male prisoners claimed that a correctional officer fondled their genitalia and sodomized them. A federal district court in the Southern District of Mississippi ruled that fondling and sodomy did not constitute an "injury" within the meaning of the PLRA. Thus, that court granted summary judgment against the inmates. In another case, *Benfield v. Rushton*, an inmate lawsuit regarding rape was dismissed because the inmate had not properly exhausted the state grievance process. According to the inmate, he did not file a grievance in time because he "didn't think rape was a grievable issue."

While not pertaining exactly to sexual assault or rape, another case, *Latham v. Pate*, illustrates how correctional officers might manipulate the PLRA process to their advantage. In that case, an inmate filed suit claiming that he was beaten while in custody. Ultimately, the suit was dismissed because the inmate had not filed grievance forms in time. However, the inmate claimed that the reason he was unable to file the forms in time was that he was being housed in administrative segregation. As a result, grievance forms were not available to the inmate until after the deadline to file had passed.

Due to the conflicts between the PLRA and the PREA, the *Prison Abuse Remedies Act of 2007* was introduced in the House of Representatives as H.R. 4109 (110th Congress) and sponsored by Representative Robert Scott (D-Virginia). Hearings were held on the bill on April 22, 2008. The bill sought to amend the PLRA so that it better complied with the PREA. Among the proposed changes was eliminating the requirement that a prisoner must show a prior physical injury before bringing a claim for mental or emotional injury suffered while incarcerated. Additionally, the legislation proposed a 90-day stay of nonfrivolous claims relating to prison conditions, so that prison officials could consider these claims through the administrative process. Furthermore, the proposed amendments sought to exclude inmates under the age of 18 from the restrictions of the PLRA when reporting sexual assault or rape. Last, the bill sought to treat indigent prisoners the same as indigent defendants awaiting trial in the federal court system. The practical effect of this would have been to restore attorneys' fees and alter filing fees for indigent prisoners, thus allowing them easier access to filing lawsuits. Ultimately, the bill did not pass. Two years later, the Prison Abuse Remedies Act was proposed as H.R. 4335 (111th) and again sponsored by Representative Scott. The bill had similar language and once again did not pass.

Antiterrorism and Effective Death Penalty Act of 1996

Not all limits on the federal courts are the result of simply clearing court dockets. In the wake of several notable terrorist attacks in the United States during the 1990s (Oklahoma City, the Unabomber, and the first attacks on the World Trade Center), many people in the United States demanded more stringent punishments for the perpetrators of these and other similar types of attacks. As a result, Congress passed and President Bill Clinton signed the *Antiterrorism and Effective Death Penalty Act of 1996 (AEDPA)*. The Act expanded both the number of crimes that could make a person eligible for the death penalty in the federal court system and attempted to expand the reach of prosecutions of terrorist crimes. In particular, this allowed federal prosecutors to prosecute alleged terrorists who committed their crimes beyond the borders of the United States (McGarvey, 1998).

Despite the name of the legislation, the AEDPA included other issues that went beyond mere prosecution of terrorism. Indeed, much of the AEDPA seemed to be directly linked to reforming habeas corpus procedures. For instance, Section 104(3) of the AEDPA stated that a writ of habeas corpus could not be granted for a person who was incarcerated in a state court unless the decision in state court proceedings "resulted in a decision that was contrary to, or involved an unreasonable application of, clearly established Federal law, as determined by the Supreme Court of the United States." As Steinman (2001) states, such a provision seems to target former habeas corpus procedures by the courts, in particular, the precedent set by the 1953 Supreme Court decision *Brown v. Allen*. This case ushered in what some people have referred to as the "golden age" of federal habeas corpus relief, as it established a *de novo* standard in federal habeas corpus petitions. That means that whenever a federal court granted a writ of habeas corpus, instead of considering the previous rulings of state courts on the legal matter, the federal court was free to essentially reevaluate and discuss constitutional questions and disregard state findings and rulings. In *Williams v. Taylor*, the Supreme Court developed a two-prong test to comply with the AEDPA's new standards for habeas corpus reviews: (1) a habeas corpus motion would be granted if a state court opinion was contrary to a previous Supreme Court ruling; or (2) a habeas corpus motion would be granted if a state court opinion involved an unreasonable application of a previous Supreme Court ruling.

Another way in which the AEDPA limited federal habeas corpus proceedings was to reduce the amount of time prisoners have to file these motions. When an inmate is awaiting execution, states may require that these inmates file a habeas corpus petition within 180 days of conviction, if they have been provided an appellant attorney (states that still use the death penalty typically require an appellant attorney be appointed for indigent death-row inmates). Furthermore, the AEDPA established a one-year statute of limitations for most habeas corpus proceedings. That issue was later considered by the Supreme Court in *Artuz v. Bennett*. In that case, Tony Bruce Bennett had filed a motion in 1995 to have his 1984 conviction vacated. Three years later, Bennett filed a habeas corpus motion alleging several of his constitutional rights had been violated during his trial. A federal district court dismissed his habeas corpus petition because it had not been filed within the one-year statute of limitation, but the Second Circuit Court of Appeals reversed. In doing so, that court noted that the one-year statute of limitations had been tolled (temporarily suspended) because Bennett had never been informed that his original 1995 motion had been dismissed. Furthermore, the Second Circuit ruled that Bennett's 1995 motion had been properly filed, even though the motions he asserted were barred by two New York statutes. Thus, his habeas corpus motion should have been allowed to proceed. Ultimately, the Supreme Court agreed with the Second Circuit.

Such a time limit can have other practical restrictions on filing habeas corpus petitions. In *Duncan v. Walker*, Sherman Walker filed a habeas corpus petition in 1996. The district court hearing Walker's petition dismissed it and ruled that Walker had not exhausted his available state remedies. Instead of pursuing state remedies, Walker filed a second federal habeas petition in 1997 without pursuing any state remedies. The district court dismissed his second habeas corpus petition because the one-year statute of limitations had passed. Later, the Second Circuit Court of Appeals reversed the district court's decision and ruled that the first federal habeas corpus petition actually counted as "other collateral review" and should have tolled the one-year statute of limitations. However, the Supreme Court disagreed. According to the Court, if Walker was allowed to file a second habeas corpus petition instead of filing in state court, this would cause most prisoners to skip filing appeals in state court altogether.

As Zheng (2002) notes, another criticism of the federal habeas corpus procedures that led to the passage of the AEDPA was that inmates would seemingly tie up the courts with endless appeals. The AEDPA limits a prisoner's right to file a second habeas corpus petition. A claim presented to the courts for a second or successive application of habeas corpus, the act declares, should be dismissed unless it relies on a new constitutional law that has been made retroactive by the Supreme Court to cases that were previously unavailable (for example, if the Supreme Court delivered a new decision that might help other incarcerated inmates, they could have the opportunity to file a new habeas corpus petition). Furthermore, a second habeas corpus petition, if granted, must be heard by an appellate panel and the decision of the panel cannot be appealed to the Supreme Court. In *Felker v. Turpin*, Ellis Felker was a death-row inmate who filed a second habeas corpus petition. Felker argued that the new requirement of the AEDPA effectively suspended writs of habeas corpus and unconstitutionally removed the Supreme Court's authority to hear these petitions. Yet, a unanimous Supreme Court disagreed with Felker's assertion. The Court ruled that the AEDPA simply transferred subsequent habeas corpus applications from district courts to an appellate panel. Furthermore, all the act did was to help remove the Court's authority to hear a subsequent habeas corpus petition; the Court still has the authority to hear original habeas corpus petitions.

Right of Habeas Corpus for Foreign Nationals

One of the consequences of the so-called "war on terror" that began after September 11, 2001, has been the increase in foreign nationals captured by the United States overseas. Many of these foreign nationals have been taken to the American military base in Guantanamo Bay, Cuba, and incarcerated for extended periods of time. In *Rasul v. Bush*, the Supreme Court considered the legal rights of these people. Several of them had family members who filed habeas corpus motions that alleged the incarceration of prisoners in Guantanamo Bay was unconstitutional and violated their Fifth Amendment right to due process. The United States government argued that the federal courts lacked the jurisdiction to hear these cases because the prisoners were not American citizens and were held in territory over which the United States lacked sovereignty. According to an agreement the United States made with Cuba in 1903, the United States leased the Guantanamo Bay base indefinitely and Cuba retained "ultimate sovereignty." Both the district court that heard the original petitions and the U.S. Court of Appeals for the District of Columbia agreed with the government's position. However, the Supreme Court ultimately ruled that the people incarcerated at Guantanamo Bay should be allowed to file habeas corpus petitions. The Court ruled that the United States essentially had "dominion" over the base and exercised "complete jurisdiction and control." Thus, Cuba having ultimate sovereignty was irrelevant. Furthermore, the Court ruled that the right to file a habeas corpus petition was not dependent on whether a person was a citizen of the United States.

Somewhat as a reaction to the decision in *Rasul v. Bush* and a similar case, *Hamdan v. Rumsfeld*, Congress passed the *Military Commission Act of 2006 (MCA)*, signed by President George W. Bush. This act eliminated federal court jurisdiction from hearing habeas corpus applications from those detained as enemies of the U.S. and combatant soldiers. The act did not seek to merely strip the rights of all detainees, but relied on procedures established in the *Detainee Treatment Act* of 2005 (DTA) to essentially replace habeas corpus petitions. The DTA was set to address many issues related to enemy combatants detainees by the United States military. As such, the DTA places restrictions on the treatment and interrogation of said detainees who are foreign born and are placed under U.S. military prison custody. Additionally, the act provides procedural protections for U.S. personnel accused of engaging in improper interrogation and as such, presented the legislative foundations for the MCA that was enacted a year later. What the Military Commission Act (MCA) attempted was to have all detainee complaints heard in military tribunals instead of federal courts. However, in *Boumedienne v. Bush*, the Supreme Court ruled that the procedures established in the Detainee Treatment Act were not adequate substitutes for habeas corpus petitions. Therefore, detainees should still be allowed to file habeas corpus petitions in federal court. This decision essentially nullified the provision within the MCA legislation that had sought to limit the rights of detainees to have access to the federal courts.

Conclusion

In this chapter, we have seen how the federal courts are allowed to consider inmate lawsuits. During the "hands-on" period, many inmates effectively used federal habeas corpus petitions to gain additional rights or protections while in custody. Such a process was viewed as superior to filing claims in state courts and grievance systems operated by state correctional systems. Many inmates believed then, as many still do now, that the states had no incentive to make rulings against facilities operated and funded by the states themselves. Thus, it was necessary to have access to the more neutral federal courts. Yet, with the introduction of the PLRA, many additional limitations have been placed on inmates' access to the federal courts. This trend continued with the introduction of the AEDPA, a law that was originally meant to combat terrorism but ended up having an effect on inmate access to the federal courts. While one cannot simply say that inmates no longer have access to the federal courts, their access to these institutions has certainly been limited.

Discussion Questions

1. Discuss the implications of the abuse of the writ doctrine in regard to the limits of prisoners' litigation. In your discussion refer to relevant cases.

2. Discuss the judicial context of the congressional passage of the prisoners litigation reform act (PLRA). What are the main concerns this bill aims to address? And how does it affect prisoners' litigation and access to the courts?

3. Discuss the importance of *Woodford v. Ngo*. How does this case relate to the PLRA, and what insights does it adds to its interpretation?

4. In your opinion, should the Supreme Court place any limitations on the PLRA? Explain while referring to relevant cases and consequent arguments made by the Supreme Court.

5. Discuss the background and context of the Prisoners Rape Elimination Act of 2003. Is there any contradiction between this act and the PLRA? Explain.

6. What changes did the Prison Abuse Remedies Act of 2007, aimed to added to the Prisoners Rape Elimination Act of 2003 (PREA)? Explain, why such changes were essential to the judicial process, and to the enforcement of the PREA? In your opinion, why do you think the Prison Abuse Remedies Act failed to pass?

7. Explain, how does the Antiterrorism and Effective Death Penalty Act of 1996 (AEDPA) apply to judicial intervention in corrections? Specifically, what are the unique judicial provisions of such legislation to federal habeas corpus petitions and how does it affect death-row inmates?

8. Discuss and explain the context of the Military Commission Act of 2006 (MCA). Why was such act needed? How does this act relate to the Detainee Treatment Act of 2005?

List of Cases Cited

Artuz v. Bennett, 2000. 531 U.S. 4.

Benfield v. Rushton, 2007. No. 8:06-CV-2609, WL 30287.

Booth v. Churner, 2001. 532 U.S. 731.

Boumedienne v. Bush, 2008. 553 U.S. 723.

Brown v. Allen, 1953. 344 U.S. 443.

Brown v. Plata2011. 563 U.S. 493.

Brown v. Sikes, 2000. 212F. 3d 1205

Burns v. Ohio, 1959. 360 U.S. 252.

Coleman v. Wilson, 1995. 912 F. Supp. 1282

Curry v. Scott, 2001. 249 F.3d 493.

Duncan v. Walker, 2001. 533 U.S. 167.

Ex parte Hull, 1941. 312 U.S. 546.

Jones v. Bock, 127 S. Ct. 910, 549 U.S. 199, 166 L. Ed. 2d 798 (2007).

Felker v. Turpin, 1996. 518 U.S. 651.

Handan v. Rumsfeld, 2006. 548 U.S. 557

Hancock v. Payne, 2006. No. 1:03-CV-671, WL 21751.

Latham v. Pate, 2007. No. 1:06-CV-150, WL 171792.

McCleskey v. Zant, 1991. 499 U.S. 467.

Martin v. Hadix, 1999. 527 U.S. 343.

Massiah v. United States, 1964. 377 U.S. 201.

Miller v. French, 200, 530 U.S. 327

Porter v. Nussle, 2002. 534 U.S. 516.

Rasul v. Bush, 2004. 542 U.S. 466.

Riccardo v. Rausch, 2004. 375 F.3d 521.

Smith v. Bennett, 1961. 365 U.S. 708

Spano v. New York, 1959. 360 U.S. 315.

Strong v. David, 2002. 297 F. 3d 646.

Williams v. Taylor, 2000. 529 U.S. 362.

Woodford v. Ngo, 2006. 548 U.S. 81.

Chapter 12

Community Supervision and the Law: Probation and Parole

Community supervision is designed, among many other things, to alleviate prison overcrowding while promoting the rehabilitation and reintegration of convicted offenders to normative society. Probation and parole are the two primary forms of community supervision in the United States, and while many people use the terms interchangeably, they are not the same. Specifically, *probation* is a sentence by which the court requires offenders to serve a period of correctional supervision in the community in lieu of incarceration, as discussed earlier in Chapter 3. Accordingly, convicted offenders are placed under the care of community agents of supervision, namely probation officers, who are responsible for an offender's compliance with a set conditions in lieu of any period of incarceration, which is considered to be suspended as long as the offender complies with the conditions set forth by the court and probation agency. The aim of probation is to offer young, first-time, or low-risk offenders the opportunity of rehabilitation while avoiding the harmful consequences and stigmatization of incarceration. As such, probation is also aimed at harm reduction, as it allows convicted offenders to remain in their communities with their families and thus avoid unnecessary disruption to these support networks. *Parole* is a period of conditional supervised release in the community following an active imprisonment term. In that regard, it is a conditioned release—a conditional freedom—in which prisoners are released early and serve their remaining sentence in the community under the supervision of a parole officer. It is similar to probation, however, in that the aim of early release is improved reintegration into society. At the same time, parole aims to protect the public by monitoring parolees, controlling their behavior, and helping them adjust to the world outside prison.

Because parole and probation occur at different points in the judicial process, judicial interventions in these two matters will receive different attention in certain circumstances. For example, the decision to grant or deny early release on parole has been determined by the courts to be a matter of institutional and executive discretion. This means that the courts decided not to interfere in administrative decision-making. While there is no constitutional right to parole or sentence commutation, the Supreme Court has held that when parole is a possibility, correctional administrators should follow due process in making their decision. This merely requires that a parole board hold a hearing and provide inmates with written reasons for its decision to grant or deny parole. When it comes to revocation of parole, a similar process to that of revocation of probation, the courts have focused their attention more closely on issues of due process as these relate to changing the conditions of punishment.

Of importance and relevance to the discussion is the 13th Amendment to the Constitution. While the Amendment aimed to abolish slavery, it also created a condition by which those convicted of a crime may forfeit their rights to the state, as if they were slaves. The Amendment reads as follows:

> *Neither slavery nor involuntary servitude, except as a punishment for crime whereof the party shall have been duly convicted, shall exist within the United States, or any place subject to their jurisdiction.*

It is within these parameters that revocation proceedings should be viewed, as often the courts are confronted with the requests to evaluate the legality of various processes that lead to revocation hearing. The argument set forth by the Thirteenth Amendment is that offenders who are sentenced to probation have been duly convicted of a crime and as such, lose some of their constitutional rights and in particular, those rights that pertain to privacy and search and seizure. Such an argument also applies to offenders that were granted early release on parole. However, due process must be followed to enable justified revocation.

Legal Rights of Probationers

In addition to their duties of supervision, probation officers are responsible for completing presentence investigation reports (PSIs) on every person who has been convicted of a crime. Indeed, completing these reports is often more time-consuming for probation officers than their supervision duties. These reports document an offender's criminal history, determine whether any treatment is necessary (especially mental health or substance abuse treatment), and most important, provide judges with the necessary information for sentencing, and even a recommendation for best practices that will fit the offender and his or her crime, within the limitations of the prescribed penal code. Thus, PSIs are extremely important to the sentencing process, yet it is not a given that offenders or their legal representation will be able to view these reports. This causes concern when an offender believes that an inaccuracy or a downright falsehood may be included in a report that carries weight in a judge's sentencing decision. Therefore, the courts have heard several cases concerning PSIs.

In *Williams v. New York*, a jury in a New York state court convicted Williams of first-degree murder and recommended a life sentence. The judge, however, imposed a death sentence. In doing so, the judge noted the findings of the jury, as well as the findings of the probation department, but did not disclose the latter findings to the defense. Williams argued that this violated his right to due process and his ability to confront witnesses, as guaranteed by the Fourteenth and Sixth Amendments, respectively. However, the Supreme Court ruled that Williams had no such right. According to the Court, the right to confront witnesses is a trial right, not a sentencing right. The Court ruled that judges have wide discretion in the sources and types of information that they use when deciding on a sentence. Furthermore, the Court ruled that even though Williams was given a death sentence, this did not give him extra rights beyond a normal offender being sentenced. Many years after the *Williams v. New York* decision, in 1977, the Supreme Court came to a slightly different conclusion in *Gardner v. Florida*. In this case, the Court ruled that, based on "constitutional developments" in which capital punishment had been given more scrutiny, when defendants faced the possible imposition of the death penalty, then any information contained in a PSI must be provided to them.

Civil Rights

One common constraint on probationers is that whenever they are asked a question by their probation officer, not only are they supposed to answer the question, but they are supposed to answer truthfully. However, it appears from the case of *Minnesota v. Murphy* that probationers should in some instances be careful about what they disclose. In that case, Marshall Murphy had been questioned by police on two separate occasions concerning the rape and murder of a teenage girl. No charges were brought against Murphy or anyone else. Six years later, Murphy pleaded guilty to false imprisonment in an unrelated case, for which he was given a 16-month suspended sentence and three years of probation. While on probation, Murphy had disclosed to his counselor, during a confidential treatment session, that he was responsible for the murder for which he had been previously questioned. Later, a probation officer, noting that Murphy was supposed to be truthful with him as a condition of his probation, asked Murphy if he had committed the murder. The probation officer did not read Murphy any Miranda warnings before asking the question. Murphy admitted to committing the crime, and was then indicted for murder. After this, Murphy challenged the introduction of the confession into evidence, arguing that this violated his Fifth and Fourteenth Amendment rights. Ultimately, the Supreme Court ruled that the probation officer did not need to read Murphy his Miranda rights, because Murphy was not in custody. Furthermore, the Court ruled that Murphy voluntarily made the statement and if he did not want the statement to be used against him, he should have invoked his Fifth Amendment right to remain silent.

In addition to having to report to a probation officer, probationers can expect to have their homes searched. In *Griffin v. Wisconsin*, the Supreme Court ruled that such a process was reasonable under the Fourth Amendment and represented "special needs" of the probation system, as probationers are still under the control and care of the correctional system. Thus, because a prison or jail inmate would have little protection from the Fourth Amendment, probationers should expect similar treatment. As the Court determined, requiring probation officers to go through the normal process of securing a warrant would undermine the system of probation supervision. Additionally, it is necessary for probation officers to respond quickly to any evidence of probationer misconduct. Requiring a warrant for such searches would be cumbersome to the process and also reduce the deterrent effect of probationers knowing that their residence could be searched at any time. Furthermore, in *United States v. Knights*, the Supreme Court ruled that not only are probation officers allowed to search probationers' homes, but law enforcement officers are allowed to do so as well. According to the Court, the law enforcement officer needs to show only reasonable suspicion that a probationer committed or was involved in a subsequent crime. However, later, in *Samson v. California*, the Supreme Court ruled that no reasonable suspicion is needed and a police officer can search a probationer or parolee simply because the person is still under the custody of the correctional system.

Legal Rights of Parolees

One issue that the Supreme Court has considered is how much notice a parole board must give inmates prior to their parole hearing. In *Greenholtz v. Inmates of Nebraska Penal and Correctional Complex*, the state of Nebraska had specific procedures for determining when inmates could be considered for parole. Inmates underwent a yearly review in which they were allowed to submit any letters or statements supporting their potential release. After this review, the parole board would determine which inmates were good candidates for release, then schedule a final hearing for those inmates. Before the start of each month, inmates would be notified if their hearing would occur during that month, but as for the precise date of the hearing, inmates would only be notified the morning of their hearing. A group of inmates filed a class action lawsuit in federal court arguing that such a process violated their due process rights guaranteed by the Fourteenth Amendment. The district court agreed with the inmates and the Eighth Circuit Court of Appeals affirmed the district court's decision. For corrective actions, the Eighth Circuit Court of Appeals ruled that the state of Nebraska must provide not only a full formal hearing date, but also, in the cases of parole denials, the evidence that the parole board made to come to the negative decision. Yet, the Supreme Court would reverse the previous decision. According to the Court, although the state of Nebraska, by allowing parole, created expectations of procedural due process, the state criteria satisfied these requirements. Another procedural due process case decision was reached in *Board of Pardons v. Allen*, when the Supreme Court determined that because the Montana Parole Statute included language that inmates "shall" be released if they meet certain requirements, procedural due process attached to the process. Therefore, the Court reasoned that the parole board did not have absolute or unlimited discretion to decide whether inmates should be paroled.

An issue that the Supreme Court has had to consider is when changes are made to the parole system. Such an issue was presented in *California Department of Corrections v. Morales*. In that case, Morales was sentenced to 15 years to life in prison for the murder of his wife, which took place in 1980. Morales became eligible for parole 10 years into his sentence. At his first parole hearing, Morales was denied parole. The board reasoned that because Morales had committed the murder of his wife while on parole for a previous murder, he was not the best candidate for early release. In 1980, offenders going up for parole were allowed a hearing every year after their first eligibility, until either they were released or their sentence expired. However, in 1981, California passed a law that changed this procedure to every three years for inmates who were convicted of more than one unlawful homicide. Morales filed a habeas corpus petition, arguing that the ex post facto clause of the United States Constitution prevented this procedure from being applied to him because he had been convicted a year before the law went into effect. However, the Supreme Court ruled that no violation occurred because no change had been made to his sentence, just how often he could be considered for parole. In a subsequent decision, *Garner v. Jones*, the Supreme Court elaborated a bit on whether changes in the intervals in which parole decisions will be heard could be prohibited by the ex post facto clause. In this case, the state of Georgia changed the time period for subsequent parole hearings from every three years to every eight years. In a 6–3 decision, the Supreme Court ruled this was constitutionally permissible, but changes should not be allowed if these changes will inevitably result in inmates staying in prison for longer periods of time and thus, receiving more severe punishment than was intended at sentencing. Such a situation had occurred in *Lynce v. Mathis*, when the state of Florida changed the manner in which inmates accumulated provisional release credits. The Supreme Court ruled that canceling inmates' provisional credits awarded before the change took place violated the ex post facto clause.

Commutation and Clemency

Slightly different from the process of parole is the process of commutation or clemency. Awarding commutation or clemency is not like the risk assessment done by parole boards; instead, it is a process through which an inmate argues that certain circumstances may mitigate their guilt and potentially justify an early release. Such a process is derived from the common law process of seeking a commutation or clemency from the king. Within the United States, such an appeal can be made to the president or within the individual states to a governor or a board of pardons. In some states, parole boards have the dual functions of both parole and clemency or pardon (Lavinsky, 1965).

In the case *Connecticut Board of Pardons v. Dumschat*, Dumschat was an inmate serving a life sentence in a Connecticut state prison. After filing an unsuccessful application to the Connecticut Board of Pardons for a commutation of his life sentence, Dumschat filed a Section 1983 motion arguing that the process of commutation should have procedural due process safeguards. As a result, Dumschat believed he was entitled to a written statement that included the reasons for the denial of his commutation application. Ultimately, the Supreme Court disagreed with Dumschat's argument and the Court ruled that Dumschat had a right only to seek commutation. Beyond that right to file an application, he could hold no further expectations or constitutional protections. Additionally, in *Ohio Adult Parole Authority v. Woodard*, the Supreme Court ruled that inmates do not have procedural due process safeguards in clemency hearings. Additionally, allowing inmates the opportunity to voluntarily testify at these hearings does not violate inmates' Fifth Amendment protection against compelled self-incrimination.

Revocation of Probation and/or Parole

Probation officers alone cannot revoke probation; a formal hearing is needed to make such a determination. In *Mempa v. Rhay*, Jerry Mempa had been placed on probation for a term of two years after pleading guilty to joyriding. During his probation period, the county prosecutor moved to revoke Mempa's probation based on Mempa's role in a burglary. At the hearing, Mempa was not represented by counsel and he was never asked if he wanted counsel present. Mempa pleaded guilty to the charge of burglary. As a result, Mempa had his term of probation revoked and was sentenced to 10 years in prison. However, the Supreme Court ruled unanimously that the right to counsel guaranteed by the Sixth Amendment extends to any post-trial proceedings for either the revocation of probation or deferred sentencing. Thus, to revoke anyone's probation, a court must give a person the opportunity to procure counsel and the state needed to provide counsel for indigent probationers.

As we previously mentioned, probation and parole are different criminal sanctions and forms of supervision. Yet, according to Nahari (1988), the courts and the protections that should be given to probationers and parolees, are essentially the same. Indeed, in *Gagnon v. Scarpelli*, the Supreme Court stated that these two different sanctions are "constitutionally indistinguishable." Thus, two Supreme Court decisions decided in consecutive years, *Morrissey v. Brewer* and the aforementioned *Gagnon v. Scarpelli*, together laid the foundation for the process by which revocation hearings should operate for both probation and parole. In *Morrissey v. Brewer*, the Supreme Court ruled that due process required that parole revocation procedures should include at a minimum the following: (1) written notice of the claimed violations of parole; (2) disclosure to parolees of any evidence against them; (3) the opportunity to be heard in person and to present evidence and documentary evidence; (4) the right to confront and cross-examine witnesses (unless the hearing officer has a good reason not to allow it); (5) a neutral and detached hearing body, such as a traditional parole board; and (6) a written statement by the fact finder as to the evidence relied on and reasons for revoking parole. The court reasoned that after an inmate is granted parole, to withdraw it is a "*grievous loss of freedom*," and thus merits due process protection. In the following year, the Supreme Court considered probation hearings in *Gagnon v. Scarpelli*, and somewhat limited these rights and the previous decision in *Mempa v. Rhay*. In *Gagnon*, the Court ruled that the Constitution did not require a probationer be provided "proper representation." As for whether a court should appoint an attorney, that should be decided on a case-by-case basis. Such a determination ought to be made at the initial hearing, in which it is also determined if a probationer or parolee must be incarcerated while awaiting the final hearing. The Court did not provide any real guidance as to why a person should be denied counsel for a revocation hearing, but did seem to indicate that for a probationer or parolee to receive counsel, there must be some question of fact or expertise needed that would make an attorney necessary to the process.

Some decisions do not have to be made at a hearing. In *Jago v. Van Curen*, Van Curen pleaded guilty to embezzlement and several other related crimes. After his guilty plea, Van Curen was given a sentence of six to 100 years in prison (meaning that the sentence should not be less than six years but not more than 100 years). Two years prior to Van Curen's parole eligibility, the state of Ohio passed what was called a "shock parole" statute, which allowed for the early release of nonviolent offenders after six months of incarceration. Van Curen applied for early parole under the new statute, and it was granted. However, after the parole board learned that Van Curen had made false statements to the parole board and regarding his proposed parole plan, the parole board terminated Van Curen's early parole without a hearing and before Van Curen had been released. He argued that this violated his due process rights guaranteed under the Fourteenth Amendment, but the Supreme Court ruled that no such liberty interest was attached to early parole. However, in a slightly different case, *Young v. Harper*, the Supreme Court ruled differently on another pre-parole program. In that case, whenever prisons in the state of Oklahoma became overcrowded, a varying number of inmates needed to be released on conditional release. The pardon and parole board of the state established criteria for these decisions, including the requirement that inmates must have served at least 15% of their sentence. Leroy Young was released under such a program after serving 15 years out of a life sentence. However, five months after Young was released, the governor denied Young's parole and he was ordered back to prison. Unlike the decision in *Jago*, in *Young v. Harper*, the Supreme Court sided with Young ruling that the pre-parole program was sufficiently like a parole program, and thus, an offender facing parole revocation was entitled to the same protections as anyone else applying for normal parole.

In addition to the process of revocation, the Supreme Court has also had to determine for what periods of time probationers could serve in prison or jail after having their probation revoked. In *United States v. Granderson*, Granderson had been convicted of mail destruction. Under the United States Sentencing Guidelines, a defendant convicted of this crime could face an imprisonment period of zero to six months. However, instead of being incarcerated, Granderson was given a sentence of five years of probation. While on probation, Granderson tested positive for cocaine. According to the United States Penal Code, if anyone serving probation is found in possession of illegal drugs, probation shall be revoked and that person must be incarcerated for not less than one third of their sentence. The district court hearing Granderson's case sentenced Granderson to one third of the five years of probation (a total of 20 months), rather than one third of the zero-to-six months of incarceration term in the sentencing guidelines, which would have only been two months. Granderson appealed his sentence to the Eleventh Circuit of Appeals, which ruled that the period of incarceration should be controlling, rather than the period of probation, so Granderson should have been sentenced to two months instead of 20. The Supreme Court agreed with the Eleventh Circuit and affirmed its judgment.

The Supreme Court has also ruled on what ought to be considered when revoking probation. In *Black v. Romano*, Nicholas Romano pleaded guilty in a Missouri state court to several drug offenses. He was given a suspended prison sentence and placed on probation. Two months afterward, Romano was charged with leaving the scene of an automobile accident, which in Missouri is a felony. At a revocation hearing, a judge revoked Romano's probation and sentenced him to the originally suspended prison sentence. After Romano exhausted his state court remedies, he filed a habeas corpus petition and argued that rather than sentence him to prison, the judge in the case should have considered other alternatives to incarceration. Romano argued that this failure constituted a violation of his due process rights. The district court hearing Romano's habeas corpus petition agreed and ordered Romano released from prison. Furthermore, the Eighth Circuit Court of Appeals affirmed the decision of the district court. However, the Supreme Court ultimately reversed the decision and ordered Romano back to prison. The Court ruled that although the sentencing judge could consider other alternatives to incarceration when hearing a probation violation, no judge is under any obligation to make such a consideration.

Another way in which probation and parole revocation hearings are different from criminal trials is in regards to the exclusionary rule. For defendants in a criminal trial, if evidence is illegally obtained, it cannot be introduced at trial. Yet in *Pennsylvania Board of Probation and Parole v. Scott*, the Supreme Court ruled that illegally obtained evidence could be used during probation and/or parole hearings. In that case, both a state court and the Pennsylvania Supreme Court ruled that evidence used against Keith Scott had been illegally obtained. However, the Supreme Court of the United States ruled that the exclusionary rule was a judicially created remedy and did not come directly from the United States Constitution. According to the Court, state probation and parole authorities must have greater latitude to search probationers and parolees. Thus, evidence illegally obtained could still be introduced at these hearings.

One issue the courts have considered is when a probationer or parolee can challenge a conviction with a federal habeas corpus petition. In *Jones v. Cunningham*, Claude Jones had been convicted in 1953 for his third crime, which resulted in his being sentenced to 10 years in prison. Eight years later, Jones filed a habeas corpus petition for a 1946 conviction (which had played a part in his aforementioned 10-year sentence). The petition alleged that he had been deprived of counsel. As Jones' case was being processed, he was paroled and still under the court's supervision. Jones wanted to continue his lawsuit, but the state objected because it believed that because Jones was no longer incarcerated, he was no longer in the custody of correctional authorities. To them, the whole purpose of a habeas corpus petition was for them to explain why they held Jones. Therefore, the state believed the case was moot. However, the Supreme Court ruled that any time a person is under the correctional authority of the state, whether in a jail or prison or on probation or on parole, that person is still within the custody of the state. Thus, any of these offenders should be allowed to file a habeas corpus petition.

Use of Fines

Often, fines will be imposed alongside other sentences and may also be a requirement for fulfilling the conditions of supervision. Yet, in many instances, the courts are asked to evaluate the ethical conundrum by which revocation of community supervision is handled and in particular, when an offender is experiencing economic hardship and is unable to pay a fine. In *Williams v. Illinois*, Williams was convicted of petty theft and given the maximum sentence for that crime of one year of imprisonment, a $500 fine, and $5 in court costs. As prescribed in the statute, if an offender had not paid the fine, he or she had to remain in jail to work off the rest of the fine. For each day in jail, an offender earned $5. Williams, who claimed that he was indigent and had no means to pay the fine, argued that incarcerating him in this fashion violated his rights under the equal protection clause of the Fourteenth Amendment, as he was essentially being incarcerated because he was poor. Ultimately, the Supreme Court agreed with Williams and ruled that although states had "considerable latitude" in deciding punishments for state crimes and may develop many different forms of alternative sanctions, states cannot punish indigent defendants by sentencing them to periods of incarceration more than the maximum sentence that is prescribed by state statute. In a similar case, *Tate v. Short*, an indigent defendant in Texas was convicted of a traffic offense and fined a total of $425. According to Texas law, only fines can be given for such an offense. If an offender does not pay in time, however, they can be incarcerated until they have served enough time to satisfy the debt. Just as in the previous case of *Williams v. Illinois*, in *Tate*, the state of Texas imposed that a day in jail was worth $5; thus, the defendant was expected to serve an 85-day jail term for an offense that is not supposed to punishable by incarceration. Based on the previous decision in *Williams v. Illinois*, the Supreme Court ruled in *Tate* that this was a violation of equal protection.

After the Supreme Court ruled that a state cannot threaten a person with incarceration when they are unable to pay a fine, in *Beardon v. Georgia*, the Court provided additional criteria for such situations. In that case, Beardon pleaded guilty to burglary and theft by receiving stolen property. Based on the Georgia First Offender's Act, Beardon was allowed to have his judgment of guilt deferred so long as he paid restitution ($250, in this case) and a fine ($500). The terms of this agreement specified that Beardon had to pay $100 when he entered the deferred guilty verdict, $100 the next day, and then the balance of $550 within four months. A month after Beardon made the agreement, he was laid off from his job and, despite continued efforts, was unable to find another. As a result, Beardon informed his probation officer that he would not be able to pay the $550 that was coming due. Furthermore, Beardon did not have any assets from which payment could be taken. After the deadline passed, Beardon's probation was revoked, his previous plea of guilty was entered, and he was sentenced to prison. Unlike the decision in *Tate*, Beardon's crime did merit prison time and unlike the decision in *Williams*, Beardon had not already served the maximum amount of time prescribed by statute. Thus, the state court was giving Beardon a sanction that was justified by law. However, the Supreme Court ruled that because

Beardon was poor and making good faith efforts to pay his fines, his probation should have been revoked only if he had shown bad faith, either by hiding the means to pay his fines or not actively looking for work.

Employment Issues Concerning Probation and Parole Officers

Turning from probationers and parolees to employees in community supervision programs, the courts have also had to consider who is allowed to be a probation officer. In *Cabell v. Chavez-Salido*, the Supreme Court ruled that restricting the hiring of probation officers to people who are only United States citizens is not a necessary restriction on employment, but it is a valid one. As the Court noted, merely restricting lawful resident aliens from having employment is not a valid job restriction and should have strict judicial scrutiny, but for positions within government that include responsibility for enforcing "the sovereign's power," such a restriction is a valid job requirement.

Another issue that has affected the employment of probation and parole officers is when they can seek damages for discrimination suffered during the scope of their employment. In one case, *Forrester v. White*, Cynthia Forrester was an adult and juvenile probation officer in Illinois. Within that state, probation officers are considered court employees and have judges as their supervisors. After being fired from her job, Forrester alleged that her supervising judge, Howard White, had engaged in sexist discrimination against her. Forrester filed a Section 1983 motion against White. However, the lawsuit was dismissed because judges have absolute immunity from lawsuits against them for any decision they make. This absolute immunity, however, was a defense against inevitably disappointed defendants suing judges and arguing that they had suffered from judicial decisions. Noting this, the Supreme Court ruled that Forrester's case was an entirely different matter, as the judge was being sued for his alleged discrimination as a supervisor. Thus, the Court ruled that a judge's absolute immunity did not protect him or her from employment discrimination lawsuits.

While probation officers may be able to sue their immediate supervisors in some instances, suing the state in which they work can be more difficult. In *Alden v. Maine*, a group of probation officers sued their employer, the state of Maine, in state court, alleging that their rights had been violated under the federal Fair Labor Standards Act. The lawsuit was dismissed because both the state trial court and the state supreme court ruled that Maine had sovereign immunity and could not be sued within their own courts. Alden and the other probation officers argued that the passage of the Fair Labor Standards Act had essentially superseded the sovereign immunity. However, the Supreme Court would rule that Congress had no such authority to abrogate or supersede a state's sovereign immunity.

Conversely, the courts have also had to consider the liability of probation and parole officers from lawsuits. In *Martinez v. California*, Richard Thomas had been convicted of attempted murder and was committed to a mental institution for a suggested one to 20 years. Yet, Thomas was paroled after only five months. Five months later, he murdered a 15-year-old girl named Mary Ellen Martinez. Mary's family filed a negligence lawsuit against the parole officer who supervised Thomas; however, the lawsuit was dismissed because California had a statute that gave parole officers immunity from lawsuits for actions in the scope of their employment. The Martinez family believed that this was a violation of the due process clause of the Fourteenth Amendment and as such, challenged the legitimacy and public safety associated with parole supervision. A unanimous Supreme Court ruled that no such protection existed. The Court reasoned that being a parole officer is a difficult job and that in many instances, parole officers need to make difficult decisions. Parole programs were necessary to rehabilitation, but if the state wanted to abolish parole, that was a state decision, not one to be made by the courts.

Conclusion

The perceived freedom that accompanies community supervision, whether on probation or parole, is not without its limits. Although the Thirteenth Amendment, discussed earlier in this chapter, suggests that those convicted of a crime should expect that some of their liberties and constitutional rights will be revoked, such revocation has limits and while under community supervision, offenders are still protected by the Constitution. Such protection may be seen as the moral responsibility of the government and states, as enforcers of the law. According to *Immanuel Kant*, punishing the offender is a moral obligation and is justified simply by the fact that the individual broke the law, yet we must also be fair in the way in which we punish the offender. While fairness toward the offender was not one of Kant's main ideas, *Georg Wilhelm Friedrich Hegel* argues that in punishing offenders, society honors them as equal members of society, and as members of society, they share common interest. It is within this context that the courts have decided to protect the rights of those sentenced to community supervision. However, while doing so, the courts have also acknowledged that not all the constitutional rights reserved for those who obey the law may be equally reserved for those who broke it. When the decision comes to a point when those supervised may have their limited freedom revoked, the courts are perceived as guardians of fairness.

On the other side of the equation are those men and women who do the tough work of correctional supervision. As representatives of the state and government, they are protected by these bodies and, as previously discussed, protected from many lawsuits brought against them. What penological aspect this serves is far greater than a mere discussion of individual goals of punishment, as they provide society with a clear system of penological "checks and balances" that provides feedback to the somewhat gray area of punishing offenders while not removing them, or in the case of parole, reintegrating them back to normative society. It is in this context that we must not abandon the main goals of probation and parole: rehabilitation and reintegration. Within these contexts lies the importance of the discussed landmark cases. Each in its own manner addresses the needs and risk of the offenders at hand while also aiming to protect the safety of their relative and perspective community.

Discussion Questions

1. Discuss the difference between probation and parole and explain the important judicial implications of such differences.

2. While both probationers and parolees are supervised in the community their civil rights may be limited. Discuss the judicial implications of the 13th Amendment on offenders supervised in the community, and explain the logic of these offenders restricted rights.

3. Discuss some of the civil rights issues arise during community supervision that required judicial intervention. In your opinion, should offenders remanded to the care of community supervision agencies enjoy such rights? Explain your response while referring to relevant cases.

4. How did the cases of *Morrissey v. Brewer* and *Gagnon v. Scarpelli* changed the revocation process? In your response, discuss the minimum requirements for revocation set forth by the courts and explain their due process context.

5. Discuss the issues that revolve around collections of fines from offenders' supervised in the community. In your discussion refer to the relevant cases and explain the logic that directed the judicial decision in these cases. In your opinion, was the court right to decide the way it did in each of these cases?

6. In your opinion, should probation and parole officers be protected by law from litigation? In your response, discuss the *Martinez* case, and explain its importance.

7. Discuss the relevance of Kant and Hegel's justification of punishment to some judicial decisions made in regard to cases of violations of due process rights of probationers and parolees. In your discussion, explain the main idea of community supervision on its goals, as discussed earlier in the chapter, and how they correspond with these justifications.

List of Cases Cited

Alden v. Maine, 1999. 527 U.S. 706.

Beardon v. Georgia, 1983. 461 U.S. 660.

Black v. Romano, 1985. 471 U.S. 606.

Board of Pardons v. Allen, 1986. 482 U.S. 369.

Cabell v. Chavez-Salido, 1982. 4545 U.S. 432.

California Department of Corrections v. Morales, 1995. 514 U.S. 499.

Connecticut Board of Pardons v. Dumschat, 1981. 452 U.S. 458.

Forrester v. White, 1988. 484 U.S. 219.

Gagnon v. Scarpelli, 1973. 411 U.S. 778.

Gardner v. Florida, 1977. 430 U.S. 349.

Garner v. Jones, 2000. 529 U.S. 244.

Greenholtz v. Inmates of Nebraska Penal and Correctional Complex, 1979. 442 U.S. 1.

Griffin v. Wisconsin, 1987. 483 U.S. 868

Jago v. Van Curen, 1981. 454 U.S. 14.

Jones v. Cunningham, 1963, 371 U.S. 236

Lynce v. Mathis, 1997. 519 U.S. 433.

Martinez v. California, 1980. 444 U.S. 277.

Mempa v. Rhay, 1967. 389 U.S. 128.

Minnesota v. Murphy, 1984. 465 U.S. 420.

Morrissey v. Brewer, 1972. 408 U.S. 471.

Ohio Adult Parole Authority v. Woodard, 1998. 523 U.S. 272.

Pennsylvania Board of Probation and Parole v. Scott, 1998. 524 U.S. 357.

Samson v. California, 2006. 547 U.S. 843.

Tate v. Short, 1971. 401 U.S. 395.

United States v. Granderson, 1994. 511 U.S. 39.

United States v. Knights, 2001. 534 U.S. 112.

Williams v. Illinois, 1970. 399 U.S. 235.

Williams v. New York, 1949. 337 U.S. 241.

Young v. Harper, 1997. 520 U.S. 143.

Chapter 13

Law and Incarcerated Offenders with Special Needs

Effective punishment, argues *Cesare Beccaria*, is to be swift, certain, and proportionate to the crime if it is to prevent individuals from future offending. Yet the principle of proportionality must also address the characteristics of the offender and not just those of the crime. Today, we know and understand that offenders vary in their individual characteristics, which determine their needs and risk in a correctional setting. Putting public sentiment aside, individuals who are convicted of a crime and sentenced to confinement become the responsibility of the government (federal, state or local) that executes and delivers the punishment. As such, incarceration as a punishment meted out by the government is meant to incapacitate individuals convicted of a crime, but it can also prevent them from seeking adequate care, medical or other, for their specific needs. If there is denial of care and failure to address the needs of incarcerated individuals, this may amount to cruel and unusual punishment. Denial of appropriate care may also create public health concerns, particularly when convicted and sentenced offenders are at high risk of contracting infectious disease such as tuberculosis, HIV/AIDS, or hepatitis.

Considering the fact that more than two-thirds of offenders sentenced to jails and prisons have histories of substance abuse (Chaiken, 1989; Chavarria, 1992; Gideon, 2010; Inciardi, 1995; Inciardi et al., 1997; Welsh, 2011), reentry and reintegration practices become even more of a challenge. Nevertheless, this is not the sole problem that current correctional institutions and practitioners face. A worrisome increase is observed in convicted inmates under the age of 18 (Seiter, 2008; Sickmund, 2003; Snyder & Sickmund, 2006). Many scholars have noted, with alarm, that the juvenile offender population is growing in correctional facilities, especially in adult correctional facilities (Bilchik, 1998; Griffin, Torbet, & Szymanski, 1998; Kuanliang, Sorensen, & Cunningham, 2008). Another noticeable growing population in correctional facilities is convicted female offenders (Pollock, 1998, 2001, 2004; Morash & Schram, 2002). In fact, Stohr, Walsh, & Hemmens (2009) argue that "the number of incarcerated and supervised women under the correctional umbrella has never been larger" (p. 570). Female offenders pose new challenges to current classification practices (see Van Voorhis & Presser, 2001). For example, Baunach (1992), Henriques (1996), and Rocheleau (1987) present the challenges posed by incarcerated mothers, and the social consequences of their incarceration for broader social issues (Dodge & Pogrebin, 2001; Pollock, 2004).

An equally important growing challenge in recent years is that of senior inmates (Aday, 1994, 2003; Aday & Webster, 1979; Moritsugu, 1990; Kerbs & Jolley, 2009). Scmalleger and Ortiz-Smykla (2009) have observed an 85% increase in elderly inmates in the nation's correctional facilities since 1995. Many of these inmates require expensive medical treatment. Drummond (1999) questions whether it is necessary for such offenders to remain in custody after they become old and frail, and indeed according to Clear, Cole, and Reisig (2009), newly released inmates are now not only older and have served longer periods of imprisonment, but also have higher levels of substance abuse and other medical issues that require community monitoring.

Hammett, Roberts, and Kennedy (2001) examine the health-related issues in prisoner reentry and demonstrated the need for adequate health care for those inmates with infectious diseases that can threaten the community. Specifically, Hammett, Kennedy, and Kuck (2007) discuss the potential harms of infectious diseases such as HIV/AIDS: more than 23,000 infected inmates were documented at year-end 2004, with an estimated 10% more unconfirmed. Other diseases the researchers identify as significant are tuberculosis as well as sexually transmitted diseases, such as syphilis, gonorrhea, chlamydia, genital herpes, and hepatitis. A study conducted on Rikers Island found that the rates of these diseases increased during 2000, particularly among females and inmates in juvenile detention centers (Brown, 2003). Corzine-McMullan (2011) argues that such health challenges need to be addressed, as do mental health issues of incarcerated inmates, as these inmates pose new challenges for correctional officials as well as for those interested in reintegration.

In addition to inmates with health issues, there are other significant segments of the prison population that are overlooked by current research and available textbooks. For example, Knickerbocker (2006) estimates that based on the last national census of 2000, more than 8.7 immigrants entered the United States illegally. The United States Border Patrol union reports a much higher number, between 12 million and 15 million. Such numbers are sure to be reflected in our prison system, resulting in a new segment of inmates that require special attention. Miller (2002) argues that the massive numbers of undocumented immigrants and refugees of color have prompted an increasingly punitive response from the U.S. government, including punitive policies that have traditionally been reserved for extreme circumstances in which any notion of justice has been abandoned. Such policies are destined to receive the Supreme Court's attention as more cases and petitions will surface, especially fueled by detentions inspired by the post 9/11 fear of immigrants and refugees from Middle Eastern countries.

Based on the previous examples, we can understand that special-needs offenders are those offenders, both men and women, with unique circumstances and requirements within the corrections system. Anderson (2008) describes these populations as "those incarcerated ... with unusual or unique requirements stemming from their physical or mental age or other disabilities" (p. 361).

A more punitive approach in recent decades has inspired mandatory minimum sentences, "three-strikes" laws, truth in sentencing, and the abolishment of parole in the federal system and in many states. This in turn has led to a sharp increase in the prison and jail population, which has itself resulted in new challenges for prison officials and administrators. The prison population has changed while increasing the visibility of certain special-needs populations, mainly the mentally ill, chronically ill, and the elderly. As a result, the courts have been called to examine and discuss practices that pertain to the handling of such populations. In most cases involving special-needs offenders, the courts have made their decisions based on whether prison officials and administrators have acted with deliberate indifference, thus violating the Eighth Amendment. While many of the cases focusing on the Eighth Amendment have been discussed in previous chapters, the current chapter focuses more on the policy aspects that relate to such decisions as they pertain to special-needs incarcerated individuals.

The courts have generally made the argument that failing to address the needs of incarcerated offenders does not serve any penological purpose, and that suffering from such neglect is inconsistent with evolving standards of decency, as manifested in current legislation aimed to guarantee basic health standards for incarcerated individuals. Specifically, these standards codify the common law principle according to which the public is required to care for prisoners who, due to their status of incapacitation, cannot care for themselves. Thus, failure to serve the special needs of certain prisoners who are in need of medical, mental, or any other form of care and consideration may be considered *deliberate indifference* on the part of the prison staff. This judgment is a direct product of early cases such as *Trop v. Dulles*, *Estelle v. Gamble*, and *Gregg v. Georgia*, in which the court held that punishments that are deliberately causing suffering and pain are violation of the Eighth Amendment.

At times, the American correctional system has housed more than 2.4 million people; in recent years some decline in the number of incarcerated individuals has been observed, with the last data available from 2015 indicating that about 2.2 million people are incarcerated in American correctional institutions. Most of these people, prior to their confinement, led an unhealthy risky lifestyle. Consequently, the prevalence of somatic and mental health issues among these individuals is much higher than those found in the general population (Gideon, 2013), and as such is the focus of many lawsuits. While we cannot address all issues concerning incarcerated individuals and their special needs, the current chapter focuses on the following special needs populations and corresponding cases that have had an effect on correctional management:

1. Mentally ill prisoners;

2. Chronically ill prisoners in particular those with HIV/AIDS;

3. Women with special needs;

4. LGBTQ; and

5. The elderly.

Mentally Ill Prisoners

Historically, many mentally ill people were confined to prisons and jails simply because no other social reaction was available to their behavior and mental condition. Interestingly, correctional observers and reforms acknowledged that placing mentally ill individuals in the care of jails and prisons was not an adequate solution, and thus special hospitals were built and designed to hold and treat mentally ill individuals. However, such institutions were subjected to harsh public criticism that spearheaded the deinstitutionalization movement calling for the release of mentally ill individuals to the community based on the argument that mentally ill holding facilities and hospitals are not humane. With the deinstitutionalization movement of the 1950s and 1960s, facilities for the mentally ill reduced the number of beds available for the hospitalization of such people, leaving many of them drifting and roaming the streets of big cities. This situation led to increased encounters with law enforcement and subsequently to arrests of more mentally ill individuals. According to Torrey and colleagues (2010), by incarcerating mentally ill people in higher numbers, the American correctional system has returned to the conditions that characterized prisons more than 200 years ago, when a large number of mentally ill offenders were placed behind bars instead of treatment facilities. It is not surprising that many scholars refer to modern prisons and jails as the "new asylum" (Arrigo, 2002; Fagan & Ax, 2011).

Such an increase in mentally ill inmates requires a high level of professionalism to detect and assess different issues and how they can be addressed while the inmate is incarcerated. Moreover, mentally ill inmates are often more difficult to handle, as they tend to be more violent and also tend to have more disciplinary infractions. Consequently, offenders sentenced to jail or prison must be evaluated in an intake process, in which they are screened for mental illnesses. Most intakes, however, are based on self-reporting by the offenders on previous mental health conditions, and some may not report (or know) their true conditions. This can place the psychological staff at an initial disadvantage that may result in erroneous assessment of the offender's needs and risk and may also impede the ability of correctional authorities to tailor an appropriate treatment and reentry plan.

Another important consideration is the fact that most mentally ill offenders tend to be violent and as such, pose more risk to jail and prison staff and other inmates. Such a risk usually requires a higher level of security, which in turn typically places many mentally ill offenders with high-risk offenders who are not mentally ill. In a recent study, Frazier, Sung, Gideon, and Alfaro (2015) found that about 77% of incarcerated offenders in New York State supermax facilities and special housing units (SHUs) suffered from some form of mental illness, and that such a condition was associated with the decision to place the inmate in these highly secure and restrictive environments. Placement in high-security institutions poses additional challenges for mentally ill offenders, and often the conditions of their incarceration are not conducive to their desired treatment. Nevertheless, most inmates with identified mental health issues do receive some level of treatment, usually provided by the institutional psychologist.

As discussed in a previous chapter, the landmark case for all inmate treatment claims, whether medical or mental treatment, is *Estelle v. Gamble*. This case established the deliberate indifference standard, through which all claims of inmate mistreatment or neglect have been considered while establishing the necessary steps to prove violation of Eighth Amendment rights under Section 1983 of the Civil Rights Act. In *Bowring v. Godwin*, a decision by the Fourth Circuit Court of Appeals made shortly after *Estelle*, the Supreme Court stated that there is "no underlying distinction between the right to medical care for physical ills and its psychological or its psychiatric counterpart."

As for the precise standards of minimum mental-health care, *Ruiz v. Estelle*, though only a district court opinion, is one of the most widely cited cases. It established six essential criteria. First, when inmates are first admitted to a correctional facility, they must receive some systematic screening for mental illness that may require treatment. Second, inmates cannot be treated through mere segregation and by closer supervision by correctional officials than is afforded to other inmates. Third, correctional facilities must not only employ trained mental health professionals, but there must be a sufficient number of employees to adequately care for the inmate population at a particular correctional facility. Fourth, all treatment must be documented in "accurate, complete, and confidential records." Fifth, administering "dangerous amounts" of behavior-altering medications is "an unacceptable method of treatment." Sixth, in addition to mental-health screening, correctional facilities must have a basic program to identify inmates with suicidal tendencies.

Yet, as we documented in the due process chapter and a discussion of *Vitek v. Jones*, an inmate who needs mental-health treatment cannot be transferred to a state hospital without a hearing, even if the officials in charge of a correctional facility argue that they cannot give the proper care to that inmate. In *Vitek*, the Supreme Court determined that an involuntary transfer of an inmate to a mental hospital is protected by the due process clause of the Fourteenth Amendment. To make such a transfer, a correctional facility has to establish procedural protections that include giving an inmate notice of such a transfer and an adversarial hearing to determine whether the transfer should occur. However, as was then decided in *Washington v. Harper*, inmates can be medicated against their will if they represent a threat to institutional security. Such a decision can be made by a medical professional and does not require a hearing.

Another subset of the prison population requiring special care are people with mental disorders and disabilities. Until the *Americans with Disabilities Act* of 1990 (ADA), many of these people had few protections from involuntary treatment. A 1999 case decided by the Supreme Court, *Olmstead v. L.C.*, involved two women, identified as L.C. and E.W., who were mentally disabled; L.C. suffered from schizophrenia and E.W. suffered from a personality disorder. While both women originally voluntarily submitted to treatment at Georgia Regional Hospital of Atlanta (GRH), the women were later involuntarily held against their will. One of the provisions of the ADA is that all programs make reasonable accommodations for people with disabilities. L.C. and E.W., while being involuntarily treated, later learned that they were eligible for community treatment, yet had not been placed in a program. Both sued to be placed in community treatment, but the state of Georgia claimed that a lack of funds prevented such a transfer. Ultimately, the Supreme Court ruled that being held involuntarily represented per se discrimination, and a lack of funds was not an appropriate reason to block such a transfer. This is an example of a case in which the Court was reluctant to support measures that may be perceived as more punitive in the presence of more adequate treatment that could also benefit the individual offender, and the community.

Chronically Ill Prisoners and Prisoners with HIV/AIDS

The stereotypical image of a strong, young male inmate is no longer the reality. Many incarcerated offenders have practiced unhealthy and risky behavior, by abusing alcohol and drugs, smoking, or engaging in unprotected sex, often with multiple partners. These behaviors, combined with a lack of health insurance and regular physical checkups, often result in deteriorated health conditions. Accordingly, research indicates that those entering correctional facilities are characterized by higher rates of chronic medical conditions, such as asthma, hypertension, and diabetes, as well as highly infectious diseases such as sexually transmitted infections (STIs), hepatitis, tuberculosis. These chronic illnesses are evident in correctional facilities in much higher rates than in the general population (Freudenberg, 2001). Wilper et al. (2009) found that about 39% of federal inmates and a similar percentage of local jail inmates have at least one chronic illness. In state prisons, the researchers found this percentage to be even higher, at about 43% of all state inmates.

Such medical conditions pose a major impediment for successful rehabilitation and reintegration and may also affect the inmate during the course of incarceration. Infectious diseases (e.g., hepatitis, HIV/AIDS, tuberculosis, and other STIs) are also a challenge for correctional administrators and pose a risk to other inmates and the staff. While most of those conditions were discussed in regard to the Eighth Amendment, it is important to review some of these cases again from the angle of special needs.

The right to privacy for those infected with HIV/AIDS is an important public health issue. Yet the question of privacy poses a challenge to corrections personnel in their daily dealings with infected inmates. In *Woods v. White*, Donald Woods, a prisoner at Wisconsin's Waupun Correctional Institution, filed a Section 1983 lawsuit arguing that his constitutional right to privacy was violated when his diagnosis was discussed with nonmedical staff and other inmates at the facility. The district court judge determined that citizens have a constitutional right to privacy in their medical records and in the doctor-patient confidential relationship, and that this right is not automatically relinquished upon incarceration. Thus, individual prisoners diagnosed with HIV/AIDS have a constitutional right to privacy in their medical records as well. This decision provides inmates who have tested positive for HIV/AIDS with some degree of protection, as they retain privacy where their medical records are concerned.

Another early case involving an HIV-infected inmate is that of *Doe v. Coughlin*, which was decided by the Court of Appeals of the State of New York (which is the court of last resort for the state of New York). In this case, after the petitioner was diagnosed with HIV, the Auburn Correctional Facility denied him the conjugal visits to which he was entitled. John Doe argued that this denial violated his right to due process and equal protection, as well as his fundamental marital privacy. The court ruled that no violation of the Fourth and Fourteenth Amendment rights occurred, as being married does not automatically qualify an inmate for participation in the conjugal visit program. Further, the Court of Appeals took an important public health stand by arguing that denying an HIV-positive person to engage in conjugal visits advances New York's interest in preventing the spread of infectious and contagious diseases, and as such is more important than any equal protections the petitioner may have. The court made it clear that the interests of the free public took precedent over those of the individual inmate, and by doing so help in contain the deadly disease from spreading to the outside community.

In a later case, the Tenth Circuit Court of Appeals discussed another public health concern involving HIV/AIDS. In *Dunn v. White*, the court judged whether a non-consensual blood test for HIV/AIDS violates an inmate's right to privacy as guaranteed under the Fourth Amendment. Terry Dunn argued that the prison's required blood test for the detection of HIV/AIDS was against his religious beliefs. His argument was dismissed by the U.S. District Court in the Northern District, and this dismissal was later affirmed by the Tenth Circuit Court. According to that court, a nonconsensual blood test for AIDS is reasonably related to the legitimate penological objectives of reducing the spread of a contagious and deadly disease within a prison and as such, does not constitute an unreasonable search and seizure. In reaching this decision, the Tenth Circuit compared the mandatory HIV/AIDS blood test with involuntary urine tests for drugs given to prisoners for safety and security concerns. This case is also important as it strengthens the overall concern for harm reduction and public health, which goes far beyond specific inmates' rights to address the needs of the population in the actual facility as well as outside in the free community. In another similar case, *Harris v. Thigpen*, Carmen Harris filed a complaint against the Alabama Department of Corrections challenging its policy of mandatory HIV testing. After she tested positive, she was segregated in a separate unit. Here as well, the plaintiff claimed that her due process rights were violated, as was her protection from cruel and unusual punishment, as guaranteed by the Eighth Amendment. She also cited *Section 504* of the *Rehabilitation Act*, which guarantees certain rights to people with disabilities and prohibiting them from being excluded from participation in, denied the benefits of, or subjected to discrimination under any program or activity receiving federal financial assistance. The Eleventh Circuit Court of Appeals found that the testing and consequent segregation did not violate any prisoner's right and that there was no deliberate indifference in placing Harris in segregation. In fact, the Alabama Department of Corrections' segregation policies were consistent with previous cases that related to the dangers posed by HIV-positive prisoners. Once again, the court made it clear that the greater good, safety, and public health of others exceed that of individual inmates.

Five years after *Dunn v. White*, in *Gates v. Rowland*, an action was brought under Section 1983 to challenge deficient medical and psychiatric care, indecent confinement conditions, overcrowding and insufficient staff, and poor treatment and segregation of HIV-positive inmates at the California Medical Facility (CMF). The plaintiff alleged that inmates' constitutional rights had been violated when they were denied access to medical and mental-health care and to attorneys, and the HIV-positive inmates had been segregated from the general population. A subclass of HIV-positive inmates made claims under Section 504 of the Rehabilitation Act of 1973. During a mediation process, it was agreed that the defendants would develop a pilot program to determine the feasibility of placing HIV-positive inmates in the general population at CMF. The stated goal of the pilot program was "to demonstrate that such placement is possible consistent with medical, behavioral, and security considerations."

While these cases concerning HIV/AIDS demonstrate an approach by which prisoners are found at somewhat of a disadvantage in arguing for their rights due to their diagnosis, a different decision was made in *Roe v. Fauver*. In that case, Roe, a female prisoner diagnosed with AIDS and held in the New Jersey prison system, argued that her continued confinement in isolation without an individual hearing to show that she was at risk to herself or others violated her Fourteenth Amendment due process rights, as well as her Eighth Amendment rights. A New Jersey state court was able to contain some of the panic surrounding HIV/AIDS by looking at more scientific and concrete evidence about the disease and how it spreads. The district court distinguished this case from previous ones, when not much was known about HIV/AIDS and thus segregation was not considered a violation of constitutional rights. Here, the court focused on the procedures and justifications for segregation by looking at the following: (1) the reasons for isolating females with HIV/AIDS in a manner that deprives them of recreation, education, work, and legal access without a hearing; (2) evaluating the conditions of confinement and if they are violating any of the HIV-positive females' equal protection of the law compared with male inmates; (3) if the confinement constitutes cruel and unusual punishment; and finally (4) if the hospital to which the prisoner was confined acted with deliberate indifference. Compared with previous cases, which focused on the greater community and public health, this case was more concerned with care, treatment, and the rights of prisoners diagnosed with HIV/AIDS. In its decision, the New Jersey court determined that prisoners with similar status, regardless of their gender, must be treated equally. Further, the district court made it clear that having a medical condition does not infringe on that inmate's right to file a claim for inadequate medical care. This was also a result of another claim by Roe and other petitioners, who claimed that they were not always given the correct dosage of AZT (a cocktail drug used to treat AIDS) when needed.

Roe v. Fauver demonstrates the complex issue of dealing with inmates diagnosed with HIV/AIDS. The prison's aim is to provide public safety and maintain the safety of staff and other inmates, but it must balance that with the concerns and rights of those infected with a potentially deadly virus and maintain their dignity and address their needs.

Similar to the issues revolving around HIV/AIDS, tuberculosis (TB) is also the subject of many legal cases. The spread of TB is of utmost concern for many correctional institutions, as overcrowded conditions provide fertile ground for the virus. Such a concern is magnified in the presence of HIV that was discussed previously. In *Lareau v. Manson*, a group of pretrial detainees and inmates brought suit against the Hartford Correctional Center for exposing them to tuberculosis and other infectious pathogens. A Connecticut district court ruled that failure to screen detainees for communicable diseases not only violated the due process clause to protect pretrial detainees, but also constituted cruel and unusual punishment for all other inmates. Here again, the court made a statement about the level of punitiveness that correctional facilities practice. In other words, to not provide testing and a secure, healthy environment for prisoners and pretrial detainees exceeds any reasonable punishment. About a decade later, in 1992, a group of inmates from Pennsylvania argued that their prison's lack of adequate TB-control strategy violated their rights guaranteed under both the Eighth and Fourteenth Amendments. A federal district court ruled in their favor, mandating the immediate implementation of an effective TB-control program. Yet, similar to the issues of HIV/AIDS testing discussed previously, cases objecting to TB testing have been brought before the courts. In *Langton v. Commissioner of Correction*, the court ruled that the Massachusetts corrections commissioner had the responsibility to protect the health of all inmates and staff. Therefore, mandatory TB testing to all inmates was a lawful and justified course of action, and any inmate could be disciplined for refusing to be tested.

Women with Special Needs

The growth of female prisoners has outpaced that of male prisoners (West, 2010). According to the *Institute on Women and Criminal Justice* (IWCJ), the women's population in American prisons has risen by an astonishing 757 percent from 1977 to 2005, compared to a moderate decline in the male incarceration rate (Women Prison Association, N.D.). Correctional facilities that house women must deal with many issues that do not occur in facilities that incarcerate men. To begin with, women suffer from many health issues, such as those related to their reproductive systems, that simply do not occur in men; and of course, women can be or get pregnant while incarcerated. In addition, women have significantly different life experiences that relate to their criminal conduct. In particular, women are more likely than men to be victims of physical and sexual abuse (Snell & Morton, 1994), as well as have histories of psychological problems and substance abuse, and are at a higher risk of contracting HIV and other deadly infectious diseases as a result of their dire experiences. These issues not only lead to differences in needed health care, but there is also the question of how to deal with pregnant women and the children they bear.

One case that dealt with the plight of pregnant inmates was *Monmouth County Correctional Institution Inmates v. Lanzaro*. A group of women inmates alleged that Monmouth County Correctional Institution (MCCI) had denied them essential health care, including a lack of counseling for, access to, and funding for abortions. According to the inmates, this violated their rights under the constitutions of both New Jersey and the United States. Of particular concern was a policy that required inmates to obtain a court-ordered release if they wanted to obtain an abortion. The district court judge overseeing the case (Harold Ackerman) noted that such a policy would most likely prevent an inmate from being able to obtain an abortion. While noting that this seemed to conflict with *Roe v. Wade*, the women also sought to have MCCI pay for the abortions. Judge Ackerman noted that there did not seem to be any federal requirement that would mandate that MCCI pay for inmate abortions, but relying on New Jersey law, Judge Ackerman ruled that MCCI was financially responsible. In all, Judge Ackerman made six rulings regarding the case: (1) Monmouth County had to end the practice of requiring women inmates to obtain a court-ordered release for an abortion; (2) Monmouth County was required to inform inmates of laboratory results after a pregnancy test and their related rights (including their right to an abortion), and the county was responsible for the expenses of all medical care; (3) Monmouth County needed to provide professional counseling services, including medical and social counseling, to aid women inmates in deciding whether to terminate a pregnancy or carry a fetus to term; (4) if an inmate decided to have an abortion, MCCI medical department staff needed to make the necessary arrangements at an appropriate medical facility as soon as possible; (5) Monmouth County was responsible for the full cost of all inmate abortions; and (6) Monmouth County needed to provide a copy of these regulations to any inmate after a positive pregnancy test.

One issue that the Eighth Circuit Court of Appeals considered was if jailers have qualified immunity from lawsuits for a lack of adequate medical care for pretrial detainees who are pregnant. In *Boswell v. Sherburne County*, Wanda Boswell was arrested after midnight for driving under the influence of alcohol and taken to the Sherburne County Jail in Elk River, Minnesota. While Boswell was being booked, she notified her jailer, Valerie Lero, that she was six and a half months pregnant and that three days earlier, she had suffered abnormal vaginal discharge and had fainted, and was under the care of a physician. Boswell provided Lero with the phone number for her physician. Later, Boswell informed Lero that she was bleeding. Lero provided a sanitary pad to Boswell before she was locked into her cell for the night. Lero did not call Boswell's physician. Furthermore, Lero did not give this information to the next jailer, Nancy Riecken, who took over Lero's duties at 6:00 a.m. Around 7:00 a.m., Boswell informed Riecken that her condition had worsened. Boswell was suffering cramps and bleeding and later passed blood clots, which she actually showed to Riecken as proof that she needed medical attention. Riecken and later, the chief jailer both informed Boswell that she was required to post bail before she could get medical attention. After communicating with Boswell's mother and being informed that Boswell had suffered problematic pregnancies in the past, Riecken still refused to allow Boswell treatment until she posted bail. Around 10:00 a.m., an Elk River police officer, Thomas Tyler, arrived at the jail to begin his shift. Riecken, knowing that Tyler was an emergency medical technician, began to question Tyler about the signs of a miscarriage. Tyler, becoming concerned, asked what was happening. Tyler went to see Boswell, who at that point was crying in pain and pounding on the bars of her jail cell. After a quick examination, Tyler directed Riecken to call for an ambulance. Boswell began giving birth during the ambulance ride. Ultimately, she gave birth at the hospital, but the baby died 34 minutes later.

Wanda Boswell filed suit against her jailers, arguing that her Eighth and Fourteenth Amendment rights had been violated. In trying to avoid liability, Boswell's jailers argued that they had immunity because "their conduct does not violate clearly established statutory or constitutional rights of which a reasonable person would have known." They tried to argue that because Boswell was merely a pretrial detainee instead of a convicted prisoner, what protections or care Boswell should expect were not clear. However, the Eighth Circuit noted that as established in *Bell v. Wolfish* in 1979, pretrial detainees should receive "at least as great" protections as convicted prisoners. Therefore, while the Eighth Circuit did not rule that the jailers in the case would be liable, the court did rule that these claims should be allowed to go to trial because there was evidence to support the claim that Boswell's jailers acted with deliberate indifference.

Another issue specific to women inmates is breastfeeding of infant children. The Fifth Circuit Court of Appeals determined in *Dike v. School Board* that women have a fundamental interest in their decision to breastfeed their children. In that case, the Fifth Circuit ruled that a schoolteacher should be allowed to breastfeed her child during a duty-free lunch hour. However, in *Southerland v. Thigpen*, the Fifth Circuit ruled that the Mississippi Department of Corrections was allowed to deny women inmates the right to breastfeed their children. According to the Fifth Circuit, the accommodations that would need to be made would be both costly and a threat to institutional security. Furthermore, the court ruled that to allow women inmates a temporary suspension of their sentence to breastfeed infants would undermine principles of deterrence and retribution. However, in *Berrios-Berrios v. Thornburg*, Judge Forester of the Eastern District of Kentucky ruled that female prisoners should be allowed to breastfeed their children during visitations. As Judge Forester noted, the prison in question allowed inmates to bottle-feed during visitation and correctional officials had "failed to make the court aware of a single rational interest that the government might possess in preventing Berrios or other female inmates from breast-feeding their children during regular visitation hours." However, Judge Forester specified that correctional facilities did not have to provide Berrios with a refrigerator so that she could pump breast milk to provide to the caretaker of Berrrios' infant child. According to Judge Forester, with an average of 50 pregnant inmates at the facility, accommodating that would require an unfeasible amount of refrigeration space.

LGBTQ in Prison

In the general population, homosexuality is now accepted or at least tolerated, but inside correctional facilities, engaging in such behavior is forbidden and considered a violation of prison rules and regulations. This is mainly due to the potentially coercive nature of such relations and the problems these relationships may cause in controlling the inmate population and the operations of the facility. Although it is difficult to identify the actual scope of sexual activity in prison and homosexual activity in particular, such behavior certainly exists. In fact, all prisons have policies against any type of sexual behavior between inmates and if caught, inmates can be sanctioned and punished.

Inmates are typically expected to be tough and demonstrate self-control but openly gay inmates can be perceived as weak and may become the target of harassment and victimization (as can straight inmates, for that matter). For any inmate, fears of being sexually assaulted during incarceration are not conducive to successful rehabilitation and later reentry and reintegration. Inmates who have been sexually assaulted during their incarceration take this horrific experience with them when they leave prison. Some may have even contracted sexually transmitted diseases as a result of their attack and will be exporting them back to the community upon release.

Consequently, homosexuality behind bars and gay and lesbian inmates have received increased attention in recent years, particularly after the passage of the *Prisoners' Rape Elimination Act (PREA)* of 2003, which was discussed in Chapter 11. However, the challenges faced by gay and lesbian prisoners received some attention from the court before the enactment of the PREA. One of the cases, discussed earlier, is the 1994 case of *Farmer v. Brennan*, in which Farmer, a transsexual prisoner who identified as female, was beaten and raped by a fellow inmate; the Supreme Court ruled in Farmer's favor, affirming the claim of deliberate indifference and cruel and unusual punishment. One of the first cases brought under the PREA was that of Neon "Sandy" Brown (*Brown v. Patuxent Institution*, 2015), who identified as female and was serving a five-year assault sentence at the Patuxent Correctional Institution in Jessup, Maryland. Brown also alleged that the guards routinely taunted her, encouraged her to commit suicide, and watched her in the shower. The judge found that the prison guards' alleged voyeurism amounted to sexual abuse and awarded $5,000 in damages to Brown. Further, Judge Shaffer, a Maryland administrative judge, ruled that the prison should establish new policies for transgender inmates regarding strip searches, housing, and guard interactions. Specifically, Judge Shaffer determined that the behavior of the Patuxent correctional institutions was a clear violation of the national standards established under the federal Prison Rape Elimination Act of 2003 and required the State of Maryland to establish clear policies and mandatory training for corrections officers regarding the treatment of transgender inmates. The Maryland Department of Public Safety and Correctional Services adopted the judge's ruling, and now requires state prisons to adopt new policies and training for housing transgender inmates (Francis-Ward, 2015).

Transgender prisoners are another subset of the inmate population and they present particular challenges and a rapidly evolving court response. One example is the case of *Kosilek v. Spencer.* Michelle Kosilek, who was born in 1949 as Robert Kosilekis, was an anatomically male prisoner in her mid-sixties who suffers from gender identity disorder ("GID") and self-identified as a woman. Michelle was convicted of first-degree murder and sentenced to life in prison without parole for killing her spouse. During her incarceration, she attempted suicide and self-castration, both of which failed. This case raises many security issues as well as issues brought by the plaintiff against the Massachusetts Department of Corrections. Yet, the court ruled that no violation of the Eighth Amendment was proven and that the Massachusetts Department of Corrections operated within its means and abilities to provide the best care possible, by providing mental health and psychiatric care, hormonal care and other services relevant to the plaintiff's issues. Just a year later, however, the standards had changed in the case of *Michelle-Lael B. Norsworthy v. Jeffrey Beard et al.* Michelle, formerly known as Jeffrey Bryan Norsworthy, was convicted of murder in the second degree and sentenced to 17 years to life in prison. Michelle was diagnosed with gender identity disorder (GID), now known as gender dysphoria, a medical condition characterized by incongruence between one's experienced gender and assigned sex at birth, and clinically significant distress or impaired functioning as a result. The condition is associated with severe and unremitting emotional pain; if left untreated, people with gender dysphoria experience anxiety, depression, suicidal tendencies, and other mental-health issues. Such symptoms intensify with age. Accordingly, Michelle Norsworthy explained that she is a women trapped in a man's body and according to her deposition, argued that her spirit is imprisoned in a way that causes excruciating pain and frustration to a point that therapy and other remedies are the only way to relieve her agony. Therefore, she requested sex-reassignment surgery, to be paid for by the California Department of Corrections. This treatment is recommended by the World Professional Association for Transgender Health ("WPATH") under its Standards of Care for the Health of Transsexual, Transgender, and Gender-Nonconforming People, recognized as authoritative by the American Medical Association, the American Psychiatric Association, and the American Psychological Association. U.S. District Judge Jon Tigar ruled that refusing to pay for the surgery denied the plaintiff her constitutionally adequate medical treatment and issued an injunction compelling the state of California to provide the surgery, which could cost up to $100,000.

Taking into consideration the suffering and sensitivity of transgender prisoners, the courts have placed themselves as the guardians of these populations. Accordingly, a federal judge in Wisconsin struck down as unconstitutional a state law that reportedly is the only one in the nation banning prison inmates who were born biologically male but identify as female from receiving hormone therapy. In his decision, U.S. District Judge Charles Clevert stated that such a law violates the equal protection clause and is an unconstitutional form of cruel and unusual punishment, thus violating the Eighth Amendment. Judge Clevert also cited the ban for being cruel and unusual because it denies hormone therapy without considering individual inmates' medical needs or the judgment of their doctors (Neil, 2010).

Elderly Prisoners

As the general population of the United States is aging, so does the incarcerated population — but this is also the result of mandatory sentences, "three-strikes" laws, and longer sentences, which result in more offenders spending longer periods of time behind bars. Data from the Bureau of Justice Statistics indicate an increase of more than 40% in male inmates over the age of 50 between 1998 and 2009 (Aday & Krabill, 2013). For incarcerated women over age 50, the increase is much more acute, at 139% over the same time period. Such statistics provide a clear picture of the age of the American prison population increasing, bringing a host of new challenges.

According to Seiter (2011), one of the most pressing issues is the high cost of medical care associated with elderly inmates, who present a number of illnesses and health problems due to both general aging and particular lifestyle choices. Older inmates' health problems are different from those shared by younger inmates, which puts jail and prison clinics at a major disadvantage as health-care providers. Many services that are available to the elderly population outside prison walls may not be as accessible inside. Additionally, many facilities are not equipped to deal with chronically ill inmates and many of the infectious diseases that they carry. As noted earlier, prisons were not designed to hold ill and dependent populations. Most facilities are designed to hold young and physically active inmates who can work and be involved in prison routine and activity. The cells, beds, and other facilities are designed for inmates with good physical stamina. Imagine, for example, an older inmate who has difficulty walking being placed in a cell block on the second or third floor. This inmate must share a cell with another person and may even be required to sleep on the upper bunk of an already small bed. While most elderly offenders tend to comply with prison rules and regulations, they also tend to be easy prey for younger and violent inmates. Such conditions are not optimal for rehabilitation and preparation for reentry and reintegration. Furthermore, many older inmates have spent long years behind bars, so when they are released back to the community, they have very little knowledge of how to seek and receive the care they need. Consequently, the level of attention directed at managing the elderly inmate population has increased while efforts by correctional administrators and facilities are slowly catching up. While there is a lack federal case law (see for example *United States v. Carey, United States v. Harrison,* and *United States v. Tolson*) that has focused on the right to consider old age as mitigating factor in sentencing, there have not yet been major cases specific to elder care in prisons. Their growing representation among prison population suggests that litigation revolving around the needs of the incarcerated elderly is inevitable. Correctional speculators that focus their study on such issues further warn and advise of the magnitude of this growing population and the litigation potential that threatens to become a big issue in the near future.

Conclusion

The American incarceration binge of the 1980s up to 2010, along with changes in sentencing polices that became more punitive and less compromising, resulted in the mass incarceration of several new breeds of offenders. As this chapter discussed, more women and chronically ill individuals are being placed under correctional care, with more prisoners sentenced for very long periods of time. This spike in incarceration also brought into prisons a substantial number of individuals with substance abuse issues, mentally ill offenders, and offenders with comorbidity of substance and health issues. These groups of people have presented a major challenge to many institutions that are not equipped to deal with the increasing demands presented by these individuals. Many facilities are overcrowded and understaffed, making it all the more difficult for correctional administrators and managers to properly address the needs of individuals with special needs and those requiring special considerations and protections. In this atmosphere, it is no surprise that many individuals with special needs perceive their conditions of confinement as highly punitive and constituting cruel and unusual punishment. It is within this context that judicial intervention in correctional management becomes essential. As discussed throughout the cases presented in this chapter, the court examines whether correctional authorities have acted with deliberate indifference, resulting in inmates suffering intentional and deliberate discriminatory treatment by correctional staff who have purposely ignored their needs. The courts have sought to uphold civil and human rights of the incarcerated while avoiding nonutilitarian goals of punishment such as unnecessary retaliation and torture. By using this approach, judicial intervention has signaled that sentencing offenders to imprisonment should uphold the penological goal of prevention and incapacitation, without the infliction of any additional suffering. It is not surprising that the judicial pendulum swung toward the "hands-on" approach during the 1980s as more individuals were sentenced to longer periods of imprisonment, which in turn pushed many discriminatory civil rights issues to the surface.

Discussion Questions

1. What are the correctional challenges that resulted from the quadrupled incarceration rate of the past three decades? How did this affect judicial intervention in correctional management?

2. Discuss the effects of the changing makeup of the prison population across the nation and the challenges it presents to correctional institutions in their ability to protect the constitutional rights of inmates. How did the change affect prisoner litigation?

3. In your opinion, when considering the punishment of offenders, should judges give consideration to their special needs? What considerations must be addressed in order to provide just and proportionate punishment while minimizing the risk of later litigation?

4. Discuss the clause of cruel and unusual punishment as it pertains to prisoners with special needs. What should correctional institutions do to minimize the risk of being sued for violating this clause?

5. What is the standard used by the courts to determine if the treatment of prisoner with special needs was done in malice or not?

6. What role do the health needs of incarcerated individuals play in their punishment? Discuss the health-related issues that result in prisoner litigation.

7. What is the overall penological stand taken by the courts when deciding cases of prisoners' with special needs?

8. What are the *common-law* standards used by the courts when deciding in cases of prisoners with special needs? Discuss the ways in which these standards uphold the aims of corrections.

9. What are the main cases that established the standard of *deliberate indifference*? Explain what that standard means and how the courts evaluate its presence or lack thereof.

10. Discuss the importance of *Ruiz v. Estelle*. What are the different criteria this case established, and how are they related to the standard of deliberate indifference?

11. Discuss the implication of *Woods v. White*. In your opinion, should medical records of prisoners be shared with nonmedical correctional staff?

12. Discuss the case of *Doe v. Coughlin*. Do you think that maintaining an individual's right to privacy should be more important than upholding public health? What are the standards examined by the court to evaluate this balance?

13. Is forcing incarcerated individuals to take invasive medical examinations, such as blood tests, a violation of their rights? Do such procedures constitute cruel and unusual demands? Discuss this issue in regard to the case of *Dunn v. White*, and it importance to the overall goals of corrections.

14. Should incarcerated individuals with HIV/AIDS be segregated from the general prison population? Discuss the relevant cases and their penological implications.

15. Based on cases discuss in this chapter, do you think correctional institutions should pay for abortions? Discuss this issue with the goals of corrections in mind.

16. Discuss the case of *Boswell v. Sherburne County*. Should pretrial female detainees receive the same level of treatment as females who are sentenced to prison? What are some implications of this case for the manner in which other detainees are treated?

17. Discuss some of the correctional challenges that led to the Prison Rape Elimination Act of 2003. In your opinion, should homosexual and transsexual inmates be housed with the general population? Discuss the controversy of this issue.

18. Discuss the correctional challenges presented in the cases of *Michelle-Lael B. Norsworthy v. Jeffrey Beard et al.* What are some of the considerations given by

the court in this case regarding the health of the inmate, and the responsibility of the correctional institution to provide services?

19. What challenges may arise from the aging prison population? Discuss potential litigation that might come from aging prisoners, and how the court may view such cases.

List of Cases Cited

Bell v. Wolfish, 1979, 441 U.S. 520.

Berrios-Berrios v. Thornburg, 1989. 716 F. Supp. 987.

Boswell v. Sherburne County, 1988. 849 F.2d 1117.

Bowring v. Godwin, 1977. 551 F.2d 44.

Brown v. Patuxent Institution, 20152015. DPSC-IGO-002V-14-33232.

Dike v. School Board, 1981. 640 F.2d 783.

Doe v. Coughlin, 1988. 697 F. Supp. 1234.

Dunn v. White, 1989. 880 F.2d 1188.

Estelle v. Gamble, 1976. 429 U.S. 97.

Gates v. Rowland, 1994. 39 F.3d 1439.

Gregg v. Georgia, 1976. 428 U.S. 153.

Harris v. Thigpen, 1991. 941 F.2d 1495.

Langton v. Commissioner of Corrections, 1993. 614 N.E.2d 1002.

Lareau v. Manson, 1981. 651 F.2d 96.

Michelle-Lael B. Norsworthy v. Jeffrey Beard et al. 2015, 87 F. Supp. 3d 1104.

Monmouth County Correctional Institution Inmates v. Lanzaro, 1987. 643 F. Supp. 1217.

Olmstead v. L.C., 1999. 527 U.S. 581.

Roe v. Fauver, 1988. 3:88-cv-01225-AET (D.N.J.).

Roe v. Wade, 1973. 410 U.S. 113.

Ruiz v. Estelle, 1980. 503 F. Supp. 1265.

Southerland v. Thigpen, 1986. 784 F.2d 713.

Trop v. Dulles, 1958. 356 U.S. 86.

United States v. Carey, 1990. 895 F. 2d 318.

United States v. Harrison, 1992. 970 F. 2d 444.

United States v. Tolson, 1991. 760 F. Supp. 1322.

Vitek v. Jones, 1980. 445 U.S. 480.

Washington v. Harper, 1990. 494 U.S. 210.

Chapter 14

The United States Constitution and Its Relevance to Correctional Management

"The autonomy of corrections has diminished over the years. Wardens are no longer omnipotent administrators. Correctional staff are more professional and sophisticated. This has been necessary in order to survive. Wardens and correctional administrators are more policy oriented today than in the 1970s."

—Reginald Wilkinson, former director of the Ohio
Department of Rehabilitation and Corrections
(as cited in Riveland, 1999, p. 171)

Jacobs (1980) supports that notion by arguing that many of the correctional improvements that are apparent today are a direct result of prisoner litigation. The shift that Wilkinson describes, from autonomy to policy-driven professionalism, did not occur overnight, and it owes a lot to prisoner litigation and the due process movement led by federal courts. Litigation woke the correctional giant from its slumber and drove years of long-needed changes in correctional practices and management. Although such litigation provoked many internal and external reactions from all over the social and legal spectrum, it has forced citizens, lawyers, politicians, and judges to examine the conditions of confinement, how offenders are punished, and how the conditions of punishment reflect social beliefs in civil rights. Above all, prisoners' litigation has forced correctional administrators, who initially opposed and resented such involvement by the courts (Riveland, 1999), to reevaluate their profession and practices. Administrators were legally obliged to adopt court orders to improve conditions of confinement, and by that, promote safer institutions (Crouch & Marquart, 1990; Riveland, 1999). As a result, prisoners are now safer, enjoy better services, and tend to have more of their needs addressed during their period of incarceration (Barkel, 1986; Crouch & Marquart, 1990; Feeley & Hanson, 1986).

Today's prisons are cleaner and have better air, medical treatment, educational and other treatment programs, as well as risk and needs classification system that provide correctional officials with the ability to perform a more accurate intake and correspondingly deliver adequate treatment. These could not have happened without prisoners' litigation that challenged the status quo of the traditional correctional system and practice. Of course, not all problems have been solved and further reforms are needed. Just as previous reforms were made, new reforms will most likely be won by future litigation and court orders. Litigation has made correctional practices more effective and more efficient, which has benefited inmates, and also strengthened prisons and their administration, increasing their legitimacy by providing them with more adequate legal tools that have shaped current and evolving correctional policies. Thus, this chapter will focus on the bureaucratic development of correctional organizations as a by-product of prisoner litigation and the manner in which such litigation has affected the correctional profession and management.

Bureaucratic Approach to Correctional Management

According to Gottschalk (2006), correctional management should be based on three principles: incapacitation as the sole purpose of punishment, resocializing incarcerated offenders so they can reintegrate upon release, and managing the prison in accordance with constitutional guarantees that assure a humane and dignified environment to those housed within its walls. However, prison as a total institution is designed to operate within a set of predetermined rules that must not be challenged. Such rules create a bureaucratic environment that depersonalize those individuals who reside within its walls. Individuals lose their identities by being referred to as "prisoners"/"inmates" and assigned identification numbers. Their identity is stripped from them, and they are expected to follow strict rules and procedures that serve the interest of the institution. The basic managerial model of correctional facilities is that of separation and power, it is one that inspired and follows external bureaucratic organizational style and regime. Guards, prison administration, and other staff hold the power to control the movement, life, and liberty of the inmates, who are kept separate from the staff. Such control is legitimized by legislation, whereas use of force is available to those working in the institution to maintain order and control while enforcing the law and other institutional regulations. Such an approach also suppresses local culture by enforcing general principles, protecting civil rights, and constraining power. In the words of Feeley and Swearingen (2003: 467) it can be perceived as the "iron fist cloaked in the velvet glove."

As mentioned earlier, in Chapter 4, correctional institutions operate in two levels. According to Goffman (1961; 1968), correctional institutions operate on both the formal and informal level. The formal level is also the more visible one, the one that all must abide by. This level directly corresponds with Weber's definition of bureaucracy, which manifests itself in today's correctional institutions in a defined organizational structure with a clear division of power and responsibility, a rationalized set of rules to be followed, a management class of professional administrators who specialize in corrections, and a rigid classification system for all individuals involved (see Feeley & Swearingen, 2003). Simply put, the formal level that operates inside correctional institutions, also known as total institutions, includes the rules and regulations, and the system of discipline, order, and other procedures. On the other hand, the informal level is the one that is less visible to the observer; it derives from personal interests, conflicts, and struggles between inmates and between inmates and staff. Power struggles eventually lead to changes in the administration of policies and consequent rules. Thus, it is essential to understand that as a result of competing interests between inmates and correctional staff, conflicts will arise, and lawsuits will be filed. Such actions should be viewed in a much wider context of opposition. Inmates who are perceived as powerless tend to use the legal system in an effort to gain power, while at the same time adjusting to their situation of being powerless individuals. Another argument is that inmates use litigation as a way to manifest their oppositional culture by way of harassing correctional personnel (Schlanger, 2003; Thomas, 1988). In fact, Thomas (1988) argues that such harassment is not without intent; rather, it puts a particular officer on notice that future misbehavior will receive scrutiny. Regardless of intent, such litigation and appeals to the courts can and should also be viewed in a constitutional context.

Effects of the Constitution and Bill of Rights on Correctional Management

As the supreme law of the land, the Constitution and Bill of Rights serve as a guardian of citizens and their rights when dealing with governmental institutions (DeLisi & Conis, 2013). All actions, policies, and practices implemented by governmental agencies are subject to scrutiny for adherence to the Constitution, and correctional institutions are no different (Shaw, 2015). We may assume that correctional institutions aim to uphold to the highest constitutional standards in their daily dealings with the incarcerated population, but the truth is that often the institutional environment poses major challenges. Specifically, maintaining a humane and dignified daily routine within a prison environment is not always possible because inmates tend to violate rules and manifest impulsive behavioral patterns. Indeed, many inmates are in prison because they have a problem following rules. Further, many inmates abuse their freedoms and rights, and some perceive humane, polite, and considerate treatment from the prison staff as weakness.

As discussed in the second chapter and throughout the pages of this book, the United States Supreme Court, in its role as the ultimate judicial authority, has made decisions on cases that have had a lasting effect on correctional management and staff. In particular, two types of cases have greatly concerned the Court: petitions of habeas corpus and civil rights claims invoking Section 1983 (Collins, 2015). Within these two avenues, the Court has debated and decided on numerous cases concerning the management and operations of prisons and jails, often challenging the far-reaching hand of the Constitution into these facilities in an attempt to provide prisoners with constitutional protections while limiting the unrestrained discretion of prison administration. This involvement is not to be taken lightly, as often discretion is needed to ensure the smooth operations of the facility, and to allow prison administrators and professionals to carry on the extremely difficult task of keeping both prisoners and staff safe and healthy, while effectively operating their institution. As an example, prisoners have argued violations of their Fourth Amendment rights while incarcerated, confronting both the courts and correctional administrators with the issue of search and seizure inside correctional facilities. This led to the Supreme Court's determination in *Hudson v. Palmer* that privacy of prisoners in their cells simply cannot be reconciled with the concept of incarceration and the needs and objectives of penal institutions. Specifically, the Court stated that incarcerated individuals forfeit their right to privacy under the Fourth Amendment when they are admitted to a penal institution. Such a decision is important to the management of correctional facilities and assures safety in such facilities.

The courts have also had to make numerous decisions regarding procedures and due process when it comes to depriving incarcerated individuals from their limited liberty as a result of disciplinary issues. As discussed in Chapter 8, many due process rights guaranteed to Americans under the Fifth and Sixth Amendments may pose some challenges in penological and correctional settings. For example, in the Supreme Court ruling on *Shaw v. Murphy*, Justice Thomas applied the *Turner* standard to the question of the monitoring and regulation of prisoner communications, and so upheld regulatory impingements on the constitutional rights of prisoners when the regulation is reasonably related to a legitimate penological interest. Justice Thomas took the side of prison administration in its effort to provide a safe and secure environment, even though that also limits the freedoms of those convicted of criminal conduct. The right of corresponding via written letters among inmates existed, the court declared, but allowing such activity without proper correctional supervision and control would undermine prison administration, as dangerous and incitement contents can lead to unrest, which may pose great risk to the safety of other prisoners and correctional employees.

The strong effect of prisoner litigation on correctional management is critical to our understanding of the evolution of corrections locally and internationally. The impact begins with the shift in the role of federal judges, who became policymakers as well as rule appliers (Feeley & Swearingen, 2003), and by that forced the wheels of correctional change into motion. With each ruling, federal judges examined the current correctional practice and regulation, then adopted goals and developed strategies to achieve them, and in this way forced correctional administrators into an accountability-driven system that promoted and emphasized professionalism while facilitating opportunities for a new generation of administrators and correctional professionals (Riveland, 1999) who do not possess the notion of "us versus them," but can also value the idea of prisoner rights and judicial intervention. Judges assuming the role of policymakers had another effect too, a much larger one. According to Feeley and Swearingen (2003), correctional institutions became more bureaucratic, and although bureaucracy reduces arbitrary and capricious treatment, it introduces a host of other issues, mainly infringements on democracy, freedom, and rationality and a boost to the power of the organization over that of the individual, which in turn perpetuates domination and hierarchy. However, bureaucracy also constrains power, and thus limits the ability of correctional officials to abuse their power, in effect forcing them to maintain some level of basic civil rights. Similarly, Whitty (2011: 138) argues that prison wardens are at the sharp end of human rights compliance when they are forced to preside over human rights violations they are powerless to prevent or are unaware of, but nonetheless must be held accountable for. Human rights, Whitty says, have "an increased ability to manifest as major organizational risk." Thus, it is the connection between law and correctional management, as a form of bureaucratic organization, that transformed litigation to safeguard the rights of prisoners while at the same time strengthening correctional management through revisited and newly developed policies that reduce the organizational risk of liability. Decades of correctional litigation led to judges' instructing correctional administrators, which further led to the accreditation of correctional facilities and correctional professionals, a process set in place to avoid lawsuits. In fact, many prison administrators joined the accreditation bandwagon not because they care much about inmate welfare and well-being, but because these administrators were looking for relief from litigation and by doing so, positively affected conditions of confinement. Feeley and Swearingen (2003: 474) summarize this notion: "the reforms adopted are more likely to first and foremost meet organizational needs, and only secondarily meet needs of inmate."

Business Management Approach to Corrections

With correctional institutions becoming more bureaucratic and prison wardens required to follow policies and insulate their actions from external scrutiny, many correctional administrators found themselves in a unique position in which they are required to provide humane confinement conditions in which civil rights are upheld, but at the same time face rising incarceration rates that demanded more resources. The combination of more bureaucratic structure along with a higher level of professionalism also created a businesslike approach to the management of correctional facilities. The operating budget for many correctional facilities began to increase in direct relation to the increase in cost of staffing, health care, goods, and services in an attempt to comply with court orders and legislation. Specifically, correctional administrators were expected to be more accountable to politicians as the business of corrections became an important aspect of states' annual budgets. Policymakers and chief executives increasingly demanded explanations for the significant consumption of fiscal resources, and this became a pivotal issue in correctional management. While at first look, the issue of fiscal consumption may not seem directly related to the prisoner litigation discussed previously, the two topics share a direct cause-and-effect relation; furthermore, this is aggravated by the increase in national incarceration rates. Higher incarceration rates add not just to overcrowded facilities but also to the increased demand in services and, consequently, in budgets. When the courts require prison administrators to change their practices and provide better and more adequate services to incarcerated individuals, they are essentially requiring correctional facilities to invest in treating prisoners and addressing their needs, and not just warehousing them. Such an investment requires changing policies and modes of operation, which

Figure 14.1 The Circular Effects of Prisoner Litigation on Correctional Management

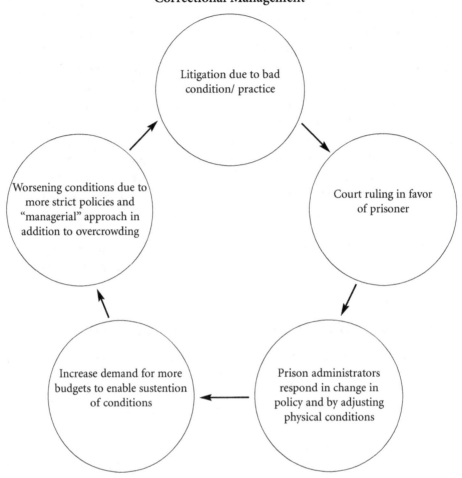

in turn affects existing budgets. As more inmates gain access to the courts and their complaints are resolved by court rulings, prison administrators must respond to the court instructions to accommodate and change operations, even when this is not something that prison administrators are keen to do. This feedback loop is not that different from any business operation module, in which managers are adjusting to demand and adjusting their operations to survive. These accommodations and changes lead to more professionalism, and professionalism translates to increased costs, costs that in turn place more strain on state budgets. When states increase their prison population—due to get-tough policies, for example—this presents renewed challenges to prison administrators, who are now faced again with overcrowded facilities in which the confinement conditions are worsening. Then worsening conditions place correctional administrators at a higher risk of being sued again for terrible and inhumane confinement conditions (see Figure 14.1). Kenneth McGinnis, former director of the Michigan Department of Corrections, states in an interview that the "high cost of what we are doing will possibly cause our criminal justice policies to 'swing back' a bit" (as cited in Riveland, 1999: 195) to an earlier state where prisons could not provide full accommodation for all prisoners' needs. This may result in increased prisoner litigation.

Prisoners' Access to Courts and Its Effect on Correctional Management

Inmates can gain access to the courts using one of three venues: (1) challenging the constitutionality of their confinement by submitting a writ of habeas corpus; (2) seeking redress of civil rights violations using Section 1983; or (3) compelling correctional officials to perform a duty by submitting a writ of mandamus. Each of these has an effect on correctional management in that correctional administrators must address such writs and respond to them, and when decided by the courts, follow their instructions and adjust conditions of confinement accordingly.

Habeas Corpus

This legal doctrine grants convicted offenders access to the courts to challenge the legality of their sentence. Habeas corpus is mentioned in the Constitution under Article I, Section 9:

> The privilege of the writ of Habeas Corpus shall not be suspended, unless when cases of rebellion or invasion and public safety may require it.

In the context of prisons, habeas corpus is an order for correctional authorities to bring the petitioner to present his or her case before the court. Inmates file habeas corpus petitions for several reasons, most often to allege the illegality of their sentence stemming from ineffective legal defense counsel, or errors by the trial court.

As we previously discussed, to comply with the *Prison Litigation Reform Act (PLRA)*, inmates need to exhaust prison grievance procedures before they are allowed to file a habeas corpus petition. Prison reform advocates may bemoan such regulations as an unjustified restriction on inmates' access to the courts, but the fact that Congress felt the need to make these reforms illustrates the power that habeas corpus petitions have. Through the grievance process and later through habeas corpus petitions, inmates are able to challenge the constitutionality of their conditions of confinement. Thus, correctional administrators are given a choice: address grievances by making certain reforms (which often cost money) or leave the decision to the courts and potentially face more costs through litigation that may have forced judicial intervention in the actual management and policies of any given correctional facility.

In response to the rise in frivolous suits by inmates, correctional officials called for the regulations and restriction of such litigation. They were joined by federal judges, who had also experienced an unmanageable rise in litigation, coinciding with the get-tough-on-crime movement. Consequently, and in response to the above,

Congress adopted the PLRA in 1996, mentioned earlier in this book. The PLRA called for the development of internal mechanisms that control and address issues of grievances. The PLRA enabled correctional officials to improve the process of addressing inmates' grievances in an attempt to prevent them from pursuing remedy in federal courts. This had an important effect on correctional management. Minor and Parson (2015) argue that the grievance procedures that formed under the PLRA reflected both the staff and prisoner subcultures of correctional facilities. Further, the PLRA forced both prisoners and staff to work to solve disputes between these two competing and opposing groups, in an attempt to achieve a more workable and safe environment. The outcome of this act was a decline in complaints filed by individual inmates (Schlanger, 2003).

Section 1983

Prison life is fruitful ground for civil lawsuits. There is enormous potential for individual inmates to initiate a civil procedure against the state (Turner, 1979). Accordingly, prisoners may use their constitutional right to file suit against their jailers, and by doing so to challenge the states and local government, in an attempt to obtain compensatory damages and relief and even to generate reform that will benefit themselves and future prisoners. Not surprisingly, Section 1983 is a major portion of the federal courts' civil caseload. In fact, according to Hanson and Daley (1995), one in every 10 cases is a Section 1983 lawsuit. Prisoners tend to use Section 1983 to file lawsuits that allege the conditions of their confinement in local and state correctional facilities. In particular, such lawsuits allege that correctional staff and administrators, in their capacity as state officials, deprive inmates of their constitutional rights guaranteed under the Constitution. The challenges by prisoners range from basic things such as access to law libraries, adequate food, and use of force, to more complex issues such as poor medical care and violation of their due process rights in disciplinary hearings. The volume of prisoner-initiated Section 1983 cases is substantial by any standard, and these cases have increased dramatically. During the 1960s, Riveland (1999) states, when the U.S. Supreme Court first ruled that prisoners have constitutional rights and can sue under Section 1983, there were few Section 1983 lawsuits. However, by the beginning of the 1970s, the number of Section 1983 lawsuits had increased to 3,348, whereas in 1996 the number went up to 41,592, and had it not been for the PRLA that same year, these numbers would have mushroomed by 2015 to a catastrophic caseload. In 1995, Hanson and Daley noted that one in every 30 inmates file Section 1983 lawsuits, which at today's incarceration rates would translate into 76,000 cases per year. However, this catastrophic volume of cases was prevented by correctional administrators alerting the courts to frivolous lawsuits, and the fact that Congress agreed with them, thus bringing about the regulation of prisoner lawsuits. The surge in Section 1983 cases had a direct effect on correctional management as these cases require the correctional administrators named in the suit to defend the allegations against their management style and institutional policies. So the wealth of Section 1983 lawsuits created a demand from the court that correctional administrators examine existing policies and protocols and change as needed to enhance the professionalism of correctional staff and improve conditions of confinement. These adjustments, however, usually translate into an increased demand on future budgets. For example, the adjustments required to battle tuberculosis include improved air circulation and quality, better medical care, and reduction of crowding. All these things call for budget increases, especially the last demand, which would require the state to allocate more of its budget to building new correctional facilities.

Writ of Mandamus

A writ of mandamus is not a new legal challenge. Rather, it is simply a judicial order from a superior court to an inferior governmental agency requesting its compliance with the previously handed down judicial orders and instructions. Specifically, writ of mandamus (i.e., order or command) is a direct instruction that a person or persons (in this context, correctional officials) comply with already established legal orders. After federal or state courts make rulings that give inmates certain benefits or rights yet correctional officials fail to comply, inmates may sue to have these rules or regulations enforced. To comply with such writs, new correctional polices have been developed and adopted, as discussed earlier in this chapter. While correctional administrators were not initially happy to comply with such demands and court orders, they reached a point at which they could no longer ignore the fact that their environments are changing, and thus learned to accept such legal orders as drivers of change. As described in the opening quote of this chapter by Reginald Wilkinson, wardens and correctional administrators have become more policy-oriented than they were prior to the hands-on era, which led to an overall change in the number of writ of mandamus. While in some states the volume of such writs decreased, in others it rose. Such difference is a direct by-product of local correctional state departments level of compliance with judiciary orders, and their responsiveness to court ordered policies.

The National Institute of Correction: Correctional Response to Legal and Political Pressure

Norman Carlson, former director of the Federal Bureau of Prisons, noted that correctional practices changed dramatically after the Attica prison riot in 1971, which brought the conditions of confinement to the attention of the public. In one interview, Carlson argued that the events prompted the politicization of corrections and turned the attention of elected politicians to correctional management and policies, which became a "safe subject to campaign on" (as cited in Riveland, 1999: 172). One of the political responses was the establishment of the *National Institute of Corrections (NIC)*, with a stated mission to provide technical assistance and advice to state and local correctional departments (National Institute of Corrections, n.d.). About a decade later, in 1980, Congress passed the *Civil Rights of Institutionalized Persons Act (CRIPA)* to provide a legal basis for federal involvement in litigation that challenges conditions of confinement and treatment inside correctional institutions. The CRIPA further established federal operational standards for state and local correctional institutions in an attempt to protect the civil rights of incarcerated individuals. As such, the CRIPA demonstrated a genuine governmental interest in improving conditions of confinement, while also planting the seed of correctional management. Specifically, the act authorizes the use of Department of Justice resources to challenge confinement conditions that are horrendous or flagrant enough to deprive inmates of any rights, privileges, or immunities secured or protected by the Constitution of the United States (Feeley & Swearingen, 2003). Through the passage of the CRIPA, Congress signaled that correctional institutions nationwide should take a strong interest in management and its compliance with constitutional safeguards, or risk being subjected to governmental oversight. The CRIPA also legitimized the role of the courts in pressing for improvements in the management of such institutions. However, the CRIPA has never been used vigorously, although its deterrent effect is surely felt, as it does have the ability to impose far-reaching changes in correctional institutions nationwide. Nonetheless, that deterrent effect is not so strong that it dissolved all litigation, so there are still numerous cases of Eighth Amendment violations brought before federal judges regarding insufficient medical care and inhumane confinement conditions, as discussed in both chapters that dealt with the Eighth Amendment.

Conclusion

Prison administration has changed dramatically over the past few decades. If two decades ago the warden was the ultimate authority of everything that went on in a prison or jail, wardens now must manage a complex personnel system, overcrowded institutions, and technological advances, all with increased public and political scrutiny and close legal oversight (Riveland, 1999). This has had a strong effect on all correctional personnel and administrators. Yet one of the more important lessons learned from riots such as the one at Attica is that correctional administrators and their style of organizational management are crucial when it comes to reducing institutional frictions that can later lead to litigation (DiIulio, 1991). As courts began to oversee the correctional system, many facilities introduced new standards that changed the operational systems across the United States, improving physical conditions and equipping staff to deal with new medical challenges (such as tuberculosis, hepatitis, and HIV/AIDS) as well as mentally ill inmates and other medical issues. Although such concerns are far from resolved, court intervention was a major breakthrough, and many jurisdictions have complied simply to ward off further intrusion by the courts.

The passage of the CRIPA in 1980, and the PLRA (in 1996), along with a close legal oversight by state and federal supreme courts, helped strengthen prisoners' rights but also strengthened prison administration and supported those who work in correctional institutions. In fact, forcing correctional institutions to adhere to legal standards and uphold more civil and humane conditions benefitted not only the inmates but also institutions, as it enhanced their ability to control those residing within its walls. Stronger prison organization, under a rational-legal bureaucratic regime, resulted in a better delivery of punishment and the administration and execution of justice. This has been understood by all parties involved — inmates, correctional professionals and administrators, lawyers and judges. Unfortunately, increased incarceration numbers and subsequent overcrowding is threatening to jeopardize past achievements, taking correctional administrations and court involvement back to the end of the 1980s to revisit once-resolved issues. According to the former Federal Bureau of Prisons director Norman Carlson, the enormous growth in prison population escalated and exasperated all the problems that previous litigations aimed to solve (as cited in Riveland, 1999). Evidence of this may be seen in the *Brown v. Plata*, discussed earlier in this book. This case cited the Eighth Amendment clause of cruel and unusual punishment to fix California's overcrowded prisons, which had prevented inmates from receiving adequate mental-health treatment. This brings us back to Chapter 2, in which we discussed the pendulum of court intervention in correctional management. Once again, we are witnessing a shift away from the policy brought on by the PLRA, which limited prisoners' access to the courts by requiring them to address their grievances within their correctional institutions. Now we are seeing renewed court intervention as programs and opportunities become scarcer in correctional institutions as a result of overcrowding, legislation, and a hostile political climate against prisoners that limits budgets.

Discussion Questions

1. Describe the overall effect of prisoner litigation and judicial involvement in correctional management. What are the main benefits achieved by such litigation? How has it helped develop modern correctional systems and how they administer administration punishment?

2. What effects have prisoner litigation had on the authority of correctional managers? Was the effect negative, positive, or both? Explain.

3. What is the bureaucratic paradox that Gottschalk describes, and how may it help us better understand prisoner litigation?

4. How does Goffman's description of formal and informal levels of operation help us understand the competing interests inside total institutions, such as prison, as they relate to prisoner litigation?

5. Why is it difficult for correctional administrators to uphold the highest constitutional standards in their institutions? Discuss the unique characteristics of individuals and institutional environments and their effect on the daily dynamics inside.

6. Some argue that federal judges have assumed the role of correctional policymakers. Discuss this argument while explaining the shift from rule enforcers to correctional reformers.

7. According to Feeley and Swearingen, correctional institutions became more bureaucratic during the "hands-on" era. What role did the federal judicial system play in this transformation, and how was it perceived as better serving justice and the goals of punishment?

8. Discuss the negative effects of bureaucratization on correctional institutions and their ability to uphold the goals of corrections—mainly to manage, control, confine, and administer sentences.

9. How did the judicial interference in correctional matters affect correctional administrators' managerial style and focus? Discuss the shifting challenges in the face of rising demands for additional resources.

10. What are the managerial challenges associated with increased incarceration rates, and how may this rise put a new burden on the judicial system?

11. According to Kenneth McGinnis, former director of the Michigan Department of Corrections, the increasing coast of correctional management jeopardizes the effectiveness of correctional services. What are some of the issues that McGinnis refers to, and how are they exacerbated by high rates of incarceration?

12. What is the circular effect of prisoner litigation? In your opinion, does prisoner litigation, along with judicial intervention, have the ability to improve conditions of confinement in the long run?

13. Discuss the importance of Section 1983 in prisoner litigation. What are the legislative and Constitutional premises associated with Section 1983?

14. Discuss the importance of *writs of mandamus*, and how such writs contribute to change in the correctional environment.

15. How did external political pressure affect the correctional industry? In your opinion, has such pressure improved the American correctional system? Explain.

List of Cases Cited

Brown v. Plata, 2011. 131 S. Ct. 1910.

Hudson v. Palmer, 1984. 468 U.S. 517.

Shaw v. Murphy, 2001. 532 U.S. 223.

Chapter 15

Conclusion:
The Importance of Judiciary
Involvement in Correctional
Management

Prison policies can limit the constitutional rights of prisoners, so long as these limits can be justified logically and rationally as supporting a legitimate penological interest. As discussed through the pages of this book, the complex relationship between the courts and correctional management has helped reshape corrections and forms of punishment in the decades that followed the Attica riot. Prior to the 1970s, judges followed a "hands-off" doctrine, allowing correctional administrators to run their facilities as they saw fit and avoiding interference in how correctional facilities were managed. But the years that followed changed that approach. Yet the courts also acknowledge that they cannot always impose their opinions and policies on correctional administrators, at least not without recognizing them as the authority in their correctional domains, as they are the ones who run the facilities and are the front line of the penological enterprise. A somewhat recent example of this dynamic is found in the case of *Giano v. Senkowski*, which examined whether prison administration could censor seminude photos sent to an inmate by his wife. The Court's decision in favor of the prison administration empowered correctional officials as holders of the final word on how prisons should be managed and operated. Citing the reasoning established in *Turner v. Safley* in 1987, the Court ruled that if prison officials are to justify practices that would in free society be deemed unconstitutional, they must prove the following four conditions: (1) a rational connection between the prison regulation and the reason put forward to justify it; (2) alternative means of exercising the right; (3) a situation wherein accommodating the right would have a negative impact on guards and other inmates; and (4) an absence of reasonable alternative to the regulation. Further affirmation was found in the case of *Goff v. Nix*, in which the Court determined that mandatory visual body cavity searches after visitation are reasonably related to legitimate security goals of the facility and that such a search outweighs the Fourteenth Amendment privacy rights that prisoners may otherwise have. These cases were not decided in a vacuum, but were a by-product of almost two decades of legal and political ping-pong in which the courts directed correctional officials to develop more sustainable policies and procedures, while advancing the correctional profession and consequent professionalism.

Yet, the effect of judicial intervention in correctional management has not always been so smooth and positive. Long periods of struggle between the courts and state correctional administrators have sometimes resulted in worsening relations between the courts and state department of corrections, as with the Texas Department of Corrections (TDC) during the years following the decade-plus-long case of *Ruiz v. Estelle*, which was finally decided in 1980 and set the standards for minimum mental-health care. As you recall *Ruiz v. Estelle* dealt with the *totality of confinement conditions* and found that the TDC had violated constitutional rights of prisoners guaranteed under the Eight Amendment. As a result of this case, the judiciary appointed a special master to ensure that the TDC would comply and operate its prisons in accordance with constitutional principles (see Anderson, Mangels & Dyson, 2010). As discussed in the previous chapter, the explosion of prisoner litigation during the "hands-on" period forced many states to reevaluate their modes of operations. Judges were interested in making change, but also understood the limits of correctional administrators, and gave them some leeway. The fruits of all this discourse was some success in changing the organization operations at correctional institutions. These changes took place gradually, as the learning period was lengthy.

While prisoner litigation and judicial intervention had an effect on actual conditions of confinement, other cases made it clear that prisoners necessarily lose some of the conveniences of a free society once convicted and placed behind bars. *Wilson v. Seiter*, which addressed conditions of confinement, was a case in which the Supreme Court emphasized that the conditions of confinement may be restrictive and harsh, but they are part of the penalty that convicted offenders ought to pay for their offenses against society. A similar Supreme Court opinion from the same year, *Johansen v. Ozim*, reiterated that comfort and convenience are not elements that need be supplied to incarcerated offenders. Justice Warren Burger stated that federal judges should not be dealing with prisoners' often minor complaints; any well-run institution should be able to resolve them fairly, without the involvement of the courts (as cited in Clear & Cole, 1997). In other cases, the courts have also made it clear that incarcerated individuals should not expect to enjoy all constitutional rights that are the domain of free individuals. As James Q. Wilson (1975) argued, the function of the correctional system should be to isolate and to punish, which by default provides inmates with unfavorable conditions and deprivation of some rights. For example, in *United States v. Hitchcock*, the Ninth Circuit Court of Appeals held that prisoners should not have a reasonable expectation of privacy or Fourth Amendment protections against unreasonable searches and seizures in their prison cells. Further affirming the limitation of prisoners' constitutional rights, *Hewitt v. Helms* was a Supreme Court ruling that within the context of correctional settings, due process may be limited by the needs of the facility. The judgment identified the safety of guards and other inmates as the most fundamental responsibility of prison administration, and this responsibility outweighs due process claims. Examining such cases, Wright (1973) identifies an apparent paradox within correctional institutions. He describes this as *liberal totalitarianism*, in which all-controlling correctional institutions seemingly adopt a very progressive approach to dealing with prisoners. Correctional institutions, as their name suggest, promote the goal of "correcting" (rehabilitating) offenders, yet they exert totalitarian control over inmates' movements and every other aspect of their daily lives, all for the greater good of public safety. Even through their seemingly liberal programs, correctional institutions serve to control the prisoner population in a totalitarian manner, requiring, for example, urine and blood tests and strict adherence and compliance to rules and standards for continued participation. Prisoner litigation can be viewed as another part of this liberal totalitarianism. Prisoners have the right to challenge their oppressive environment through litigation—the very definition of playing by the rules—whereas the controlling system of the administration and the courts helps maintain the status quo of such institutions as agencies of control, as long as the prisoners actions are viewed in a professional manner and justifying their final decisions on the basis of the revered aim of public safety.

As noted earlier in this book, the courts are more likely to decide issues regarding prison safety and regulation in favor of prison administrators. Such was the case in *Block v. Rutherford*, in which the Supreme Court stated that courts "should play a very limited role since such considerations are peculiarly within the province and professional expertise of corrections officials." This suggests that the courts allow prison administrators great discretion in managing their facilities and the inmate population that resides within them. This is all the more true when the issues brought before the courts relate to safety and security. DiIulio (1991: 33) reinforces this notion by stating that it is up to correctional managers and their managing style to ensure that their facilities are safe and civilized. Specifically, he argues that "whether prisons and jails are safe and civilized, on the one hand, or riotous and wretched, on the other, depends mainly on how they are organized and managed—on what corrections officials at all levels think and do, and on how ... they coordinate their activities around the fundamental task of handling incarcerated citizens." Therefore, no combination of political, legal, architectural, or any other external intervention in corrections can improve correctional management unless correctional administrators are strong leaders who uphold the policies and adequately organize and manage their facilities. In fact, DiIulio further argues that difference in character of organization and management style explains most, if not all, variances in prison conditions, regardless of their level of overcrowding or how recently a facility was constructed or last renovated.

Regardless of the courts' decisions and involvement in correctional management, it is now clear to all correctional professionals that prisoner litigation and court decisions have helped shaped current correctional policies and practices. It did so as a reactive problem-solving mechanism that grew out of practical experience (Garland, 2001). It is also what Michel Foucault (1977) explains as an emerging response not to reflect an idea of reform but rather than to reflect changes in social institutions and governmental power. Such changes were best ordered by the courts in the name of the most sacred document in the United States, the Constitution.

Understanding Legal Challenges of Inmates: Punitiveness in a Political Context

Sentencing offenders is a political act. It represents the use of physical force by the government to control the lives of those who have violated a government's rules and laws (Wright, 1973). Similarly, prisons, in any political system, are the enforcers of the state's penological policies, and as such, they have a mandate to protect the existing social order by controlling those who defy it. To this end, sentencing has become an increasingly political issue in the past 40 years, as legislators have gained more control over the length of sentences and other related policies. This control is a result of the perceived increase in crime, as portrayed by the media and exacerbated by politicians who have called for tightening punitive policies in the name of public safety (Bottoms, 1995; Garland, 2001; Pizzarro, Stenius, & Pratt, 2006).

For most incarcerated individuals, the authority of the correctional system has no democratic legitimacy, so they perceive prison administrators and staff as aggressors in a totalitarian regime. This view, by itself, is the preliminary condition that legitimizes prisoner lawsuits against various aspects of the criminal justice system, and in particular, against correctional practices, where due process may be less visible than it is in other criminal justice practices. However, some argue that prisoners make use of the judicial system not necessarily to improve the conditions of their confinement or to negotiate their status, but in an attempt to show contempt and disrespect toward correctional officials and the legal system (DeWolf, 1996).

If we are to lean on certain aspects of the traditional strain theory, as explained by Merton in his famous strain theory (Merton, 1938), then those individuals who cannot achieve the goals of society will rebel against it and develop and engage in illegitimate activities to achieve the goals or simply retreat and give up all together. For incarcerated individuals, the goal is freedom, or at least to feel they are still free. It is also a manifestation of their desire to rebel against the capitalist upper class, and against the criminal justice system, which they view as the oppressor. Most incarcerated individuals tend to perceive the power base for correctional authority as the outside middle-class and free society (Wright, 1973). This is achieved by using the external legal system to challenge prison authority and the government that is perceived as captivator. It is inmates' way to challenge, rebel, and beat the system (Steinmann, 1999); it is crucial for them not to lose hope and retreat into despair. At the same time, challenging the system using normative means, such as the legal system, becomes an important component of their rehabilitation and a crucial step toward future release and reintegration. By filing lawsuits, incarcerated individuals learn to use legitimate means to improve their personal situation, and amend various perceived wrongdoings by the correctional system and further by the government. Such a process adds to the transformation of those individuals who previously did not obey or follow the rules.

Allowing prisoners to engage in petitioning their conditions of incarceration to the government through the use of the courts is in and of itself an important constitutional right guaranteed under the First Amendment. In that regard, prisoners are signaled, in a way, that although they are being punished for their wrongdoing, they are still members of a democratic society and their well-being is not neglected.

As discussed earlier in this book, court involvement in correctional management may be viewed as a swinging pendulum. These changes reflect the penological ideology in which such decisions were made. It is not surprising that during times of unrest and social upheaval, practices will be challenged for their aims and outcomes. It is also no wonder that the emergence of new criminological and penological theories that reflect and capture social change will have an effect on the courts' involvement and on how prisons are managed and run. DiIulio (1991) argues that the radical shift in judicial philosophy brought about a "shotgun wedding" between the courts and corrections, and was a result of the political appointment of many liberal activist judges who pushed the correctional pendulum toward a more hands-on approach to the management of correctional facilities. Such liberal judges took it upon themselves to bring change to local and state correctional facilities by aggressively enforcing sweeping changes in the country's penal system. These judges received strong support from the *American Civil Liberties Union* (ACLU) that gained increasing leverage during the second half of the 1960s and the early 1970s.

It is nonetheless true that fundamental change in any correctional system, be it local, state, or federal, must involve legislative alteration or reversal of previously existing penological policies, policies that are a result of political negotiation. The courts, argues Smith (1973), cannot simply change the way in which correctional facilities manage themselves and run their operation without the proper backing of the political arena. Changes in penological climate and correctional policies are in direct response to a high level of publicity—such as the one experienced in Attica during and after the riot—that demanded legislatures to enact some kind of change in the prison system. Yet change cannot be accomplished without proper activist groups, such as the civil rights activists and other prison reform interest groups, demanding change. Accordingly, most judges who have presided over correctional cases have approached institutional penal reform cases with the approach that court intervention in correctional management is a necessary evil (DiIulio, 1991). In granting a motion for summary judgment, justices hearing a case in the Seventh Circuit Court of Appeals stated in *Harris v. Flemming* that while judges are not wardens, they must act as guardians of the constitution even for people who reside within prison walls, and they must intervene when the constitutional rights of incarcerated individuals are infringed upon. Such judicial intervention forces the courts to become active players, and federal judges to make sure that such unconstitutional conditions will not manifest again. However, any change that will come of such a process will not be in contradiction to a political agenda that may be perceived as weak on crime, or endangering public safety. Thus, while court intervention in correctional management seems to be interested in protecting the constitutional rights of convicted individuals confined to correctional institutions, this concern still needs to acknowledge public sentiments and maintain the delicate balance between public outcry, politicians' demagoguery of fear from increasing crime rates, and basic human rights.

Judicial Intervention and Correctional Management

Prisoner litigation has had a major effect on correctional management and administration. More specifically, the pendulum of court involvement in correctional management, discussed in Chapter 2, drove correctional administrators and staff to develop better policies and management practices, which has reshaped the correctional landscape from the 1970s until the present day. By doing so, the shift of the pendulum also had an effect on the way in which correctional officials viewed the goals of punishment and how they administered those punishments. We cannot ignore the effects of prisoner litigation on the shift in goals of punishments and trends in punitive philosophies. As mentioned earlier in this book, litigation using Section 1983 challenges the conditions of confinement as well as the discriminatory correctional practices in lieu of violation of basic civil rights. Such litigation is expected to gain further momentum as prison population increases and is characterized by a disproportionate number of African Americans and Hispanic individuals. Indeed, this expected increase has been observed since 2010, but coming days will show the effect of this increase on actual prisoner litigation. It is also possible that our corrections system will face international challenges of human rights (Whitty, 2011) violations that target our increasing incarceration rates; rates which are the highest in the world (Feeley & Swearingen, 2003). These challenges will, without a doubt, require our judiciary system to reevaluate our goals of punishment and the corresponding punitive policies as they are currently practiced.

The PLRA of 1996 placed some restraints on prisoner litigation and in many aspects, caused the pendulum to shift in the direction of the "hands-off" era. Although the PLRA did not terminate prisoners' access to the courts, the legislation shifted some of the powers back to correctional administrators, who by that time had become more professionalized and adhered more to clear policies. In many ways, such shift may be seen as a signal from the courts that correctional officials, administrators, and staff are capable of handling their institutions and the individuals confined within them. It may also be seen as an acknowledgment that those in the field of corrections should enjoy more public and legislative trust in the delivery of punishment. However, if judges are to intervene in correctional matters, they should do so in a judicious manner. This should be done by advancing changes in incremental steps while trying not to step on the toes of experienced correctional administrators, who, after all, understand correctional institutions better and know them from the ground up. As DiIulio (1991: 176) states, judges "must seek to reform, not to revolutionize, the institutions ...". Further, if judges wish to engage in the reform of correctional environments and how correctional institutions are managed, they would be wise to descend from the height of their judicial bench and observe firsthand what correctional management is all about. DiIulio (1991) further suggests that judicial intervention must take into consideration the complex dynamics of correctional organizations and management.

DiIulio's Views of Judicial Intervention

We have already established that the pendulum of court intervention in correctional management is swinging in response to changes in the political climate that have affected penological ideologies and practices, and reflects public sentiments toward crime and social response to it. Yet such a swing of the pendulum is of great importance for students of corrections, as court intervention has consequences on the safety, civility, and cost-effectiveness of correctional environments in terms of institutional safety, civility and cost-effectiveness. It is in this context that John DiIulio, in *No Escape: The Future of American Corrections* (1991), presents three basic schools of thought on the impact of judicial intervention on correctional practices and institutions:

> One thought argues that judges are responsible for the increase in institutional violence, as their interference in correctional management upset the informal order keeping arrangements among prisoners and between prisoners and staff. Specifically, by intervening in what is going on inside correctional facilities, judges signal to inmates that they are entitled and should challenge the system. Citing Engel and Rothman (1983), DiIulio argues that such an approach undermines the complex relationships among inmates that help maintain order and solidarity.
>
> The second thought holds that activist liberal judges have forced correctional administrators and practitioners to make sure that constitutional rights of the incarcerated are being secured. Under this approach, federal judges do not aim to interfere with the way in which correctional institutions and facilities are managed and run, but rather are using their power to force prison administrators to operate in ways that secure prisoners' rights and well-being. Indeed, such an approach seems to have support among many correctional scholars, who can point to the many improvements that were introduced to the prison environment as a result of federal court decisions. For instance, we can now identify better delivery of medical and mental-health services, and more acknowledgements of prisoners with special needs, as discussed earlier in this book.
>
> The last thought believes that the courts have encouraged correctional workers and in particular administrators to become more professional and manage their facilities in greater compliance with transparent policies and procedures. Such a view led to the bureaucratization of correctional institutions, which made jails and prisons more orderly and humane. This view is strongly supported by the work of Feeley and Swearingen (2003), as discussed in greater detail in the previous chapter. Further, in its end result, this last view is not that different from the second approach.

No matter what view one holds of the effect of judicial intervention on correctional practices, an agreement exists that judicial intervention (and the funds required to make needed reforms) have exerted additional pressure on already limited correctional budgets. Yet, such an agreement is lacking on the cost-effectiveness of such budgetary increases. One thing is certain: judicial intervention brought with it more profes-sionalism in response to an increased demand for services and improved conditions, which made correctional officers' work more challenging as they are required to adhere to higher professional standards. Judicial intervention also changed the correctional profession and correctional institutions forever. If such change is good or bad is hard to tell. As one of the new trends in criminal justice calls for evidence-based practices, and similarly the measurement of the effectiveness of prisoners' litigation on correc-tional operations is overdue. Correctional scholars ought to clearly identify the aims of punishment and how these aims are being addressed by the courts, and in turn, how such aims are being implemented from the courts to corrections. Only then will we be able to clearly identify the full magnitude of judicial intervention in correctional administration and the management of facilities and prisoners. With this in mind, it is important to acknowledge that judicial intervention in corrections is all but im-possible to control in a pure experimental design. Judges' characteristics and the effect of external media on public opinion may pose some serious methodological issues when it comes to isolating the effect of a specific court ruling and cases on correctional management and reform.

Race and Its Effect on Prisoners' Litigation and Correctional Management

The two-decades-long increase in prison population, from the middle of the 1980s till around 2005, reflects the racial segregation that existed in the United States many years ago (Alexander, 2012). Alexander further argues that mass incarceration in the United States emerged as a stunningly comprehensive and well-disguised system of racialized social control that functions in a manner strikingly similar to Jim Crow. As such, prisons have a long history of maintaining and perpetuating segregation and racial discrimination. Indeed, a report that was published in 1971 — entitled *Struggle for Justice* — brought awareness of the discriminatory use of power to punish, via incarceration, and repress Blacks, the poor, and other cultural minorities (Garland, 2001). It is within this context that we must examine the potential effect of dispro-portionate incarceration rates of racial minorities on the conditions of confinement, the litigations that result from them, and the corresponding correctional policies and management. Jacobs (1979: 1) argues that since the late 1950s, race relations have precipitated enormous changes in prisoner subcultures and in prison organization. Jacobs argues that "Black Muslims challenged the hegemony of White officials and prisoners and their legal activism led to the intervention of the federal courts in prison administration." Indeed, racial discrimination in correctional facilities was one of the main sparks that fueled prison riots during the late 1960s and early 1970s, of which the Attica riot was the most notorious and brought about massive change in litigation and correctional management. Today, prisons capture such racial and religious po-larization and conflict even more, as the dominance of African Americans, Hispanics, and other inner-city dwellers representing racial minorities now constitute the majority of state prison populations. Such a grim picture receives further support from Marc Mauer (2006) who, in his well-known book titled *Race to Incarcerate*, suggests that the entire increase in prison population between 1980 and 2001 can be explained by changes in sentencing policy that targeted inner-city minority populations. This disproportionate representation of minorities in our prison system, without a doubt, is expected to challenge the Constitution (Riveland, 1999), and in particular the Eighth Amendment clause of cruel and unusual punishment, as more minorities from poor inner-city neighborhoods are disproportionally sentenced to longer confinement periods, some without the possibility of parole. Consequently, prisoner race relations cannot be separated from the racial context that exists within our nation's prison system, the racial context in which all the actors in the prison organization relate to one another, and in which correctional practices are carried out. Unfortunately, nowadays racial discrimination is not in the past; it is very much alive, and threatens to widen social cleavages.

Conclusion: A Penological Context

Today's prisons are a result and reflection of the many permutations of social change, fear of crime, and consequent get-tough policies. The development of supermax facilities is a prime example of the shift in cultural sensibility in American society toward greater punitiveness (Pizzaro et al., 2006). It seems that we have long neglected the other goals of punishment—mainly rehabilitation and restoration—as we became more concerned with sheer revenge and deterrence. Overcrowded prisons have become the norm in most states, and these institutions reflect the falsely perceived yet politically promoted fear of crime. The skyrocketing correctional population is the direct result of losing faith in the rehabilitation of individual offenders and communities, faith that gave way to long mandatory sentences and abolishment of parole, and dangerous risk assessment models that demand prison officials and administrators toughen standards and existing confinement environments. Wilson (1975: 173) argued that the weakening rehabilitative ideology "is also a frank admission that society really does not know how to do much else," and that any investment in social welfare policies would not reduce crime, and thus the one governmental resource that could address the crime problem is a wise administration of imprisonment. These changes in the scope of imprisonment and confinement conditions have contributed to the increase in problems within correctional facilities, making their management more difficult and dangerous (Wooldredge, Griffin, & Pratt, 2001). An increase in problems and a reduction in safety and services also translates into more lawsuits, federal oversight, and other challenges for correctional administrators (Haney, 2003; Riveland, 1999). The specter of rehabilitation failures haunts modern criminology and penology and causes many to believe that nothing else really works in corrections (Braithwaite & Mugford, 1994). Not surprisingly, the past 40 years of correctional enterprise are characterized by an enormous change in penal policies as well as in court intervention. Such changes reflect not just how the public, policy makers, politicians, and correctional administrators think and respond to crime and punishment, but also how penologists attribute the shift in penal policy to factors such as the decline in rehabilitation and the politicization of crime control and the commercialization of correctional facilities (Caplow & Simon, 1999; Feeley & Simon, 1992; Garland, 2001; Roberts et al., 2002; Pizzaro et al., 2006).

Indeed, new managerial styles and policies that reflect false public sentiments about crime came to govern correctional policies and practices. Specifically, the neglect of the rehabilitative ideal while at the same time the increased fear of crime, with the subsequent war on drugs, had a detrimental effect not only on the public but also on criminologists and penologists, who were raised to show what does not work in corrections. Such approaches and attitudes have been dysfunctional to correctional practices and management (Cullen & Gendreau, 2001). Feeley and Simon (1992) further argued that such changes in correctional policies were a very negative development in criminal justice and penological practices. According to Feeley and Simon, who dubbed their developmental observations *"new penology,"* the techniques of identifying, classifying, and managing groups of offenders according to their perceived dangerousness result in neglect of other, more important punitive goals, and is expected to inspire a renewed flood of prisoner litigation that will challenge such practices. Not only will such penological approaches have an effect on sentencing policies and practices (Bottoms, 1995; Marvel, 1995; Tonry, 1987), these approaches will also have a detrimental effect on the operation of prisons through the increase of bureaucracy, as discussed in the previous chapter.

Penological research suggests that the shift in crime prevention politics and consequent sentencing policies toward tougher penal policies have gained overwhelming popularity. It seems that in recent years we have abandoned rehabilitation, or any real effort to genuinely "correct" offenders' behavior. Thus, the weakening of rehabilitation, as part of the penological discussion, forced our policies to become more vengeful and as such more punitive than ever before. With the self-fulfilling belief that rehabilitation is a lost cause, Cullen and Gendreau (2000) argue that, it is no wonder that our current correctional policies and practices bring prisoners' confinement conditions into the spotlight and as a result to the restoration of judicial involvement in correctional institutions. We have seen such involvement in recent years with the PREA and the recent, 2011, court order to release 40,000 prisoners from the California prison system due to overcrowding and violation of the Eighth Amendment. Pizzaro and her colleagues (2006: 17) further suggest that such punitive popularity became visible via the mushrooming of supermax prisons across the country. Specifically, they argue that "[d]uring the past 3 decades, the United States has experienced a shift in the purpose of the prison: the decline in the rehabilitation ideal and the adoption of a retributive discourse that emphasizes managerial efficacy and controlling the unruly." Such a punitive political climate, characterized by massive incarceration, overcrowded prisons, and dilapidated confinement conditions, along with the increased visibility of special needs populations behind bars, as discussed in Chapter 13, will most likely result in the judicial pendulum swinging once more, forcing the courts to further examine conditions of confinement and sentencing policies (see Simon, 1999). Within this context, Steinmann (1999) suggests that the longer sentences that are now the norm will further create a climate susceptible to prisoner litigation, in an attempt to challenge their conditions of confinement. With longer sentences and the options of litigating and filing Section 1983 suits, prisoners have something to help pass the time of their confinement. Such a litigation climate becomes possible in the wake of civil rights movements and activists. It seems that the wheel has completed a full cycle, as we are experiencing a reemergence of civil rights activism and unrest. One important development in the past several months of 2016 is that of the Black Lives Matter movement; this movement is responsible for bringing civil rights and racial disparity issues into public discourse again. It is too early to predict the effects of these events, but they have the potential to stimulate another wave of change. However, any change to come will not be possible without congressional support. Judiciary involvement in correctional management and punitive policies will not be able to drive a meaningful change and proper legislation that address current and pressing issues of sentencing, and their intentional goals. In his last few years in office, President Barack Obama addressed the pain caused by mandatory sentences and their effect on overcrowded correctional facilities, and promised to address the dire situation. Yet at the time of writing this book, not much is happening, and after the presidential elections of November 2016, the future seems grimmer than ever before. As a society we must convey to our representatives that simply locking people away and shunning them from society is not the only way to deal with the crime problem. There are many other ways, better ways, to deal with offenders in a manner that will also benefit their communities and our overall society.

Discussion Questions

1. Discuss the potential effects of judicial interference on correctional management and policies.

2. What effect did the cases of *Giano v. Senkowski* and *Turner v. Safely* have on correctional management?

3. Why are the cases of *Wilson v. Seiter* and *Johansen v. Ortiz* different in the landscape of judicial intervention in correctional practices? Discuss the penological aspect that is associated with this case.

4. Discuss the term "liberal totalitarianism." How does it relate to some of the cases discussed in this chapter (e.g., *Hewitt v. Helms*, *United States v. Hitchcock*, *Wilson v. Seiter*, and *Johansen v. Ortiz*), and how are they serving the penological goal of rehabilitation?

5. According to the premise of liberal totalitarianism, what is the rationale for prisoner litigation?

6. Discuss the effects of sociopolitical climate on prisoner litigation and judicial involvement in correctional management. What are some of the main sociopo-

litical forces that drove the courts to reestablish a "hands-on" approach for correctional issues?

7. Explain the desire of incarcerated individuals to challenge correctional administrators and the system by litigating its officials. How do Merton's modes of adaptation help us understand the social process that is associated with such litigation?

8. What does DiIulio mean by suggesting that the shift in judicial intervention in the correctional management is like a "shotgun wedding"?

9. Discuss DiIulio's views of judicial intervention in correctional management. Specifically, how does judicial intervention affect correctional professionalism, and the manner in which prisons are currently managed?

10. Discuss the effects of mass incarceration on racial tensions and the effect it had on prisoner litigation and judicial involvement in correctional management. In your opinion, will racial disparity inside correctional institutions provoke more litigation from prisoners? Explain.

11. Discuss the effect of the shift in perceived penological ideology on prisoner litigation and judicial intervention in correctional management. What effect did the punitive sentences that have dominated judicial decisions and sentencing since the 1980s have on conditions of confinement? Can they predict a new wave of prisoner litigation?

List of Cases Cited

Block v. Rutherford, 1984 468 U.S. 576.

Giano v. Senkowski, 1995. 54 F. 3d 1050.

Goff v. Nix, 1997. 113 F.3d 887.

Harris v. Flemming, 1988. 839, F.2d 1232.

Hewitt v. Helms, 1983. 459 U.S. 460.

Johnsen v. Ozim, 1991. 804 S.W.2d 179.

Ruiz v. Estelle, 1980. 503 F. Supp. 1265.

Turner v. Safley, 1987. 482 U.S. 78.

Wilson, v. Seiter, 1991. 501 U.S. 294.

References

Abadinsky, H. (2008). Probation and parole: Theory and practice. (9th Edition). Upper Saddle River, NJ: Pearson Publication.

Abadinsky, H. (2013). Probation and parole: Theory and practice. (13th edition). Upper Saddle River, NJ: Pearson Publication.

Aday, R., & Krabill J.J. (2013). Older and geriatric offenders: Critical issues for the 21st century. In: Gideon, L. (ed.), 203–32, *Special Needs Offenders in Correctional Institutions*. Thousand Oaks, CA: Sage Publishing.

Aday, R. H. (1994). Golden Years Behind Bars: Special Programs and Facilities for Elderly Inmates. *Federal Probation*, 23, 162–172.

Aday, R. H. (2003). *Aging Prisoners: Crisis in American Corrections*. Westport, CT: Praeger.

Aday, R. H., & Webster, E. L. (1979). Aging in prison: The development of a preliminary model. *Journal of Offender Rehabilitation*, 3(3), 271–82.

Adler, F., Mueller, G.O.W., and Laufer, W.S. (2006). Criminal Justice: An Introduction. New York: McGraw Hill.

Amar, A.R. (1994). Fourth Amendment First Principles. *Harvard Law Review* 107(4): 757–819.

Anderson, J.F., Mangels, N.J., & Dyson, L. (2010). *Significant prisoner rights cases*. Durham, NC: Carolina Academic Press.

Andrews, D. A., & Bonta, J. (2000). The level of service inventory-revised. Toronto, Canada: Multi-Health Systems.

Arrigo, B. (2002). Transcarceration: A constructive ethnology of mentally ill offenders. The Prison Journal, 81(2), 162–186.

Baldus, D.C., Pulaski, C., & Woodworth, G. (1983). Comparative review of death sentences: An empirical study of the Georgia experience. *Journal of Criminal Law and Criminology*, 74(3): 661–753.

Ball, E.F. (1978). Good Faith and the Fourth Amendment: The "Reasonable Exception to the Exclusionary Rule." *The Journal of Criminal Law & Criminology*, 69(4): 635–657.

Barak-Glantz, I. L. (1981). Toward a conceptual schema of prison management styles. *The Prison Journal*, 61(2), 42–60.

Barkel, S. (1986). Prison reform litigation: has the revolution gone too far? *Judicature* 70(1), 1–8.

Barnes, R. (2008). High Court Reject Death for Child Rape: Penalty Reserved for Murder and Crimes against State. *The Washington Post.* Page A01. Published on June 26.

Baunach, J. P. (1992). Critical problems of women in prison. In I.L. Moyer (Ed.), *The Changing Role of Women in the Criminal Justice System: Offenders, Victims, and Professionals* (99–112). Long Grove, IL: Waveland Press.

Bayens, G., & Ortiz-Smykla, J. (2013). Probation, Parole & Community-Based Corrections: Supervision, Treatment & Evidence-Based Practices. New York, NY: McGraw Hill Publishing.

Becker, H.S. (1963). Outsiders: Studies in the Sociology of Deviance. New York: Free Press.

Belbot, B. & Hemmens, C. (2010). *The legal rights of the convicted.* El Paso, TX: LFB Scholarly Publishing LLC.

Berman, H. J. (1986). Religion and Law: The First Amendment in Historical Perspective. Emory Law Journal, 35(4), 777–793.

Bilchik, S. (1998). A juvenile justice system for the 21st century. *Juvenile Justice Bulletin,* May 1998. Washington, DC: U.S. Office of Juvenile Justice and Delinquency Prevention.

Binswanger, I. A., Krueger, P. M., & Steiner, J. F. (2009). Prevalence of chronic medical conditions among jail and prison inmates in the United States compared with the general population. *Journal of epidemiology and community health,* 63(11), 912–919.

Bohm, R. (2003). *Death quest II: An Introduction to the Theory and Practice of Capital Punishment in the United States.* Cincinnati, OH: Anderson Publishing.

Bottoms, A. (1995). The philosophy and politics of punishment and sentencing. In Clarkson, C., & Morgan, R. (Eds.) *The politics of sentencing reform,* (Pp. 17–49). Oxford, UK: Clarendon.

Bouffard, J., Mackenzie, D., and Hickman, L., (2000). Effectiveness of vocational education and employment programs for adult offenders: A methodology-based analysis of the literature. Journal of Offender *Rehabilitation,* 31(1/2), 1–41.

Bouffard, J.A & Muftic, L.R. (2006). Program completion and recidivism outcomes among adult offenders ordered to complete community sentence. *Journal of Offender Rehabilitation,* 43(2), 1–33.

Braithwaite, J. (1989). Crime, Shame and Reintegration. Cambridge University Press. New York.

Braithwaite, J., and Mugford, S. (1994). "Conditions of Successful Reintegration Ceremonies: Dealing with Juvenile Offenders." *British Journal of Criminology,* 34(2): 139–171.

Branham, L. S. (2013). The law and policy of sentencing and corrections in a nutshell. (9th edition). St Paul, MN: West Academic Publishing

Branham, L.S., and Hamdan, M.S. (2005). *Cases and materials on The Law and Policy of Sentencing and Corrections.* (7th Edition), Thomson/West: West publishing Company, MN.

Briar, K. H. (1983). Jails: Neglected asylums. *Social Casework.* 64(7), 387–393.

Brown, K. (2003). Managing STIs in jails. *Infectious Diseases in Corrections Report.* Providence, RI: Brown University. Retrieved August 26, 2016 from http://www.idcronline.org/archives/april05/article.html.

Bureau of Justice Statistics (2008). "Prison Statistics." Retrieved from http://www.ojp.usdoj.gov/bjs/prisons.htm Sep. 18, 2008.

Bureau of Justice Statistics (2010). "Prison Statistics." Retrieved from http://www.ojp.usdoj.gov/bjs/prisons.htm Nov. 25, 2010.

California Department of Corrections. (No date). "Visiting a Friend or Loved One in Prison." Retrieved on October 4, 2015 at: http://www.cdcr.ca.gov/visitors/docs/inmatevisitingguidelines.pdf.

Call, J.E. (1995). The Supreme Court and prisoners' rights. *Federal Probation,* 59(1), 36–46.

Caplow, T., & Simon, J. (1999). Understanding prison policy and population trends. *Crime and Justice,* 26(1), 63–120.

Carlson, P.M., & Dilulio, J.J. (2015). Organization and management of the prison. In: Carlson, P.M. (Ed.), pp. 269–84, *Prison and Jail Administration: Practice and Theory.* Burlington, MA: Jones & Bartlett Learning.

Chaiken, M. R. (1989). *In-prison Programs for Drug-involved Offenders.* Rockville, MD: National Institute of Justice.

Chavarria, F. R. (1992). Successful drug treatment in a criminal justice setting: A case study. *Federal Probation,* 56, 48–52.

Chemerinsky, E. (1995). Eliminating Discrimination in Administering the Death Penalty: The Need for the Racial Justice Act. *Santa Clara Law Review,* 35(2), 519–533.

Clear, T.R., & Cole, G.F. (1997). *American Corrections* (4th edition). Belmont, CA: Wadsworth.

Clear, T. R., Cole, G. F., & Reisig, M. D. (2009). *American Corrections* (7th Edition). Belmont, CA: Thomson/Wadsworth.

Clear, T.R., Cole, G.F. & Reisig, M.D. (2013). *American Corrections.* (10th Edition). Belmont, CA: Cengage.

Clear, T.R., Reisig, M.D. & Cole, G.F. (2016). *American Corrections.* (11th Edition). Boston, MA: Cengage.

Cole, F. (1987). The impact of Bell v. Wolfish upon prisoners' rights. Journal of Crime and Justice, 10(1), 47–69.

Coleman, D. L. (2005). Storming the Castle to Save the Children: The Ironic Costs of a Child Welfare Exception to the Fourth Amendment. *William and Mary Law Review* 47: 413–540.

Collins, W. C. (2015). Prisoner access to the courts. Carlson, P.M. (3rd ed.), *Prison and jail Administration: Practice and Theory*. Pp. 499–516. Burlington, MA: Jones & Bartlett Learning.

Cornelius, G.F. (2008). The American jail: Cornerstone of Modern Corrections. Upper Saddle River, NJ: Pearson/Prentice Hall.

Corzine-McMullan, E. (2011). Seeking medical and psychiatric attention. In L. Gideon & H. E. Sung (Eds.), *Rethinking Corrections: Rehabilitation, Reentry, and Reintegration* (253–278). Thousand Oaks, CA: Sage Publishing.

Cripe, C.A., Pearlman, M. G., & Kosiak, D. (2013). *Legal aspects of corrections management.* (3rd edition) Burlington, MA: Jones & Bartlett Publishers.

Crouch, B.M., & Marquart, J.W. (1990). Resolving the paradox of reform: Litigation, prisoner violence, and perceptions of risk. *Justice Quarterly* 7(1), 103–123.

Cullen, F. T., & Gendreau, P. (2000). Assessing correctional rehabilitation: Policy, practice, and prospects. *Criminal justice, 3*(1), 299–370.

Cullen, F.T., Agnew, R., & Wilcox, P. (2014). *Criminological theory: Past to present.* New York, NY: Oxford University Press.

Cunniff, M. A., & Bergsmann, I. R. (1990). Managing felons in the community: An administrative profile of probation. National Association of Criminal Justice Planners.

Cunniff, M. A., & Shilton, M. K. (1991). Variations on felony probation: Persons under supervision in 32 urban and suburban counties. Washington, DC: National Association of Criminal Justice Planners.

Cushman, R. C., & Sechrest, D. (1992). Variations in the administration of probation supervision. Federal Probation, 56, 19–29.

Darrow, C. (1922). *Crime: Its Cause and Treatment.* Thomas Y. Crowell Company Publishers: New York.

Davies, T.Y. (1999). Recovering the original Fourth Amendment. *Michigan Law Review* 98: 547–750.

Dawson, M.A. (1992). Popular sovereignty, double jeopardy, and the dual sovereignty doctrine. *The Yale Law Journal*, 102(1), 281–303.

Death Penalty Information Center (2016). Retrieved on March 30th, 2016 from: http://www.deathpenaltyinfo.org/executions-year.

DeLisi, M. & Conis, P.J. (2013). *American Corrections: Theory, Research, Policy, and Practice.* (2nd edition). Burlington, MA: Jones & Bartlett Learning

Des Rosiers, N., Feldthusen, B., and Hankivsky, O.A.R. (1998). Legal compensation for sexual violence: Therapeutic consequences and consequences for the judicial system. *Psychology, Public Policy, and Law.* 4(1–2), 433–451.

DeWolf, G.L. (1996). Protecting the courts from the barrage of frivolous prisoner litigation: A look at judicial remedies and Ohio's proposed legislative remedy. *Ohio State Law Journal,* 57(1), 257–289.

DiIulio, J. J. (1991). *No escape: The future of American corrections.* New York, NY: BasicBooks.

Dix, G.E. (1985). Nonarrest Investigatory Detentions in Search and Seizure Law. *Duke Law Journal,* 1985(5): 849–959.

Dockar-Drysdale, B. (1953). Some aspects of damage and restitution. *British Journal of Criminology,* 4(1), 4–13.

Dodge, M., & Pogrebin, M. R. (2001). Collateral costs of imprisonment for women: complications of reintegration. *The Prison Journal,* 81(1), 42–54.

Drummond, T. (1999, June 21). Cellblock seniors. *Time,* 153, 60.

Ducat, C.R. (2013). *Constitutional Interpretation: Rights of the Individual.* Volume II. 10th Edition. Boston, MA: Cengage.

Duffee, D. (1986). *Correctional management: Change and control in correctional organizations.* Prospect Heights, IL: Waveland Press.

Duffee, D.E. (1985). The interaction of organization and political constraints on community prerelease program development. In Stojkovic, S., Kofas, J., and Kalinich, D. (Eds.) *The Administration and Management of Criminal Justice Organizations: A Book of readings.* Prospects Heights, IL: Waveland Press.

Engel, K., & Rothman, S. (1983). Prison violence and the paradox of reform. *The Public Interest,* (73), 91–97.

Erez, E. (1999). Who is afraid of the big bad victim? Victim, Impact statements as victim empowerment and enhancement of justice. *Criminal Law Review,* 46(July), 545–576.

Fagan, T. J., & Ax, R. K. (Eds.). (2011). *Correctional Mental Health.* Thousand Oaks, CA: Sage Publishing.

Fagin, J. A. (2005). *Criminal Justice.* Boston, MA: Allyn and Bacon.

Fearn, N.E. (2011). Mentally ill and mentally challenged inmates. In: Chambliss, W.J. (ed.) *Corrections: Key Issues in Crime and Punishment.* Thousand Oaks, CA: Sage Publishing

Feeley, M. M., & Hanson, R. P. (1986, October). What we know, think we know and would like to know about the impact of court orders on prison conditions and jail crowding. In *meeting of the Working Group on Jail and Prison Crowding, Committee on Research on Law Enforcement and the Administration of Justice, National Academy of Sciences, Chicago.*

Feeley, M. M., & Simon, J. (1992). The new penology: Notes on the emerging strategy of corrections and its implications. *Criminology, 30*(4), 449–474.

Feeley, M. M., & Swearingen, V. (2003). Prison Conditions Cases and the Bureaucratization of American Corrections: Influences, Impacts and Implications. *The Pace Law Review,* 24(2), 433–475

Fliter, J. A. (2001). *Prisoners' Rights: The Supreme Court and Evolving Standards of Decency.* Westport, CT: Greenwood Press.

Foucault, M. (1977). *Discipline and punish: The birth of the prison.* Vintage.

Foucault, M. (1983). The subject and power. In H.L. Dreyfus, & R. Rabinow (Eds.). *Michael Foucault: Beyond Structuralism and Hermeneutics* (2nd ed.), pp. 208–216. Chicago, IL: University of Chicago Press.

Francis-Ward, S. (2015). Transgender inmate is first to be awarded individual compensation under the Prison Rape elimination Act. *American Bar Association Journal Online,* Available at: http://www.abajournal.com/news/article/transgender_inmate_is_first_to_be_awarded_individual_compensation_under_pri (last accessed: July 15, 2016).

Frazier, B. D., Sung, H. E., Gideon, L., & Alfaro, K. S. (2015). The impact of prison deinstitutionalization on community treatment services. *Health & Justice,* 3(1), 1–12.

Freudenberg, N. (2001). Jails, prisons, and the health of urban populations: A review of the impact of the correctional system on community health. *Journal of Urban Health,* 78(2), 214–235.

Friedman, L.M. (1993). *Crime and Punishment in American History.* New York: Basic Books.

Garland, D. (2001). *The culture of control: Crime and social order in contemporary society.* The Chicago, IL: University of Chicago Press

Gelman, A., Fagan, J., & Kiss, A. (2007). An Analysis of the New York City Police Department's "Stop-and-Frisk" Policy in the Context of Claims of Racial Bias. *Journal of the American Statistical Association,* 102(479): 813–823.

Gideon, L. (2010). *Substance Abusing Inmates: Experiences of Recovering Drug Addicts on Their Way Back Home.* New York, NY: Springer Publishing.

Gideon, L. (2011). Corrections in an Era of Reentry. In: Gideon, L., and Sung, H.E. (Eds.) *Rethinking Corrections: Rehabilitation, Reentry, and Reintegration,* 1–17. Thousand Oaks, CA: Sage Publication

Gideon, L., (2011). Rehabilitation, reentry and reintegration in criminal justice education. In: Gideon, L., and Sung, H.E. (Eds.) *Rethinking Corrections: Rehabilitation, Reentry, and Reintegration,* 383–397. Thousand Oaks, CA: Sage Publication.

Gideon, L. (2013). Bridging the gap between health and justice. *Health & Justice,* 1(1), 1–9.

Gideon, L., and Loveland, N. (2011). Public attitudes toward rehabilitation and reintegration: How supportive are people of getting-tough-on-crime policies and the Second chance Act? In: Gideon, L., and Sung, H.E. (Eds.) *Rethinking Corrections: Rehabilitation, Reentry, and Reintegration.* Sage Publication, 19–36.

Gideon, L., and Shoam, E., Weisburd, D.L. (2010). "Changing prison to therapeutic milieu: Evidence from the Sharon prison". *The Prison Journal,* 90, 179–202.

Goffman, E. (1961). On the characteristics of total institutions. In *Symposium on preventive and social psychiatry* (pp. 43–84).

Goffman, E. (1968). *Asylums: Essays on the social situation of mental patients and other inmates.* Aldine Transaction.

Goldberg, I. (2015). *Prison—The challenge of managing people behind bars: Moral and managerial dilemmas of imprisonment.* Tel-Aviv, Israel: Kotarim International Publishing [*In Hebrew*].

Goode, E., and Ben-Yehuda, N. (2009). Moral Panics: The Social Construction of Deviance. (2nd Edition). Wiley Blackwell: UK.

Gottschalk, M. (2006). *The prison and the gallows: The politics of mass incarceration in America.* Cambridge University Press.

Griffin, P., Torbet, P. M., & Szymanski, L. A. (1998). *Trying Juveniles as Adults in Criminal Court: An Analysis of State Transfer Provisions.* Washington, DC: National Center for Juvenile Justice.

Guerrero, G. (2011). Prison-based educational and vocational training programs. In: Gideon, L., and Sung, H.E. (Eds.) *Rethinking Corrections: Rehabilitation, Reentry, and Reintegration.* Sage Publication, 193–218.

Hall, D.E. (1995). When Caning Meets the Eighth Amendment: Whipping Offenders in the United States. *Widener Journal of Public Law,* 4(2), 403–459.

Hammett, T. M., Roberts, C., & Kennedy, S. (2001). Health-related issues in prisoner reentry. *Crime & Delinquency,* 47(3), 390–409.

Han, B., Wilson, M., Compton, J.G., & McKeon, R. (2014). Mental health treatment patterns among adults with recent suicide attempts in the United States. *American Journal of Public Health,* 104(12): 2359–2368.

Haney, C. (2003). Mental health issues in long-term solitary and "Supermax" confinement. *Crime and Delinquency,* 49(1), 124–156.

Hanson, R. A., & Daley, H. W. (1995). *Challenging the conditions of prisons and jails: A report on Section 1983 litigation.* Collingdale, PA: DIANE Publishing.

Hardwick, V. L. (1985). Punishing the Innocent: Unconstitutional Restrictions on Prison Marriage and Visitation. NYUL Rev., 60, 275.

Harper, J. (2008). Reforming Fourth Amendment Privacy Doctrine. *American University Law Review,* 57(5): 1381–1403.

Harris, D. A. (1994). Factors for Reasonable Suspicion: When Black and Poor Means Stopped and Frisked. *Indiana Law Journal,* 69(3): 659–688.

Henriques, Z. (1996). Imprisoned mothers and their children: Separation-reunion syndrome dual impact. *Women and Criminal Justice*, 8(1), 77–95.

Hensley, C., & Tewksbury, R. (2002). Inmate-to-inmate prison sexuality: A review of empirical studies. *Trauma, Violence, & Abuse*, 3(3), 226–243.

Hicks, J.P. (1995, Sep. 10th). Seeking A.T.M.-Style Probation System. [News Article] Retrieved from http://www.nytimes.com/1995/09/10/nyregion/seeking-atm-style-probation-system.html.

Hurst, W. (1945). Treason in the United States: II. The Constitution. *Harvard Law Review*, 58(3), 395–444.

Inciardi, J. A. (1995). The therapeutic community: An effective model for corrections-based drug abuse treatment. In K. C. Haas & G. P. Alpert (Eds.), *The Dilemmas of Corrections: Contemporary Readings* (3rd ed.) (406–417). Prospect Heights, IL: Waveland.

Inciardi, J. A., Martin, S. S., Butzin, C. A., Hooper, R. M., & Harrison, L. D. (1997). An effective model of prison-based treatment for drug-involved offenders. *Journal of Drug Issues*, 27(2), 261–278.

Ingraham, C. (2015). The U.S. has more jails than colleges. Here's a map of where those prisoners live. Washington Post, January 6, 2015. Available at: https://www.washingtonpost.com/news/wonk/wp/2015/01/06/the-u-s-has-more-jails-than-colleges-heres-a-map-of-where-those-prisoners-live/ [last visited Sep. 13, 2015].

Jacobs, J. (1980). The prisoners' rights movement and its impacts, 1960–1980. In Morris, N., & Tonry, M. (2nd Edition). *An Annual Review of Research*, (Vol. 2). Chicago, Il: University of Chicago Press.

Jacobs, J. B. (1979). Race relations and the prisoner subculture. *Crime and justice*, 1(1), 1–27.

Jannetta, J., & Halberstadt, R. (2011). Kiosk supervision for the District of Columbia. The Urban Institute, January.

Johnson, R., and Tabriz, S. (Eds.) (2011). Life Without Parole: Living and Dying in Prison Today. Oxford University Press: New York.

Kansas Department of Corrections: Policies and Procedures. Available at: https://www.doc.ks.gov/kdoc-policies (last access: August 25, 2016).

Kaeble, D., Glaze, L., Tsoutis, A., & Minton, T. (2016). Correctional populations in the United States, 2014. *Bureau of Justice Statistics Bulletin (NCJ 249513)*.

Kaeble, D., Maruschak, L. M., & Bonczar, T. P. (2015). Probation and Parole in the United States, 2014. Washington, DC: Bureau of Justice Statistics (BJS), US Department of Justice, and Office of Justice Programs.

Katz, L.R. (1990). In search of a Fourth Amendment for the twenty-first century. *Indiana Law Journal*, 65(3): 549–590.

Kerbs, J. J., & Jolley, J. M. (2009). A commentary on age segregation for older prisoners: Philosophical and pragmatic considerations for correctional systems. *Criminal Justice Review*, 34(1), 119–139.

Kerle, K. E., & Ford, F. R. (1982). *The State of Our Nation's Jails, 1982.* Washington, DC: National Sheriffs' Association.

Killias, M., Aebi, M., & Ribeaud, D. (2000). Does Community Service Rehabilitate better than Short-term Imprisonment? Results of a Controlled Experiment. The Howard Journal of Criminal Justice, 39(1), 40–57.

Kleck, G. (1981). Racial Discrimination in Criminal Sentencing: A Critical Evaluation of the Evidence with Additional Evidence on the Death Penalty. *American Sociological Review*, 46(6), 783–805.

Klein, S. B. (1978). Prisoners' rights to physical and mental health care: A modern expansion of the Eighth Amendment's Cruel and Unusual Punishment Clause. Fordham Urb. LJ, 7, 1.

Knickerbocker, B. (2006, May 16). Illegal immigrants in the US: How many are there? *The Christian Science Monitor.* Retrieved August 25, 2016 from http://www.cs monitor.com.

Kosiak, D. (2011). Healthcare and medical assistance for prisoners. In: Chambliss, W.J. (ed.) *Corrections: Key Issues in Crime and Punishment.* Thousand Oaks, CA: Sage Publishing

Kuanliang, A., Sorensen, J. R., & Cunningham, M. D. (2008). Juvenile inmates in an adult prison system: Rates of disciplinary misconduct and violence. *Criminal Justice and Behavior*, 35(9), 1186–1201.

Lavinsky, M.B. (1965). Executive Clemency: Study of a Decisional Problem Arising in the Terminal Stages of the Criminal Process. *Chicago-Kent Law Review*, 42(1): 13–53.

Lennard, N. (2012). US has more prisoners, prisons than any other country. SALON.com October 15th, 2012. Available at: http://www.salon.com/2012/10/15/us_has_more_prisoners_prisons_than_any_other_country/ [last visited Oct. 10th 2016].

Lerman, A. E. (2013). *The modern prison paradox: Politics, punishment, and social community.* Cambridge, United Kingdom: Cambridge University Press.

Levitt, S. (1996). The effect of prison population size on crime rates: Evidence from prison overcrowding legislation. *The Quarterly Journal of Economics*, 111: 319–351.

MacKenzie, D.L. (2011). Probation: An untapped resource in U.S. Corrections. In: Gideon, L., and Sung, H.E. (Eds.) Rethinking Corrections: Rehabilitation, Reentry, and Reintegration. Sage Publication, 97–128.

Maruschak, L. M., & Parks, E. (2012). Probation and parole in the United States, 2011. Washington, DC: US Department of Justice, Office of Justice Programs, Bureau of Justice Statistics.

Marvell, T. B. (1995). Sentencing Guidelines and Prison Population Growth. *Journal of Criminal Law & Criminology*, 85(3), 696–709.

Mauer, M. (2006). *Race to incarcerate.* New York, NY: The New Press.

May, D.C., Minor, K.L., Ruddell, R., & Matthews, B, A. (2008). Corrections and the Criminal Justice System. Sudbury, MA: Jones and Bartlett Publishers

May, D.C., and Wood, P.B. (2010). *Ranking Correctional Punishments: Views from Offenders, Practitioners, and the Public.* Carolina Academic Press. Durham: North Carolina.

McGarvey, S.M. (1998). Missed opportunity? The affirmation of the death penalty in the AEDPA: Extradition scenarios. *Journal of Legislation*, 24, 99–110.

Merton, R.K. (1938). Social structure and anomie. *American Sociological Review,* 3, 672–678. Available at: http://users.soc.umn.edu/~uggen/Merton_ASR_38.pdf (last accessed August 25, 2016).

Miller, C. (2003). Wolf in Sheep's Clothing: Wolf v. Ashcroft and the Constitutionality of Using the MPAA Ratings to Censor Films in Prison, A. Vand. J. Ent. L. & Prac., 6, 265.

Miller, T. (2002). The impact of mass incarceration on immigration policy. In: Mauer, M. & Chesney-Lind, M. (Eds.), pp. 214–238, *Invisible Punishment: The Collateral Consequences of Mass Imprisonment.* New York, NY: The New Press

Minor, K. I., & Parson, S. (2015). Grievance procedures in correctional facilities. In: Carlson, P.M. (Ed). Pp. 353–367. Prison and Jail Administration: Practice and Theory (3rd edition). Burlington, MA: Jones & Bartlett.

Minton, T. D., & Zeng, Z. (2015). Jail inmates at midyear 2014. Washington, DC: US Department of Justice, Office of Justice Programs, Bureau of Justice Statistics, 3.

Molina, L.B. (2006). Institutionalizing the Innocent: Suspicionless Searches of Prison Visitors' Vehicles and the Fourth Amendment. *U.C. Davis Law Review*, 40(1), 261–312.

Morash, M., & Schram, P. J. (2002). The prison experience: Special issues of women in prison. Prospect Heights, IL: Waveland.

Moritsugu, K. (1990). Inmate chronological age versus physical age. *Long-term Confinement and the Aging Inmate Population.* Washington, D.C.: Federal Bureau of Prisons.

Moster, A.N., & Jeglic, E.L. (2009). Prison warden attitudes toward prison rape and sexual assault. *The Prison Journal*, 89(1), 67–78.

Moynahan, J.M. & Stewart E.K. (1980). *The American Jail: Its Development and Growth.* Chicago, IL: Nelson-Hall Publishing.

Muiluvuori, M.L. (2001). Recidivism among people sentenced to community service in Finland. *Journal of Scandinavian Studies in Criminology and Crime Prevention*, 2(1), 72–82.

Nahari, M. (1988). Due process and probation revocation: The written statement requirement. *Fordham Law Review*, 56(4): 759–782.

National Institute of Corrections. Available at: http://nicic.gov/history (last visited, Aug. 10th 2016).

Neil, M. (2010). Federal judge strikes state-law ban on hormone treatment for transgendered inmates. *American Bar Association Online,* Available at: http://www.abajournal.com/news/article/federal_judge_strikes_state_law_that_bans_treatment_for_transgendered_inmat/ (last Accessed: July 15, 2016).

Neubauer, D.W., and Fradella, H.F. (2011). America's Courts and the Criminal Justice System. (10th Edition). Wadsworth/Cengage Learning: Belmont, CA.

Noonan, M., Rohloff, H., & Ginder, S. (2015). *Mortality in Local Jails and State Prisons, 2000–2013, Statistical Tables.* US Department of Justice, Office of Justice Programs, Bureau of Justice Statistics.

Oei, L. G. (1988). New Standard of Review for Prisoners' Rights: A Turner for the Worse-Turner v. Safley, The. Vill. L. Rev., 33, 393.

Ostermann, M. (2015). How do former inmates perform in the community? A survival analysis of rearrests, reconvictions, and technical parole violations. Crime & Delinquency, 61(2), 163–187.

Petersilia, J. (1997). Probation in the United States. In: Tonry, M. (Ed.), Crime and Justice: A Review of the Research (Vol. 22, Pp. 149–200). Chicago, IL: University of Chicago Press

Petersilia, J. (2017). Reentry: Saving Offenders from a life in crime. In: Cullen, F.T., & Jonson, C.L. (eds.). *Correctional Theory: Context and Consequences* (2nd Edition), 206–239. Thousand Oaks, CA: Sage Publication.

Pizzaro, J.M., Stenius, V.M.K., & Pratt, T.C. (2006). Supermax prisons: Myths, realities, and the politics of punishment in American society. *Criminal Justice Policy Review,* 17(1), 6–21.

Pollock, J. M. (1998). *Counseling Women in Prison.* Beverly Hills, CA: Sage Publishing.

Pollock, J. M. (2001). *Women, Prison, and Crime.* Belmont, CA: Wadsworth.

Pollock, J. M. (2004). *Prisons and Prison Life.* Los Angeles, CA: Roxbury Publishing.

Preyer, K. (1982). Penal measures in the American colonies: An overview. *The American Journal of Legal History,* 26(4), 326–353.

Ratansi, S., & Cox, S. M. (2007). Assessment and validation of Connecticut's salient factor score. Connecticut, USA: Central Connecticut State University.

Riveland, C. (1999). Prison management trends, 1975–2025. *Crime and Justice,* 26(1), 163–203.

Robbins, I.P., & Buser, M.B. (1977). Punitive conditions of prison confinement: An analysis of Pugh v. Locke and federal court supervision of state penal administration under the Eighth Amendment. *Stanford Law Review,* 29(5): 893–930.

Roberts, J. V., Stalans, L. J., Indermaur, D., & Hough, M. (2002). *Penal populism and public opinion: Lessons from five countries.* Oxford, UK: Oxford University Press.

Rocheleau, A. M. (1987). *Joining Incarcerated Mothers with Their Children: Evaluation of the Lancaster Visiting Cottage Program* (Pub. No. 14,886-149-250-6-24-87). Milford, MA: Massachusetts Department of Corrections. Retrieved August 6, 2011, from the Executive Office of Public Safety and Security: http://www.mass.gov/eopss/docs/doc/research-reports/inmate-eval/eval-309B.pdf.

Samaha, J. (2012). *Criminal Procedure*. (8th Edition). Belmont, CA: Cengage.

Schlanger, M. (2003). Inmate litigation. *Harvard Law Review*, 16(6), 1555–1706.

Schlanger, M. (2015). Trends in prisoner litigation, as the PLRA enters adulthood. *University of California at Irvine Law Review*, 5(1), 153–178.

Schmalleger, F., & Ortiz-Smykla, J. (2009). *Corrections in the 21st Century* (4th Edition). New York, NY: McGraw Hill.

Seiter, R.P. (2008). *Corrections: An Introduction* (2nd Edition). Upper Saddle River, NJ: Prentice Hall/Pearson Publishing.

Seiter, R.P. (2011). *Corrections: An Introduction*. (3rd Edition). Upper Saddle River, NJ: Prentice-Hall.

Sickmund, M. (2003). *Juvenile Offenders and Victims—National Report Series: Juveniles in Court*. Rockville, MD: Office of Juvenile Justice and Delinquency Prevention.

Siegel, L., & Bartollas, C. (2016). Corrections Today. (3rd edition). Boston, MA: Cengage learning.

Simon, K. (1999). Are inmate lawsuits out of control? No! In Fields, C.B. (ed.) *Controversial Issues in Corrections*. (Pp. 247–255). Upper Saddle River, NJ: Allyn and Bacon

Simpson, D.D., Wexler, H.K., and Inciardi, J.A. (Eds.) (1999). Special issue on drug treatment outcomes for correctional settings. *The Prison Journal*, 79(3/4), 291–293.

Shapland, J. (1984). Victims, the criminal justice system and compensation. *British Journal of Criminology*, 24(2), 131–149.

Shaw, J.R. (2015). Compliance with the Constitution. In: Carlson, P.M. (3rd ed.), *Prison and jail Administration: Practice and Theory*. Pp. 519–533. Burlington, MA: Jones & Bartlett Learning.

Sherman, L.W. (1993). Defiance, deterrence, and irrelevance: A theory of the criminal sanction. *Journal of Research in Crime and Delinquency*, 30(4), 445–473.

Shoham, S. G., and Shavit, G. (1995). *Crime and Punishments: An Introduction to Penology*. Am-Oved Publishers, Tel-Aviv, Israel.

Shoham, E. (2004) Characteristics of the interaction between women battered by their husbands and the police from the women point of view. In: Eden, L., Shademi, A., and Kim, Y. (Eds.) *Chasing Justice*, Tel-Aviv: Beit-Berel College and Chrikover Publishers: 140–160 [*in Hebrew*].

Shoham, E., Gideon, L., Weisburd, D., and Vilner, Y. (2006). "When 'More' of a program is not necessary better: Drug prevention in the Sharon prison". *Israeli Law Review Journal*, 39(1), 1–23.

Smith, J.F. (1973). Prison reform through the legislature. In Wright, E.O., *The Politics of Punishment : A Critical Analysis of Prisons in America* (Pp. 262–280). New York, NY: Harper Colophon Books.

Snell, T. L., & Morton, D. C. (1994). *Women in prison*. Washington, DC: US Department of Justice.

Snyder, H. N. & Sickmund, M. (2006). *Juvenile Offenders and Victims: 2006 National Report*. Washington, DC: Office of Juvenile Justice and Delinquency Prevention.

Steinman, A.N. (2001). Reconceptualizing federal habeas corpus for state prisoners: How should AEDPA's standard of review operate after *Williams v. Taylor*? *Wisconsin Law Review*, 2001, 1494–1539.

Steinmann, R.M. (1999). Are inmate lawsuits out of control? Yes! In Fields, C.B. (ed.) *Controversial Issues in Corrections* (Pp. 239–247). Upper Saddle River, NJ: Allyn and Bacon.

Stoffers, C. (2015). For the First Time, Vermont Will Search Prison Staffers. *The Marshall Project*. Retrieved on Nov. 24th, 2016 at: https://www.themarshall project.org/2015/07/13/for-the-first-time-vermont-will-search-prison-staffers#. BUQzlDR0V.

Stohr, M. K., Walsh, A., & Hemmens, C. (2009). *Corrections: A Text/Reader*. Thousand Oaks, CA: Sage Publishing.

Sturm, S.P. (1993). The legacy and future of corrections litigation. *University of Pennsylvania Law Review*, 142: 639–738.

Sundt, J., Cullen, F.T., Thielo, A.J., & Jonson, C.L. (2015). Public willingness to downsize prisons: Implications from Oregon. *Victims and Offenders*, 10(4), 365–379.

Thomas, J. (1988). *Prisoner litigation: The paradox of the jailhouse lawyer*. Rowman & Littlefield.

Tonry, M. (1987). *Sentencing reform impacts*. Washington, DC: National Institute of Justice.

Torrey, E. F., Kennard, A. D., Eslinger, D., Lamb, R., & Pavle, J. (2010). More mentally ill persons are in jails and prisons than hospitals: A survey of the states. *Arlington, VA: Treatment Advocacy Center*.

Turner, W. B. (1979). When prisoners sue: A study of prisoner Section 1983 suits in the federal courts. *Harvard Law Review*, 92(3), 610–663.

Van Voorhis, P., & Presser, L. (2001). *Classification of Women Offenders: A National Assessment of Current Practices*. Rockville, MD: National Institute of Justice.

Walker Jr, B., & Gordon, T. (1980). Health and high density confinement in jails and prisons. *Federal Probation*, 44(1), 53–57.

Welsh, W.N. (2011). Prison-based substance abuse programs. In: Gideon, L., and Sung, H.E. (Eds.) *Rethinking Corrections: Rehabilitation, Reentry, and Reintegration.* Sage Publication, 157–192.

Welsh, W. N. (2011). Prison-based substance abuse programs. In L. Gideon & H. E. Sung (Eds.), *Rethinking Corrections: Rehabilitation, Reentry, and Reintegration* (157–192). Thousand Oaks, CA: Sage Publishing.

West-Smith, M., Pogrebin, M. R., & Poole, E. D. (2000). Denial of parole: An inmate perspective. Federal Probation, 64(2), 3–10.

West, H. (2010). *Prison inmates at midyear 2009-statistical tables.* Washington DC: Bureau of Justice Statistics, U.S. Department of Justice.

West, H., and Sabol, W. (2008). Prisoners in 2007. Washington, DC: U.S. Department of Justice, Bureau of Justice Statistics, 2008.

Westen, P. (1980). The three faces of double jeopardy: Reflections on government appeals of criminal sentences. *Michigan Law Review*, 78(7), 1001–1065.

Whitty, N. (2011). Human rights as risk: UK prisons and the management of risk and rights. *Punishment & Society, 13*(2), 123–148.

Williamson, R.A. (1973). Federal habeas corpus: Limitations on successive applications from the same prisoner. *William & Mary Law Review*, 15, 265–285.

Wilper, A. P., Woolhandler, S., Boyd, J.W., Lasser, K. E., McCormick, D., Bor, D.H., & Himmelstein, D.U. (2009). The health and health care of US prisoners: Results of a nationwide survey. *American Journal of Public Health*, 99(4), 666–672.

Wilson, J.Q. (1975). *Thinking About Crime.* New York, NY: Basic Books.

Women's Prison Association (N.D.) Available at: http://www.wpaonline.org/institute [last visited: Nov. 14th, 2016].

Wooldredge, J., Griffin, T., & Pratt, T. (2001). Considering hierarchical models for research on inmate behavior: Predicting misconduct with multilevel data. *Justice Quarterly, 18*(1), 203–231.

Wright, E.O. (1973). *The Politics of Punishment: Critical Analysis of Prisoners in America.* New York, NY: Harper & Row Publishers

Yanai, A. (2003) Innovation in the criminal trial: Submission of sexual-assault victims' impact statement by adult probation services. In: Hovav, M., Sebba, L., and Amir, M. (Eds.) *Trends in Criminology: Theory, Policy and Implications.* Jerusalem: The Institute for Comparative Law and Legislation: Hebrew University, 235–272.

Zheng, L. (2002). Actual innocence as a gateway through the statute-of-limitations bar on the filing of federal habeas corpus petitions. *California Law Review*, 90(6), 2101–2141.

Zimring, F.E., Hawkins, G., and Kamin, S. (2001). *Punishment and Democracy: Three Strikes and You're Out in California.* Oxford University Press.

Table of Cases

Name Index

Subject Index